$39.95

D1554612

Is Language a Music?

Musical Meaning and Interpretation
Robert S. Hatten, editor

DAVID LIDOV

Is Language a Music?
Writings on Musical Form and Signification

INDIANA UNIVERSITY PRESS
Bloomington and Indianapolis

This book is a publication of

Indiana University Press
601 North Morton Street
Bloomington, IN 47404-3797 USA

http://iupress.indiana.edu

Telephone orders   800-842-6796
Fax orders   812-855-7931
Orders by e-mail   iuporder@indiana.edu

The paper used in this publication meets the minimum requirements of American National Standard for Information Sciences—Permanence of Paper for Printed Library Materials, ANSI Z39.48-1984.

Manufactured in the United States of America

Library of Congress Cataloging-in-Publication Data

Lidov, David, date
    Is language a music? : writings on musical form and signification / David Lidov.
        p.   cm. — (Musical meaning and interpretation)
    Includes bibliographical references and index.
    ISBN 0-253-34383-6 (cloth : alk. paper)
  1. Music—Semiotics. 2. Music and language. I. Title. II. Series.
    ML3845.L53 2005
    781′.1—dc22

                                                                                    2004004471

1 2 3 4 5   10 09 08 07 06 05

Contents

Preface

The new and older writings on music collected here do not comprise a system, but they are loosely coordinated by the system constructed in my *Elements of Semiotics* (1999), a work which treats *general* semiotics and reflects on musical semiotics *en passant*. A theory of general semiotics opens the doors of comparison. It holds out the prospect that we might compare a sonata with a poem, or a symphony with a painting, or a fugue with a philosophy while maintaining as much precision and attention to detail as we would expect to bring to the comparison of m. 3 and m. 17. A further promise of that wide perspective is the freedom not to specialize. A couple of the papers in this collection, I won't say which, were instigated simply by the temptation of experimenting with ideas, trusting them to explore music about which, previously, I knew almost nothing. The collection is not specialized in its repertorial interests, and I certainly hope that its mixture of theory and criticism will not suggest a specialization in method.

In this book the first chapter is new. The Introductions which precede the five parts of the book are partly new. Except for Chapter 12, extensively recast, the re-published articles do not depart substantially from their initial presentations. As for papers that were read but not previously printed, you know the drill. I have tried by means of the Introductions to make the various material, all independently conceived, a bit more clear and less repetitious. The last chapter is almost new, missing by just a few months and intended from the start for this publication, though it has now appeared in *Ex Tempore*. I owe thanks for his persistent urgings to write it to John MacKay, editor of *Ex Tempore*, a very independent journal of contemporary music theory, the author, with Robert Erickson, of a fine handbook on that composer's music (Erickson and MacKay 1995), and, as a pianist, an excellent exponent of my 1966 piano sonata. This chapter is the only essay I have ever written about my own music, a project that made me nervous for two obvious reasons. Any such undertaking invites confusion between appreciation of the art and appreciation of oneself, and any such undertaking invites a speculation that the score was inadequate to say its own piece. I don't know of any composers ever who were guaranteed immunity from those hazards. I think charitable readers can find a third, more harmless reading. I appeal to your charity. I am also pleased to have framed this collection with two invitations. The first chapter invites anyone who would be interested in a fuller account of the logic of these essays to look at my previous book. The last chapter invites anyone who would like to know more of the sensibility which informs them to explore my music.

Most of the work here first appeared in venues that may seem alien to some readers of the present volume—semiotics journals and proceedings, a Canadian music journal, and stranger still, a Canadian semiotics journal! I am grateful for those fora and the very open-minded academic communities they represent, as it was there that I found the ideas for figuring out what I was saying. We look strange only from a distance. I am also grateful to Robert Hatten, the editor of this series, who encouraged this project, not only because he did so, but because his own research, which this editorship continues, has played a key role in bringing together modes of musical inquiry that seemed radically divergent from each other two decades ago.

All of the figures of the book have been redrawn. I thank Christy DeFelice for a big head start with that job and Marcia Ostashewski and Julien Müller for help with several editorial tasks and I thank the editorial staff of Indiana University Press for their assiduity and helpful judgment.

D. L., Toronto, 2003

Is Language a Music?

1   Prelude: Is Language a Music?

We speak both of the language of music and of the music of language. The difficulty of dismissing the relationship as mere metaphor is just this reversibility, which we don't find so convenient with Achilles and lions or with teeth and pearls. A metaphor that works well both ways, not just humorously, suggests a genuine interpenetration of its two domains. Rousseau thought that music came first and language was a subspecies. Perhaps he would have been prepared to acknowledge that such a historical construction was really a rhetorical device, but perhaps there is also an insight there we should eventually acknowledge.

When I first encountered the cliché, perhaps more prevalent then than today, that "music is a universal language of the emotions," I was about twelve and did not approve. Beyond a dependable suspicion of pomposity we can count on among young persons, it was very clear to me at twelve that real music made more sense than "emotions," and "universal," though surely my sense of the word was naïve, couldn't even encompass my neighborhood playmates or certain friends of the family. Correct music—this was patently self-evident, but apparently not to everybody—was a Bach invention or a Schubert march and did not include such indigestible sound as Stravinsky or Stan Kenton—absolute values perhaps, but no universals.

Half a century later the venerable cliché that music is a universal emotional language has lost all credibility among worldly folk; yet I find myself inclined to argue for a partial and conditional rehabilitation. Of the three component notions, emotional content, universality, and linguisticity, it is now the third that warrants the greatest caution. Comparisons of music and language are the chief project of this chapter. In brief, I will argue that they can be like or unlike each other in very diverse ways, but that none of these resemblances is necessarily "of the essence." To orient that project, it will be helpful to spend a moment on the other two ingredients.

That music has a special relation with emotion is a thought that never wants to go away. I hope this book and this chapter will traffic with that matter in an honorable manner. We will never say we can explain music by regarding it as merely a direct expression of the feelings of the musicians who make it or, for its listener, merely an object of attachment or a stimulus of feeling. Music is not that simple even in music therapy or when used as a background fix. Nevertheless, I will keep on the table the idea that immediate evocation of emotion in music is an orienting moment of its discourse. There are orienting moments of emotional expression in speech, as well, but we may not see a deep parallel there. In speech, we might argue, directly contrary to Rousseau, the direct expression of emotion is a "rider" tacked onto a bill of goods with a more abstract content. In music, the evocation of emotion can constitute a kernel from which abstraction proceeds.

Regarding *universality,* we know now that "music" takes a plural. All cultures have at least one music, and we cannot discount the potential incommensurability of musics from different cultures. Granted that premise, we still see much evidence that people learn new musics more rapidly than new languages, at least to a level of competence that permits engaged and contrasted listening experiences. When Debussy heard a Javanese gamelan at the Paris Exhibition of 1898, he got something he could take home. I wouldn't suggest that he had acquired expertise, but he and his compatriots evidently felt a significance and richness in gamelan music—without translation—that was not available to them in untranslated Indonesian poetry. Is this because music is simpler than language? My music is not simpler than my speech, and neither does Ravi Shankar's seem to be, nor Louis Armstrong's. The initial engagements we establish with "foreign" musics are not expert, but it would be arbitrary and unwarranted to dismiss them as totally superficial. Furthermore—this may be the crucial point—experience and exposure, without tutelage, are frequently sufficient to nourish sophistication in a fairly short time. The same thing happens with second languages but, obviously, only after a much longer and more painful initiation. If we are honest about these facts, then we must be open to theories that understand music partly by its interaction with universal human characteristics, that is, with our physiological and cognitive biology, and not exclusively according to differences of culture.

Our main task of comparing music and language wants a bit of method. For example, we could start with the categories of linguistics and look for musical equivalents. (Does music have something like a morpheme? Like a sentence? Like a noun?) Alternately, we could start with the categories of musicology—meaning the word broadly, to encompass all forms of musical study. (Does language have something like melody? Ostinato basses? Prolongation structures?) The point of *semiotics* is to offer a more even-handed perspective, not necessarily neutral, but embracing. Semiotics is concerned with *general* problems of representation: how media are comparable and different; how reference is possible and how it is limited; how signs are biased and how they compete with their objects; and other broad questions.

It is not a matter of consensus just what semiotics would imply here regarding method. For me, a *special* semiotics, like the semiotics of music, is intellectually compelling as a framework only if it is clearly related to a *general* theory of semiotics. When I began to consider problems in musical semiotics, I got stuck because I did not find a general theory to which I could relate music. In consequence, I felt impelled to try my own hand at general semiotics. My book *Elements of Semiotics* (1999) was the fruit of my interest in establishing a genuinely comparative semiotics, not excessively biased to music or language or mathematics or any other medium. The book does not spell out a method, but it offers the perspective that guides what follows here. I compare music and language, first, with regard to their capacity to realize inflected and articulated structures; second, in relation to their simplest elements of reference; third, with respect to their manner of elaborating structure and meaning (forming what I call discourse); and finally I touch on a vast subject that greatly exceeds the scope of this essay, the differences in cultural function of music and language.

1.1. Inflection and Articulation

An inflection of sound is a shape of *continuous* change imposed on it, like a swell or an acceleration or a pitch bend. Articulation implies a point of *division*. An articulation is either one distinct segment of sound or the point of division of the stream between two distinct sounds or the action of dividing sounds into distinct units. (Inflection has another technical meaning in linguistics, irrelevant to the present discussion, which refers to variations of words such as in the inflections of a verb to show tense.)

I emphasize this opposition between inflected continuity and articulated divisions because the key move that sent structural linguistics into high gear a hundred years ago was to ignore continuity in favor of articulated segments. The latter have appeared more tractable to logical investigation and more distinctive. The same strategy holds considerable sway in music studies. It is in our interest to be aware that it is problematic. Ignoring continuity is more problematic for music than for language, an important difference that I must flesh out.

A sound stream may be regarded as continuous "by definition" if we acknowledge silences as pauses or rests as part of the stream. Insofar as the sound stream is correlated with a stream of attention, this makes perfect sense. What interests us is not the physics of continuity but both the experience of the sound and our conceptualization of it—the two not necessarily fully coinciding. In both language and music we attend to a chain of articulations, notes, phrases, words, and syllables, but there is something more. We are also caught up in the continuous inflections of the speaking voice, if it is personal or expressive, and the continuous stream of the voice may appear as independent of its words as a river is of the boats it carries. The pianist hopes to get this effect, too, and the cellist is supremely confident that she will.

Modern linguistics, as a science, seems generally to ignore the aspects of language which cannot be studied as systematic articulations. To say this is almost to say that linguists ignore what we might call the musical side of speech—the feeling tones and gestural character of speech. In part, the bias is the bias of writing, the prejudice of regarding what can be written as more essential to the medium than what cannot be. The scope of unwritable effects of speech, in maintaining authority, in asserting need, in communicating personal emotion, is in truth enormous. If these effects seem "not of the essence" in language, it may be also because compelling methods to study them are not in view. But there is another, better reason for the bias, the recognition of what language and only language can do. That special function has to do with particular types of reference (which, however, are not easy to specify). Those referential functions which can be fulfilled by *writing* and which are thus fulfilled by systematic articulations have a great claim to priority. Nevertheless, to regard this special capacity as the essence of language, as

Saussure did, is logically indefensible, hides the density, prevalence, and human importance of other, expressively referential functions of language, and also needlessly handicaps the comparison of language and music.

The ratio of articulation to inflection varies greatly among the speech of different persons and sometimes in one society among the speech of different classes. It also varies according to circumstances (more vocal inflection when joking at a party, less when reading a conference paper). This variation is substantial, but I think the ratio varies far more between styles of music than it does between different languages. There is a kind of Buddhist chant in Japan that is all inflection, made of slides and rhythmically elastic, and a kind of metalaphone music in the Philippines that is all articulation, made of tightly metrical rhythms and neat segments of melody. I see no variation among languages so extreme as those among musical styles.

The judgment that a style of music is highly articulate or highly continuous or very mixed is not a simple descriptor of the sound surface. A sense of continuity underlies the musical images of Indonesian gamelan musics, their preponderance of percussion not withstanding. Hence the magic of their ensemble accelerandos and retards in a flow which absorbs timbral and rhythmic articulations as a continuous glitter. On the other hand, the extraordinary fluidity of the sound surface in the vocal music or violin playing of the Indian subcontinent robes a complex interplay of distinctly articulated figures, often language-like in their persistent variations and concatenations. We must look past the surface, regarding musical and linguistic articulation and inflection in terms of the structures they convey.

Articulatory Structures

Articulation of the sound streams of music or language presents us with parts or sections or *units;* parts of parts—and thus *hierarchies* of parts with possibly distinct *strata*—and types of parts or *categories*. For everyday speech (leaving aside the more elaborate special forms like jokes, orations, novels, and so on) linguistics identifies the *sentence* as the largest unit reliably accounted for by structural rules. The parts of a sentence constitute a stratified hierarchy: clauses, phrases (nominal, verbal, adjectival, etc.), words, morphemes, phonemes. The terms we use for musical articulations—periods, phrases, motives, notes—reflect a linguistic borrowing of great antiquity (Powers 1980), but the hierarchy is not always similar. The parallel is so familiar that I think I can pass immediately to the differences.

Linguistic strata are distinguished from each other by different sets of rules of combination: for example, the rules for forming sentences are entirely different from the rules for forming syllables. A first difference is that musical strata are not so patly distinguished by method of organization as their supposed linguistic counterparts. The tonic-dominant relation might be equally germane to one motive or to a full period. A second difference is that linguistic categories are given with the language. For language, the most prominent category structure is vocabulary, which remains a constant resource from one conversation to the next. Music has some fixed vocabularies. An $E\flat^{11}$ chord and some of the riffs that go with it survive from one solo to another and from one performance to another, but for much music, vocabulary is created within the work—the motive, the theme—and its reappearance in other works is generally regarded as incidental and accidental. Consequences of these differences are developed in several of the chapters which follow, especially Chapters 2, 3, and 5.

A still more fundamental difference is entailed in musical continuity. Both in pitch and in time, music exhibits the type of articulatory structure that I call *dual articulation*. (Note that this is not "double articulation," a linguistics term from Martinet.) Dual articulation presents boundaries and regions. In the case of music, notes function as boundaries and intervals as regions. The terminology may seem backwards; it doesn't ultimately matter which is which, just that there are two. Some other examples of dual articulation: Time zones are regions; lines of longitude are boundaries. Climate zones are regions; lines of latitude are boundaries. Calendar days are regions (twenty-four-hour periods); clock times are boundaries. Movements are regions; positions are boundaries. In general you can name a boundary as the product of two regions—Broadway at 42nd—and you can name a region as the product of two boundaries: "From Times Square to Penn Station" specifies a region of a subway route in New York City. Dual articulation arises only in the articulation of a continuous space.

The articulated sound structure of language shows no such duality. The sounds of language are a chain. Words, like the dominant content of the visual field, are understood as distinct objects. Although we see in space, we don't normally see space itself (fog can be considered as furnishing one of the exceptions). We see the stuff in it, stuff that gets bundled as *gestalts*. Music will sometimes imitate the hierarchical forms of language and vision, which are well represented by tree graphs and which depend on the logical relation of *inclusion—X includes Y*. Language, however, does not seem to utilize the type of hierarchy most characteristic for pitch and rhythm. This other type depends on the logical relation of *between*. Chapter 6 explores this issue, which I regard as badly neglected, and contends that Schenker, whose notion of organicism has the distinctly anti-linguistic bias of his romantic sources, developed a notation resembling net graphs, not trees, and was therefore able to represent both continuity and interruption, a task ill-suited to a well-formed tree.

Interactions of Articulation with Inflection

A notated musical composition is a coherent, articulated structure which a performance realizes with inflectional nuance, just as when one reads aloud a written verbal text. In both cases the notated articulations motivate inflectional nuances (accentuation, fluctuations of tempo, and so on) without fully determining them, and in both language and music it may be possible to suggest quite different imports by choices of performance manner. This fact is so obvious as to seem trivial, but to account for it is not. It is clearly the case for language that performance nuance normally reflects an understanding of both grammar and *reference*. Some people are inclined to think that in the case of music the impact of performed nuance is entirely a matter of the understanding it conveys of the articulate syntax (voice leading, tonality, metrical relations). This is how Bruno Repp (1989) interprets computer analyses of performance nuances. But the way performers talk about music suggests that for most of them images of the music's character, that is, qualities of action and feeling, not just syntax, are of pivotal importance in shaping their inflections. The implication of this position is that in music, as in language, notated articulations are interpreted with reference to some further object of thought (such as a feeling) that can, in turn, influence, though not fully determine, inflectional traits.

A yet more delicate question that attaches to these considerations is whether we should regard the notation as an approximation of a nuanced performance or regard notated, articulate relations and performance nuances as somewhat independent channels. I often favor the second view and hold that this difference, analogous to the difference between concepts and impulses, obtains even in music that could be notated but isn't. A principal source of my thought is Goodman's analysis of notation in his *Languages of Art,* briefly reviewed in Chapter 5.

1.2. Simple Elements of Reference in Music and Language

In language, the way words mean things, whether by immediate reference as with "rug" or by a more deliriously complicated logic as with "the," is quite different from the way sentences mean things or novels mean things. Any elaborate semiotic system is going to suggest multiple levels of discursive relations. Here I consider only some of the very least parts or aspects of music that might be referential outside of its own syntax. Even at the simplest level, we note there are signs of different kinds.

Sign Classifications

The analysis of meaning in music frequently stumbles on a distinction between possessing a quality and referring to a quality—being red or sad or chaotic versus indicating red or sadness or chaos. Language is quick to construct a distinction. Chapter 7 is intended to advance the view that the distinction is not pat and not always pertinent. The question is a subtle one, and no answer can be held immune from the influence of philosophic taste. For the moment, I am deferring the debate but adopting the position that we won't need this distinction.

Roland Barthes (1967, p. 35) offers a useful concordance table which indicates how several philosophers classify the relations between signs and the objects they represent. All these theories distinguish one way or another between motivated and unmotivated signs. "Unmotivated," if we must make rough cuts, corresponds to "arbitrary" as well as to "conventional." On one side of this cut we have signs which are explicable by natural or physical relations of cause or similarity—footprints are an example—and, on the other side, signs due to social or perhaps personal conventions—like words and red octagons. Some philosophers (and semioticians) find it nonsensical to group both classes under one term. Roger Scruton (1980) offers a pithy defense of that position. In that view, music, which has only a partial and hardly thoroughgoing reliance on conventional references, cannot be at all the same sort of thing as a real language, where the arbitrary but conventional sense of words is foundational. The best support for the opposite point of view is a philosophy which emphasizes the interpretive act rather than the relation of signs to their objects.

My interest in Peirce, as should be evident in Chapter 7, is due more to his development of this second perspective than to his classifications, but like many colleagues, I find his initial classifications of the possible relations between sign and object (part of an extremely complicated scheme) are often productive. In his terminology, signs by arbitrary convention are *symbols*. Signs which have an inherent property that we identify with their objects (or, in other words, understand as resembling their objects) are *icons*. Signs attached to or in some other way controlled or determined by their objects are *indexes*. Peirce thus maintains the distinction between signs motivated or not, but it is subordinated to other considerations. In Peirce's scheme all words are symbols. Words which are pointers like "I" or "this" are indexical symbols, though I am paraphrasing his more subtle analysis and terminology. With the same qualification, words that imitate natural sounds ("meow") are iconic symbols. Unlike words, the simplest signs of music do not all belong to one general category.

Simple Signs in Music

I don't want to propose a full typology, but here are three categories appropriate to our immediate task of language-music comparison:

Topics. Following Monelle (but in his case, too, abridging many subtleties) a topic is a type of musical figure that has developed an association with a unit of thought determined by cultural tradition—moderately slow, minor-mode dotted rhythms with funerals, for example. Adopting this notion, we take advantage of a near consensus in musical semiotic theory. The notion of "topic" from the older form "topos" reentered musicological discourse with Ratner's well-known study *Classic Music* (1980; see also Noske 1977). Ratner's argument that stylistic features were understood in the eighteenth century to carry semantic weight nourished a number of studies, among them, Robert Hatten's *Expressive Meaning in Beethoven* (1994), which accorded the concept a rigorous reconciliation, till then lacking, with general theories of representation. Raymond Monelle's analysis, now available in his *Sense of Music* (2000), shows decisively that Ratner's concept of topic belongs to our time, not to the eighteenth century, and that it is a broadly applicable frame for investigating musical semantics, workable if the research is thorough, for any style of music. Topics like horn calls, sigh motives, various characteristic gallops may be the semantic units of music most similar to words. Even though the "etymology" of a musical topic uncovers an underlying icon, its appeal to convention comes to have more authority than its appeal to resemblance. Therefore, the topic is a symbol. But musical topics don't work like words. They don't fit into a subject-predicate scheme; they don't define each other. They are just a tiny bit like words.

Gesture. We can note that the discussion of the inflected dimensions of music is quick to turn referential. The results are often uninspiring. Herbert Spencer gave us a very mediocre essay, in 1857, relating speed and loudness to excitement along with many other equally uninsightful details. (But his last edition of the essay is of some interest for the rebuttal he appended of Darwin's even worse theory of music; see Spencer 1970.) It is no surprise that he finds music and language essentially identical in exploiting speed and loudness for expression. It is certainly the case that music can imitate speech melody, speech pacing, speech accent. These crude truths are important, but we needn't dwell on them here. They can only help us to understand a complex and subtle art when they are integrated with other modes of interpretation. Talking about "more" or "less" speed and loudness misses the observation, critical to all the chapters in Part III of this book, that expressive inflections are highly particular in shape and don't convey their reference unless they are just right.

A more specific locus of semantic attribution that picks up the theme of physical energy suggested by Spencer is the liaison of motive and bodily gesture. Gesture in music must be theorized as iconic and/or indexical, not symbolic. The idea of a close correspondence between musculoskeletal action and music is ancient and perhaps universal, but a detailed analysis of the relation remains problematic. Part III is introduced by a review of a theory which develops very specific questions about the relation of music to gesture and of gesture to expression. The hypothesis that will be considered there posits a vocabulary of neurological templates as underlying both muscular gesture and its auditory correlates and regards these as functionally linked to emotion expression in movement, music, and speech.

Deryck Cooke's "terms." I asserted above that much of a composition's referential vocabulary is created internally, within a single composition, though less so in improvised styles. Topics, imported to a composition from a common stock, would constitute an important minority by that rule. Cooke, in a widely noticed book, *The Language of Music* (1959), proposed that a further vocabulary of musical "terms" is understood universally within European tonal music. His term "term" suggests a parallel with words, but his theory does not justify the parallel. Table 1.1 is my summary of his "basic terms." His compilation is fascinating because of the examples, mostly of vocal music, from more than five centuries which he submits as evidence of the continuity in meaning of these formulas. The dossier is a tour de force by a musician of vast repertorial knowledge. I am not able to supply persuasive counterexamples, but that may be because he doesn't really have a clear thesis.

First, though he calls these musical skeletons "terms," he acknowledges that some of them combine in ways that render their sonic identities hard to distinguish

Table 1. Summary of "Some Basic Terms" from Deryck Cooke, *The Language of Music* (1959), pp. 113–167.

Figure—By Scale Degrees	In Major	In Minor
1–(2)–3–(4)–5	Outgoing, assertive joy	Sorrow, protest, complaint
5′–1–(2)–3	Similar, less exuberant	Tragic, with courage
5–(4)–3–(2)–1	Passive joy, consolation	Yielding to grief
8–7–6–5	Similar	Similar: passive suffering
Descending chromatic scale		Suffering and weary
5′–3–(2)–1	(Not discussed)	Passionate outburst of pain
1–(2)–3–(2)–1		Brooding, sense of doom
1–(2)–3–2		Slow—pathetic; Fast, repeated—obsessive
5–6–5	(I–IV–I)—joy	Burst of anguish
5–6–5	Other harmonies—various	
1–(2)–(3)–(4)–5–6–5	Innocence, happiness	Grievous anguish

from each other—never the case with real words. Second, the meanings proposed are not clearly distinguished from each other either except that major is euphoric and minor disphoric, upward motion assertive and downward passive. The third confusion arises with the second. It appears that rather than functioning independently, the terms are simply combinations of more basic distinctive features: mode, direction, and final scale degree, the tensions associated with each degree—no news here—having been explained in relation to scale structure. The "terms" seem in the end to be reference positions, somewhat arbitrarily selected, in a continuous field of movement and tension which turns us back toward somatic imagery and to the perceptions underlying the idea that music is tensional and gestural.

Signs of somatic experience are the kinds of elementary signs that I tend to regard as most fundamental and pervasive in music. Mark Johnson (1987) alerts us to somatic imagery that may govern schemes of relation for language, but this is not the same. Schemes of relation are a higher level of semantic content than what I call elementary references. What words refer to most simply has to do first and foremost with the actions and things we see, including other people, even if our way of conceptualizing these objects proceeds, as his work suggests, by identifying physically with them in our imagination. In its elementary references, language is most characteristically a system of articulated sounds correlated with articulated objects (gestalts), while music, a deeply continuous medium, is correlated with the continuities of the kinesphere as felt in proprioception, not as seen. Musical reference, sustained by principles of tension, direction, energy, motion, and inertia, begins with indices, not symbols. The indexical elements are only a point of departure. Elaborated music and language form discourses that convey attitudes and broadly resonant models of experience. When they are considered in their complexity, some of the distance that separates music from language is traversed.

1.3. From Simple Signs to Elaborate Discourse

I don't like to hit a man when he's down, but the following example of what we must not do is hard to pass up. It is the very worst moment in that frequently delightful book with many happy insights which I have just criticized. Cooke's panegyric on the theme of the Gloria in the *Missa solemnis:*

> Beethoven, to give vent to his sense of joy in "the glory of God," might have jumped for joy, or shouted for joy (with his violent temperament, he probably did both many times) and thus communicated his joy to a few people living in Vienna at that time. Being a composer, he felt the need to convert [his emotional energy] into a permanent, stored-up, transportable, and reproducible form of energy—a musical shout for joy. . . . The "score" is simply Beethoven's message down the years: "Pick up a D trumpet and play these notes . . . and everyone within hearing will know how I felt." (1959, pp. 209–10)

Are we to understand, then, that the composer wouldn't have needed to go to all that trouble if only he had a camcorder? There must be something else.

"Discourse" is a word used variously in semiotic, cultural, and linguistic theory. I adopt the word in a special sense to indicate those elaborated signs that we can understand as representations of active thought, signs of thinking. I don't merely mean signs that require lots of thinking to be invented, as a truck or a wristwatch does. I mean signs that evoke for us an image of mentality in its vacillations and unpredictable but rarely random unfoldings. The most radical and most interesting turn in composition in the last half century made it clear that not all music, old or new, aims to do this, but my initial motivation to explore musical semiotics came out of a tradition that did, and my personal interest has always been to understand how music can appear to think out loud.

Non-conformal Syntactic and Semantic Structures

Louis Hjelmslev (1943) proposed that a true semiotic system must have structures of expression—for our purposes let us say sound structures—that are independent of their structures of *import,* his term for meaning. He found this criterion satisfied—Surprise! Surprise!—only in language. (Hjelmslev was a linguist.) An interesting test, but is there not some question begging here?

Let us note first exactly how language passes the test. He illustrates non-conformality in this manner: /d/ + /aw/ + /g/ means [domestic] + [canine]. The sound has three elements, and they, on their own, have nothing at all do with the two elements of the meaning.

Hjelmslev knows well that the full independence of sound structure from meaning structure is characteristic of *only one stratum* of language, the *morpheme,* the smallest meaningful unit. Morphemes are sometimes words, sometimes less. "Deformation" has three morphemes, "de-" [with negative force] "-form-" [order, etc.] "-ation" [process as substantive]. The import of the combination is not nonconformal; it is systematically determined by the parts and their relations. The same holds for sentences. Meanings of sentences are not related arbitrarily to words but derive formally from the imports of words plus rules of grammar. Only the smallest referential units show non-conformality.

It is true, as Hjelmslev suggests, that the smallest referential signs in music are not predominantly arbitrary. Topics emerge from historical use. Timbres resemble or contrast qualities of the human voice. Gestures in music, though we don't yet have a specific theory on the table here, are in some way determined by a relation with the body. However, in music the meanings of longer, more complex elaborations are not so readily explained by routine rules of combination as are the meanings of sentences. The simple logic that connects sound and sense at the small level does not account in a predictable manner for the sound-to-sense relations of extended passages and complete pieces. I do not say that the relation becomes arbitrary in extended music, but it becomes at least unidirectional. We can show that certain interpretations are plausible, but we cannot suggest or even imagine a scheme that would output the music if its import or effect were specified as the sole input. Here, in diagrammatic form, is the ratio as I see it:

	Shortest elements	Extended units
Language	arbitrary	rule governed
Music	rule governed	unique, irreducible*

*Not arbitrary but not rule governed.

Complexity in music takes a role complementary to arbitrariness in language and echoes the feature so important to Hjelmslev even if it is not quite the same.

Models of Semantic Elaboration

Music elaborates meaning in limitlessly varied ways. Recent writings in musical semiotics offer us a bouquet of ideas how to get at it. Hatten (1994) pursues an aspect of discourse structure in music via the concept of *troping*, where one reference colors another, and has more recently proposed a hierarchical, developmental conception of gesture (2004). Naomi Cumming (2000), expanding a figure Edward Cone brought to music, explored the emergence of the *persona* in music. In a series of rigorously methodical papers (all of them, I believe, in French) Marta Grabocz has adopted in music the semiological models of Greimas for *narrative*, and narrative, as a model of musical discourse, is now also well known in English language musicology. Eero Tarasti (1994), also drawing on Greimasian doctrine, has borrowed his concepts of *actantiation* and *modality*.[1] Music is very dif-

---

1. For a discussion of Grabocz's work and a partial bibliography, see Lidov (1998). Tarasti's work is discussed in the same review essay.

ferent from language in its devices and strategies of discourse—I can hardly think of any way to propose an orderly comparison in such a heterogeneous territory— but the capacity of each to represent thinking suggests a unity among them. My forays into the conceptualization of discourse are one of the chief themes of this volume, especially in Chapters 4 and 8–14. There is no need for me to anticipate here the schemas essayed in these chapters, and I hope they will not be seen as conforming to one model. One subtheme often invoked is that music develops a homology between formal constraints on musical expressivity and social constraints on impulsive behavior.

1.4. Social Functions of Music and Language

Context and function cannot *explain* musical communication. For instance, I know what the words say, but what does the *tune* add? I know we are burning the goat so the god will relieve us of pestilence, but why must I sing exactly *these* notes? Would you have any difficulty thinking up a plot that would need slow music during the car chase? The music, whatever the function and context, makes a contribution of its own and demands musicological analysis that neither sociology nor anthropology can shortcut. The relations we have reviewed so far have some points of intersection with social semiotics. These remarks by way of a coda touch on a major subject that my book largely neglects.

Self-representation in Music and Language
as an Element of Ideology

In representing ourselves and our communities, music participates in ideology. Insofar as we start out from representations of felt somatic states, we can note that music has a solipsistic bias, be it the solipsism of first person singular or plural. Music abounds in idealized images of sociality (necessarily idealized because solipsistic). The range is enormous—camaraderie in Dixieland, innocuous anarchy in Cage and Cowell, fraternal triumph in Beethoven, intimate friendship in Schumann, congregational devotion in Bach's great passions, and so on. We have here a big difference from language, which objectifies ideology as a contest. We *see* others and objectify them, but in proprioception any "other" belongs to an undifferentiated environment, an exterior. This principle holds even in genres which promote differentiation of character. In a sonata we don't hear the tonic theme as first person and the dominant theme as third person. Both invite a participatory identification. The "other" here is, at least initially, another side of the self. Music has power to mobilize a community in promoting its identity or arousing its will to action, a power that may surpass language in this respect (we feel mobilization in our muscles) but fewer resources to identify an *other*. I think this difference underlies the instability of ideological interpretations of music. Yet I set no limitations on elaborated music; musical discourse is often complicated enough and precise enough to prompt a very nuanced interpretation of its modeling which contradicts or bypasses the bias toward solipsism. I think the very unalike musics studied in Chapters 11 and 13 reward our attention in this perspective.

Music as an Artistic Category

Art, where we find the idea used, is a socially constructed category. In my own social context (speaking roughly, advanced industrial society) art is cordoned off. We leave a wide gap between the genuine theater of pronouncements from the Federal Reserve Board and concert life. What I see from my personal position is a world of art that is both glorious and dysfunctional, debased by commerce or withdrawing from the public because it cannot possibly satisfy its weighty mandate to compensate for the alienation of industrial work, the impersonal quality of economic transactions, and the disruption of communities. This is the social context of absolute music and, if we may propose another category, absolute entertainment. We need the refuge of music that is wrapped up in itself, in part because we can offer adult music so little socially effective space.

It is symptomatic of our social functions for music that we are able and often inclined to obscure or cancel out its enormous potentials for reference in favor of the unconstrained play of its syntactic relations and the invention of sensual delights. The historical task of musical semiotics in recent decades was to revitalize the discussion of musical representation. We have deferred our appreciation of the other side of the coin. (It is deferred in this book until Part V.) The erasure of reference is really as pertinent to semiotics as its construction. Semiotics must distinguish that moment, the phenomenon of erasure or abstraction in music, to avoid the fallacy that music as a medium is non-referential. Within a particular social situation, we separate art from *real* (!) life, and we are forced therefore to widen the gulf between music, as abstract, and language, as practical. To generalize this difference beyond its local situation might be outrageous.

1.5. The Musicology of Language

Music and speech are not isolated from each other psychologically or socially. The musical part of speech fades into speech-song, and even string quartets have verbal discourse contexts. I need give no evidence. An hour of random browsing in ethnomusicology or cultural theory or the "new musicology" will uncover the scent. This simple fact should not discourage the search for contrasting principles, the whole exercise we have undertaken to this point, but it ought to ward off any search for purity in one medium or the other. Brains work by electricity!— They are wet!—How can thought in one medium be insulated from the others?

In 1963, when it was not yet unfashionable to speak of a "linguistics of musicology," George List, writing with too much sophistication for any such slogan, published "The Boundaries of Speech and Song," abundantly illustrating intermediate phenomena. Writing with data from the field (not from the easy armchair of semiotics, as I do) he illustrated at least three partially independent, continuous variables that situate vocal expressions in various cultures as closer to the side of speech in some respect or closer to the side of song: stability of pitch, expansion or contraction of intonations (inflections), and the development of scalar structure.

We must distinguish, therefore, between demonstrably separate functions within aural semiosis and the forms and activities—the signs—which embody those functions. Magnetic resonance imaging leaves us in no doubt that words light up one side of the brain more brightly and melodies the other, but we cannot conclude from those data that melodies and sentences are mutually isolated phenomena. To claim today that musicology should encompass linguistics rather than the reverse can only be a literary ploy. Two wrongs don't make a right. But without such a full-scale, Derridean inversion of categories, let us note that the music of language has not yet been given its full due in either musical or linguistic theory, and that to that extent Rousseau's point still merits our notice. There is a kind of traumatic aphasia in which patients cannot find the words they want but they remember the word rhythms. The musical aspect of speech is truly of its essence, whether manifested in an expressive freedom of vocal inflection or revealed by absence in the flat tones of authority or obedience; writing almost always conveys a tone of voice. We don't know yet, socially or genetically, how much language and music have to do with each other. Some of the things we don't understand about music and some of the things we don't understand about language may well be the same.

Part One: *Structuralist Perspectives*

Structuralism has a wide sense and a narrow sense. In the wide sense, musical scholarship has a celebrated history of structuralism. Everything we do or learn under the heading of "music theory" is part of it. In the narrow sense, structuralism is a movement in scholarship inspired by work at the turn of the last century. For this movement, the linguistics of Saussure is particularly emblematic. Fredric Jameson, in *The Prison House of Language,* includes Marx and Freud and Durkheim as founding figures. The structuralist movement bracketed questions of value, history, psychology, and context to postulate axiomatic schemes of elements and logical relations as the basis of understanding the forms of culture. The prominence of Saussure in defining the trend may have been due in part to accident. The key work, his *Course in General Linguistics* (1915), is a posthumous compilation of notes by his students, and it is very brief. Anyone interested can read it quickly, and the influential ideas (but not all the good ideas!) are in the first hundred pages. Here we find the pivotal proposition that language must be studied as an autonomous social system, *langue,* that is evidenced by individual utterances, *parole* or "speech," of which the essentially linguistic character can only be demonstrated by reference to the autonomous system. The structuralism which appeared in musicology in the sixties, with something of the starch and sheen and unrealistic promise that mark a novelty, was inspired by Saussure's linguistics and then, a bit later, by Chomsky's formal and mathematical linguistics. In this musicological vogue, Babbitt's structuralism (structuralism in the large sense of the term) was bypassed, Schenker's structuralism (large sense again) was filtered. The novelty was not to compare music to language, an ancient idea, but, more narrowly, to import into musicology the philosophical and methodological innovations of twentieth-century linguistics. (Indeed, enthusiasm for this program tended to obscure the criticism of language as a metaphor for music which was implicit in nineteenth-century organicism.)

Even in its widest sense, structuralism is not a panacea nor can it be exhausted. It is simply the aspect of musical knowledge that develops when we discover new models of structure that are relevant to perception or to understanding. The discovery of a new model of structure does not make older ones obsolete and does not render their unsolved problems irrelevant. Having mastered something of Schenkerian reductive analysis, it still remains informative to study how individual harmonies are effectual through their relations of sonority and tonal suggestion. Insights in motivic analysis do not substitute for other ways of appreciating embellishment. I recite these truisms to make the very same claim about structuralism. The pendulum of fashion swings quickly, but the theoretical insights that go in and out of fashion mature on a slower timescale. The next three chapters assume the Saussurian conception of articulation that regards the stream of music as a chain of discrete parts. Though I have already flagged this premise for criticism in the previous chapter, I defer reservations until Part II. We may advantageously attend first to the unfoldings that enrich and diversify segmentation within this model.

Three fundamentally different (but interacting) processes of perception contribute to our sense of music as a chain of segments: *gestalt perception,* which tends to generate a hierarchy of groups; *category formation* (taxonomy), which tends to resolve music's parts into vocabularies of types and to resolve hierarchy into differentiated strata; and *grammatical interpretation,* which tends to parse music by recognizing previously known forms and codes. Each of these processes encounters ambiguities of its own, and each may contradict or reinforce the others. As music is an art, its possibilities of ambiguation are of its essence. Structuralism celebrates ambiguity.

Segmentation

In my view, the fundamental phenomena of segmentation in music are much more complex than any currently popular theory acknowledges. The summary of the previous paragraph follows the scheme of my 1980 monograph for the Toronto Semiotic Circle. I amplify that summary a bit further here to emphasize that very different kinds of logic contribute to musical articulation. Gestalt perception is the primitive and innate cognitive capability that Köhler and Wertheimer, the founding researchers of experimental gestalt perceptual psychology, studied primarily in vision. (Wertheimer does comment in passing on music.) Mursell's *Psychology of Music* (1937) proposes gestalt rules of grouping for small groups of notes. Tenney's *Meta+Hodos* (1964) formalizes gestalt analysis to model an entire composition as nested "temporal gestalts" that form a hierarchy or "holarchy," the term he prefers as not attributing an implication of greater value to a whole than to its parts. Tenney's inspiration for his research was the music of Charles Ives, music which is recalcitrant to other segmental models because it eschews literal repetition and conventional phrasing formulae. (Gestalt music theory has a sequel in current musical research on auditory streaming.)

A further stage of analysis beyond gestalt segmentation is required either to identify categories of segments as belonging to one type or to assign independent segments (segments neither of which includes the other) to the same hierarchical stratum. A segmentation which does establish these additional relations is described in the music theory of Nicolas Ruwet. Ruwet, a professional linguist, was not the first to notice that repetition in music is instrumental in establishing the vocabulary of a composition, but he was the first to situate this analogy precisely in its relation to linguistics and thus to lay out the framework for the mode of research which Jean-Jacques Nattiez, whose work I review in Chapter 5, developed as "distributional taxonomy." Distributional taxonomy establishes a segmental hierarchy by noting repetitions in music at different strata of durations, that is, repetitions and repetitions within repetitions. Categorization and grouping can also contradict each other. (For an example, see Figure 2.5 in the next chapter.)

Neither musical gestalt analysis nor distributional taxonomy deals with the segmentation of period, phrase, and motive as determined by a cultural tradition that codes signals such as formulaic cadences, the pre-cadential hemiola, the mora, or in certain styles of jazz, the major seventh as a nearly obligatory final sonority. Normally the relations between these signals and gestalt factors are cooperative, but contradictions are a source of liveliness. When we use culturally formed intuitions to distinguish between a half phrase and a full phrase, a rich complex of criteria are evoked which neither gestalt analysis nor distributional taxonomy can supply.

Chapter 2, on repetition, is concerned both with syntactically foundational repetition, what I call "formative repetition," the repetition that contributes to a composition's taxonomy, as well as with repetition that exceeds the needs of syntactical clarity and takes on other aesthetic functions. A striking deficiency of this 1978 essay, which I certainly do not hope to fully remedy at this late date, is its failure to consider Leonard Meyer's masterful development of his concept of "conformant relations" in *Explaining Music* (published five years earlier, 1973), especially in his third chapter. His balanced, amply illustrated, and richly elaborated discussion subsumes many of my observations. The reader can decide whether I still add something to our understanding of repetition in music, but I will take advantage of the parallel to address another issue. While Meyer is a sufficiently systematic theorist, I think it will be apparent that my shorter sketch is more radical than his in its pursuit of axioms. My posture here is one that the enthusiasm of structuralism readily encouraged, and it leads easily enough to the excessively schematic accounts that post-structuralism is quick to condemn (see, e.g., Chapter 1 of Monelle 2000). I am not entirely chastened. I acknowledge that structuralism encourages a tendency to buy clarity at the price of adequacy, but we will always need that gambit. Close readings and thick descriptions must either rely on a background of more formalistic schemas or descend toward vagueness. Rich readings and schematic readings constitute a dialectic to which I see no alternative. Meyer's strength is that he often supplies both sides of this dialectic. Yet Meyer's most elegant argument in the chapter cited above is perhaps his critique of Reti's more exaggerated formalism, and there Reti's radical viewpoint is the necessary foil for Meyer's more nuanced response.

When Meyer then proceeds in that book to contrast conformant relations with hierarchic relations, he has nearly put into play the schema I develop in my third chapter. I return to his writings shortly.

Grammar and Design

Chapter 3 presents a Beethoven analysis. I had a long struggle figuring out what terminology to use for the idea that is central to this chapter and to my theory of syntactic elaboration in general semiotics. The idea is that parallel but independent principles of organization (sometimes in coordination and sometimes in opposition) are established interior to one work and as a feature of a wider style to which that work belongs. What I called "design" in this essay (in opposition to "grammar") became "pattern" in *Elements of Semiotics*. The intended sense of these two terms is absolutely identical, but I couldn't transpose my first term, "design," into a book that dealt equally with music and visual art without inviting considerable confusion. Now, when I tried changing "design" to "pattern" in Chapter 3, it walked cross-legged. For someone with my pretensions to announce *general* principles for *comparative* semiotics, it was most disconcerting not to have portable terminology! I don't like neologisms unless they have good roots. My present solution has been to leave "design" in Chapter 3 but to sprinkle the argument with an additional pair of opposed terms, *idiolect(al)* and *dialect(al)*.

A dialect is the language spoken by people across a geographical region. We typically say "dialect of" emphasizing a larger whole of which the dialect is a part, dialect of English, for example, but also, and do please note, "French and Italian are Romance dialects." Dialect, then, is simply a shared language. The same word may conventionally refer to a subdivision of a wider language (as in Meyer's usage in *Style and Music,* where dialect is a subset of style), or as here in my chapter, it may refer to the larger class which is subdivided (here, by idiolects). Idiolect is, conventionally, the language of one person, and my usage, not exactly that one but close, makes it the language of one work. The purpose of my excursion into autobiography was to alert the reader that I mean "design," "idiolect," and, elsewhere but not here, "pattern" as synonyms. Do not look for a subtle distinction. The redundancy is intended simply to allow the one idea to commute between musicology and the disciplines of other media.

Two authors I know of have come very close to my conception of grammar and design (dialect and idiolect)—close enough that specifying our differences might seem annoying. Paul Garvin (1981), whose interests focused on literature and ballet, wrote of the "structure of the language" as against "structure of the work," and Ruwet, especially in his analyses of poetry, less directly in his musicology, spoke of "deep structure" and "surface structure," terms which point out his debt to Chomsky. Leonard Meyer's distinction between *strategy* and *goal* does *not* provide a parallel, as both concern deployment of what I call grammar. Once again, we can find comparable categories in Meyer's theories, with a signal difference. Meyer defines "strategy" as a particular deployment of the possibilities chosen from those a style affords (1989, p. 20). Though the compass of "style" may be wider than what I call "grammar," the two are close enough that there is little distortion of the idea if I paraphrase his definition of strategy as a particular deployment of grammar. To reach further for a concordance of terminology, what I call "design" or "idiolect" might be characterized as a particular deployment of conformant and nonconformant relations: the temporal distribution of similarities (especially repetitions) and contrasts, a realm of relations that I think Meyer approaches but does not quite pin down as "interopus structure" and "interopus style" (pp. 24–30). The important difference between his approach and mine is that I am asserting a more aggressive distinction than he does between the logical mechanisms (and by implication, cognitive mechanisms) available at the level of the single work and at the level of the shared language, and it is in this respect that I think my mode of analysis is closer to Garvin and Ruwet than to his. The specific difference is that design proceeds from concrete instances of its elements while grammar appeals to socially established abstractions. I am trying to be emphatically careful about this matter simply because some of my best friends have already presented me with misunderstandings of my notions of grammar and design. I do not assert that design is more original, more personal, or more expressive than grammar, though it may be idiosyncratic and asocial. My argument, one of the principal lines of argument in *Elements of Semiotics*, is that because grammar and design are essentially independent principles of organization, their interplay accounts for much of the freedom and variety of elaborated texts, or here, works of music. The motivating quest behind my enterprise is not to explain coherence so much as to account for the greater degree of structural freedom and variation that artworks exhibit in comparison with everyday speech.

The way I construe the matter doubles up Saussure's opposition of *paradigm* and *syntagm*. The paradigm is a group in vocabulary or a category formed by equivalence. The syntagm is a combination of elements, such as words, chosen from different paradigms as in, for example, "the army <noun paradigm> retreats <verb paradigm>." My model of *double structure*, illustrated in this Beethoven study, supposes that the two-dimensional diagram of paradigms and syntagms is replicated on two planes. It occurs both on the plane of a single composition's *idiolect* and once more, with a different content, on the plane of its *dialect*. The idiolect is determined by repetition and variation within one composition and is potentially unique to that composition; in the idiolect, themes and motives are defined by this structure. The dialect (tonal harmony, meter, and phrase structure) needs no such elementary exposition: we have learned it in advance, we deduce it from familiar features. The logical difference is that grammar refers to socially established abstractions, while design proceeds from the concrete instance.

We must note that the opposition of idiolect and dialect is old news for music theory insofar as we already appreciate the intersection of motives with harmony. Part of my original motivation in formulating the matter in the way I did was to offer scholars in other fields the opportunity to borrow our wares. But there are also advantages to the musicologist in thinking through this familiar opposition from a more general and external perspective.

Dialect and idiolect may reinforce each other or may resist each other. A tiny case of contradiction is noted in Chapter 2 in a minuet of Bach's. In *Elements* I emphasize the cultural force of the opposition of dialect and idiolect, a theme which reappears in this book in Chapters 3 and 10. The cultural affiliations of the two planes arise from the social dimension of dialect and the potentially asocial or self-sufficient character of idiolect.

Mediations

Chapter 3 introduces a notion of *mediation* that is further elaborated in Chapter 4. The concept of mediation is crucial to the anthropological structuralism of Lévi-Strauss, whose appropriation of Saussurian linguistics was deeply influenced by the poetic structuralism of Roman Jakobson. When Lévi-Strauss elaborates the Saussurian ideas that nature is continuous and that culture advances by dividing nature into discrete units, I think he speaks for a consensus which dominated semiotic structuralism for at least a decade, though his angle is highly personal. The most eye-catching characteristic of Saussure's logic is its dependence on binary oppositions, proliferated in the *Course on General Linguistics* with ingenuity and deployed with flourish. Lévi-Strauss analyzes the elements of myths categorically by binary oppositions but with special attention to those elements that refuse easy accommodation. Ambiguous motifs, the mediating elements with partial allegiance to both of two polar categories, arise in his interpretation as solutions to problems or denouements in myths. Lévi-Strauss adds a further dimension. Mediation, besides occurring as a syntactic feature that resolves opposition, also appears as a semantic content. When the boundaries between categories are breached in a myth, he finds the myth to be representing a movement from the articulations of culture to the continuity of nature. I believe this schema is deeply revealing, as much when serving as an image of music as when it is taken as an image of literature. When we trace the working of mediation carefully, we cover some of the ground that Greimas (1984) proposed to explain in his narrative theory by his squares of contradiction. Greimas's method seems to me to dictate a much more complicated, rigid, and arbitrary artifice than my simple borrowing from Lévi-Strauss.

The form of mediation observed in the Beethoven Allegretto includes a prefiguration, in the "interlude" of that movement, of the resolutions later achieved by the principal materials themselves. The first example in the following chapter shows the same pattern in miniature. This Debussy study accepts a conception of Debussy's form suggested by the writings of Ruwet and Nattiez but also responds to a lacuna in their work through its consideration of phrase structure. I republish here an abbreviated version of the essay which was included in my collection *On the Musical Phrase* (Lidov 1975b), where the analysis of phrase structure is spelled out in more detail. We don't think of theory, especially structural theory, as preceding composition in Debussy's music, but if it ever did, then this prelude, *Voiles,* might be the candidate instance—it is almost too neat for a demonstration.

The second example, a study of mediation in a folk-song arrangement, is extracted from a paper I wrote with the musicologist Gaynor Jones in 1980 (but which we did not publish). Her contribution to the project provided, among other things, a history of the concept of *poeticity,* as an important topic of nineteenth-century aesthetics. This analysis concerns text-music relations and cites Jakobson's definition of *poeticity.* Jakobson, rejecting both the value-laden terms of that discourse and its reliance on paraphrase, recasts poeticity as a strictly structural feature which occurs when "the axis of choice" (Saussure's *paradigm*) is imposed on the "axis of selection" (or syntagm). Jakobson told me once that he knew nothing about music, but we need look no further for an example than modal mixture. According to our common practice dialect we *select* a minor or major key and other choices follow, but if we write I–iv–V–I, and thus *combine* the minor subdominant with the major tonic, the typically poetic inflection instances Jakobson's principle.

I had studied Liszt's *Tasso,* the final example in the mediation chapter, in preparation to write an article (1982) that reviewed Eero Tarasti's *Myth and Music* (1979). Tarasti's was the first book of semiotic affiliation to alert us that a serious semiotics of music could not be merely structuralist. Tarasti notes that Tasso, though he was a historical personage, functions for Liszt as a mythical figure. My analysis of this symphonic poem is very different from Tarasti's, but I am indebted to him for taking into account at face value what Liszt himself said about tone poems. If Liszt's voluminous writing is tainted either by self-promotion (Who is innocent?) or by ghost-writing, that is no excuse for ignoring the carefully considered ideas and judgments they convey. Liszt gave serious attention to the notion of the epic, a literary vehicle of myth. Thus, though it was not Tarasti's approach, it seemed to me fitting to pursue a technique from Lévi-Strauss's mythological analyses in this context. I do not think Liszt's method of thematic transformation is merely variation under another name. In this case, I describe the whole form as mediating dialectal and idiolectal structures, among other polarities. (When I went back to my review with the intention of extracting this analysis, I was dismayed to read only "Lidov, in prep." The analysis here, the fruit of a paleographic exercise, is reconstructed from notes for a lecture at the University of Montreal two decades ago.)

2 Structure and Function in Musical Repetition

We rarely regard repetition as an independent topic in musical studies. When you repeat, you have to repeat something; it seems unnatural to separate the repetition from the "something." However, we do utilize other, equally dubious divorces in music pedagogy. We even teach harmony separately from rhythm! As a laboratory exercise, I will undertake to deal with repetition independently here. Furthermore, like the harmony teacher who investigates chords by roots without considering all the difficult situations chords end up in, sometimes obscuring their identities, I will put aside much complication by ignoring many of the ambiguities which creep into my experiment at the threshold between repetition and variation and at a few other leaky boundaries. This chapter will suggest some specific correlations of types of repetition *structures* with a number of repetition *functions*. Although the conclusions will not be surprising in themselves, I think the process of extracting them (via these simplifications) turns to be more informative than one might expect.

2.1. General Observations

Before embarking on a technical classification, I summarize some general observations on repetition drawing in part on the writings of others. My purpose here is not to recapitulate the existing literature on repetition—not extensive, but some of it excellent—but rather to indicate the scope and variety of musical phenomena which a systematic theory might help us to take into account more thoroughly.

Pervasiveness of Repetition

Although the density of repetition in music varies with style and aesthetic orientation and from work to work, the sheer quantity of repetition in music is a fundamental and striking fact. Carlos Chavez dealt with this aspect of repetition in the third and fourth of his Norton Lectures (1961). He points out the intensity of repetition in certain compositions and deals with its effects on pleasure and interest. He also illustrates the compositional craft of repeating with artistry. We

This chapter was published under the same title in the *Journal of the Canadian Association of University Schools of Music* 8, no. 1 (1979).

need not be surprised that a composer has dealt so ably here with a theme that theorists are wont to neglect. Although all artistic and communicative media have aspects of repetition, I don't think any other, with the possible exception of dance, so regularly tolerates—or should we say requires—the degree of literal repetition which is normal in music.

Concreteness of Repetition

Most other formal means such as systems of harmony, tonality, meter, or phrase structure are abstract generalizations. Every work of music realizes them in a slightly different fashion. Although biological and acoustical conditions may limit and direct our musical systems, harmony and tonality as we know them, and meter too, are social facts which depend on the conventions of music agreed upon consciously or unconsciously by a musical community. Repetition, on the contrary, is a relatively concrete fact. The perception of an exact or close repetition does not seem to depend so strongly on a particular stylistic system in which it functions.

If we include variation as a kind of repetition, we must acknowledge immediately that variation clouds this distinction between abstract and concrete domains of form. Variation always includes an element of repetition, but, if the variation is sophisticated, its repeated aspect may be perceptible only to the listener who already knows its style. On the other hand, when variation is simple, an "outsider" can follow it, and furthermore, the equivalences asserted to this outsider by the variation will serve to introduce other, more abstract principles. Phrases which are repeated first with a dominant and then with a tonic ending, for example, provide the most natural expositions of the tonic-dominant opposition as an abstract principle.

The concreteness of repetition, if limited by the more sophisticated facts of variation, is also put in doubt by the less sophisticated facts of raw acoustical data. We know that the musical repetitions we call identical may actually presuppose a great deal of culturally determined listening and prior systematization of materials. For example, in listening to a string quartet we will discount certain vagaries of intonation as mistakes, if we notice them at all. Nevertheless, when we are dealing with conscious musical experience, repetition is one of the first and most solid elements of that experience, and we are still entitled to recognize repetition as holding a privileged status among formal devices on the basis of its at least relative if not absolute concreteness.

Segmental Hierarchy of Repetitions

Jean-Jacques Nattiez of the University of Montréal has exploited the distinction between repetition as concrete and other devices as abstract in developing the *distributional taxonomy* of music first proposed in 1966 by the French musicologist Nicolas Ruwet (1972). In such a taxonomy, the analysis of music begins with the segmentation of a given text into a hierarchy of longer and shorter units based entirely on a mechanical description of repetitions and partial repetitions in a selected musical text. The analysis yields both *categories* of like segments and a *hierarchy* of their combinations. Given the relative style and cultural independence of repetition analysis, it is no accident that Ruwet's method was inspired by the work of an ethnomusicologist, Gilbert Rouget, and that Ruwet's initial ideas found their richest application outside of standard classical literature. Ruwet had at first presumed that all other theoretical relationships could be reconstructed on a more scientific basis by examining the resulting parts and their orders of combination resulting from repetition analysis. Instead, as he later acknowledged (1975), it appears that distributional analysis based on repetition, although it is extremely valuable in its own right, does not recapture the abstract ideas which depend on cultural traditions.

Definitional Effect of Repetition

Whatever is repeated in a piece of music is a specific unit or, as we sometimes say, "idea" of the music. Other forms of analysis demonstrate the conformity of music. Repetition analysis vouchsafes the uniqueness of each musical composition. We all encounter the embarrassment of harmonic reductions which, in accounting for tonality, show mainly how one piece is like another. Repetition always enters the analysis (sometimes by a back door) when we want to show how one piece differs from another. Schenker's *Harmony* begins with an excellent discussion of repetition, and it develops the similar point that the association of music with external idea depends on music imitating itself (Schenker 1954, pp. 419).

Repetition as a Means of Stylistic Development

Since repetition can be perceived in an unfamiliar style, innovations which lack the support of an established musical language can appeal to repetition to clarify their vocabulary and procedures. The evidence in twentieth-century music ranges from the characteristic two-bar repetitions of Debussy's style to the camouflaged but pervasive repetitions of the tone row.

The same logic applies to the enlargement of musical language within one piece, a fact which should play a greater role in theory courses and especially in the study of Baroque polyphony. Figure 2.1A quotes a few measures from the Minuet of J. S. Bach's B-minor French Suite to show how an accented upper neighbor dissonance is set up through repetition of an initially consonant figure. There is a myth, perpetuated by harmony and counterpoint texts, that the expressive Baroque dissonance structures such as delayed resolutions and accented neighbors are simply new licenses freely added like a musical paprika to the dissonances of the older, strict style. This point of view may be justified in relation to some passages which aim at improvisatory or declamatory effects, but it ignores a crucial principle. The dissonance structures of strict style are those which, for acoustical and psychologi-

Figure 2.1A. Bach, Minuet from the French Suite in B Minor.

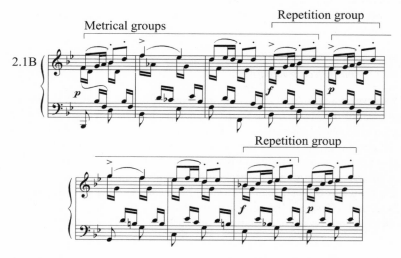

Figure 2.1B. Repetition across a segmental boundary (Schumann, Op. 20).

cal reasons, succeed in subordinating dissonance to consonance on an intervallic level. The additional dissonances of so-called free style are rationalized on other levels by their subordination to chord prolongations, to the tonic-dominant polarity, and/or, in countless instances, to repetition. Unfortunately—Figure 2.1A not withstanding—the contribution of repetition to harmony and counterpoint cannot be learned through the tiny excerpts to which textbooks accustom us. One must study whole movements or at least large sections.

Repetition as an Affective Element

All of the principles which have been mentioned above concern the syntactic role of repetition: its contribution to segmentation and hierarchy, the identification of "ideas," and the clarification of style. As we well know, the effects of repetition are not limited to its grammatical contributions. Repetition can itself be a vehicle of drama, humor, and poetic reflection. Repetition can create a hypnotic continuity which is opposite in its effect to segmentation. Meyer has noted that repetition increases tension, but that when sufficiently prolonged, the tension yields to saturation, which has its own expressive values (1956, pp. 136, 152). Because of the fact that repetitions mark off equal durations in time, abundant repetitions enhance the sensory quality of rhythmic experience, and interesting repetitions enhance rhythmic consciousness. On the other hand, repetition which is camouflaged, as in music which follows the preferences expressed in theories like Schoenberg's or Tinctoris's (the eighth of his rules of counterpoint), assists in leading the rhythmic experience into a more intellectualized domain.

2.2. A Sign-Theoretic View of Repetition

A study of repetition brings us to a junction where questions of musical structure meet questions of value and content. Is there a framework in which we can account for these phenomena in their integrity? The problem of relating communicated content to communicative structure is the central problem of semiotics, the formal and generalized study of signs and symbolic relations. Some of the concepts worked out in these studies apply very well to the specifically musical phenomena of musical repetition.

A considerable part (not necessarily the most fruitful part) of semiotics is concerned with classifying signs into types. Some chapters of this book import a coherent system, but here I will mix and match. Ideas on which I draw include the notion of a "self-referential sign," like a too-loud necktie, which figures in the semiotic theories of art of the Prague School;[1] the "formator," a term by which Charles Morris (1938) designated syntactic signs, like word order, which control the interpretation of other signs; and Charles Peirce's term "index" for a sign that locates or points, like an arrow, for a visual example, or the word "this," for a verbal example.

These three categories are neither mutually exclusive not exhaustive in relation to sign typology, but they can serve to interpret three classes of musical repetition defined according to their domains of reference: *formative repetition,* which interprets what is repeated; *focal repetition,* which is a self-referential type that focuses attention on the fact of repetition, per se; and *textural repetition,* an index which points away from the repeated material to other musical signs while, at the same time, influencing their quality. These types of referential functions—whether they occur pure or mixed—correlate in a dependable and specific way with structural factors: the number of repetitions, whether they are immediate or delayed, and, in some cases, their position. The same structural-functional categories apply in general to both long and short repetitions, although I feel some caution in applying them to single notes or to the largest sections of long pieces.

---

1. Particularly in the writings of Jan Mukařovský. See Matejka and Titunik (1976).

2.3. Formative Repetition

Formative repetition, as repetition which refers or directs attention to and marks the material repeated, is the kind of repetition which fulfills the various syntactic functions outlined so far, those of defining the units of a musical work and establishing their position in a hierarchy of longer and shorter segments. Secondarily, when varied, formative repetition establishes equivalences and oppositions between different features of the material so that it serves to identify significant differences as well as concrete units.

The normal structures for this type are a single, immediate repetition or single and multiple delayed repetitions, but we must exclude those immediate repetitions which cross segmental boundaries. Formative repetition is conventional and logical and does not attract attention. The exclusion of repetitions which cross segmental boundaries follows this principle because such repetitions are extremely striking. In Figure 2.1B there is a higher-level (four-measure unit) boundary crossing the one-measure repetition; m. 4 = m. 5.

I do not feel at all as sure of the conditions which should constrain delayed formative repetitions as I do of those for immediate repetitions. One might hold that in the same passage the delayed repetition, m. 1 = m. 4, attracts nearly as much attention as that immediate one, m. 4 = m. 5. It is an unconventional repetition. The case of immediate repetition is much more secure because it does not depend on our interpretation of convention. It can be deduced from more basic principles: A single immediate repetition is the minimum sufficient and the maximum necessary to define a musical segment. When a segment is presented twice in immediate succession, the two units will tend to form a larger group, according to the laws of gestalt perception, because they are both similar and adjacent. The defining function of formative repetition is that the material but not the repetition, per se, attracts attention. When the repetition crosses a larger segmental boundary, there is a distracting conflict between the gestalt tendencies referred to above and the hierarchical structure of the larger segments. If the repetition is hierarchically conformal, its necessity and sufficiency neutralize its interest. Interest passes to the material.

Neutralization of interest is attested by another circumstance. The absence of formative repetition has a more striking effect than its presence. Schenker's discussion, referred to above, cites several illuminating examples which prove that non-repetition is a special communicative device.

The following forms of repetition, not hard to find in music, illustrate repetitions that exceed the requirements of clear syntax:

i.   *aabcc* or *aaba* or *aabaa*
ii. *aabbcc* or *aabba* or *aabbaa*.

Since *b* is defined in (i) by the repetitions of *a* or *c*, the second repetition of *b* in (ii) is syntactically redundant. These excess duplications occupy a middle ground between the categories we study later, *focal* and *textural* repetition. As numerous *rondeaux,* waltz cycles, and song forms bear out, they contribute to an intellectually relaxed and rhythmically entrancing style, not quite attention grabbing in themselves, not quite hypnotic. But note that the examples I characterize in this way do not include any threefold or still more numerous immediate repetitions.

Transparency and Bartha's Quaternary Stanza Structure

Figure 2.2 diagrams formative repetition from "that miracle [of repetition] which still holds the world in amazement" (Chavez 1961, p. 61). I introduce this diagram to expose a further function of formative repetition, which, despite its familiarity to us, has no name in general currency. The unit lengths in these sixteen bars are 4, 4, 2, 2, 4 and comprise a very conventional pattern which Bartha (1971) calls *Quaternary Stanza Structure* (QSS). As the name suggests, Bartha has traced this pattern from poetry, and he has accumulated incontestable evidence of the movement of this structure from folk sources into art music tradition. Bartha opposes his theory to Riemann's concept of period structure in a way which I do not completely understand, for it seems to me in this case that Bartha is attributing an even tighter straightjacket to the venerable master than the one he wore.[2] This quibble aside, we must recognize Bartha's analysis of this structure and its role in classical style as a major contribution to phrase theory. He has demonstrated the pervasiveness of the pattern, its importance in identifying thematic content, and its extension to different hierarchical levels of length. Bartha's analysis is generic, not noetic (or functional), and does not mention structural reasons which make the QSS so valuable to musical form. A structural property, which I call *transparency,* animates both the QSS and other variants which might not be so well accounted for by historical precedents.

"Transparent" indicates a musical unit comprising a model and its formative, single repetition. For example, a transparent eight-measure phrase consists of two identical or very similar four-measure halves; an eight-measure phrase which does not so divide is "opaque." Formative repetition frequently characterizes its materials by contrasting transparent and opaque units of similar length. This contrast provides an essential asymmetry in otherwise symmetrical structures. In graphic analysis I use parentheses to indicate transparent units, and I use square brackets to indicate opaque units which have transparent subunits at the next level. These symbols are used in Figure 2.2. In this notation Bartha's QSS could be indicated (8) [8] or, equivalently, 4 4 (4) 4 or a a (b) c. Besides the QSS, other repetition forms such as 4 2 2 4 2 2 = 4 (4) 4 (4) or 2 2 4 2 2 4 = (4) 4 (4) 4 also take advantage of transparency.

In addition to its value as an asymmetry which marks the contents of a "square" unit, the transparency structure provides a trace which identifies odd-size phrases with symmetrical archetypes. To cite an example which is far removed from the stylistic regions of the QSS, Debussy's second prelude, *Voiles,* employs a highly

---

2. See Reimann's appreciation of repetition options within the period in *Rhythmik und Metrik,* p. 212.

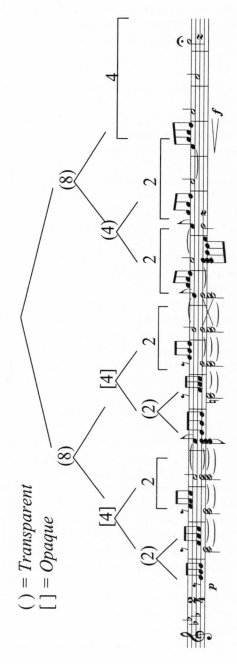

() = *Transparent*
[ ] = *Opaque*

Figure 2.2. Hierarchic formative repetition, Beethoven, Symphony No. 5.

structured phrase architecture which hinges on this identity (discussed in Chapter 4). Related and very striking examples have been discovered by James McKay, who has found asymmetrical phrases in *Pelléas et Mélisande* which are derived from symmetrical phrases in the earlier manuscript drafts (McKay 1977). When the transparent/opaque contrast remains as a trace in the final version, it can evoke the structural "norm" of the symmetrical form and function in tension with it.

The interplay of transparent and opaque units in Figure 2.2 may be extended hierarchically to encompass the whole exposition of that symphony (given, also, a representation of phrase extensions). In this enlarged use, as in the Debussy example, it seems inappropriate to insist on the QSS model. With x standing in for 2 or 4 or 8 or 16, the generalized rules which cover these formulas are the following:

1. Either the first or second half of an opaque unit is a transparent unit (not both).

   Mathematical notation: [x] à [½] (½) or (½) [½]

2. The two identical (similar) halves of a transparent unit are opaque.

   Mathematical notation: (x) à [½] [½]

These are descriptive, not prescriptive, rules; they summarize a recurrent structure of music that is formulaic, not obligatory. The opposite rule also has a function.

3. The two identical (similar) halves of a transparent unit are transparent.

   Mathematical notation: (x) à (½) (½)

While the "hard" rules (1) and (2) are typical of Mozart's *Teutsche* and Joplin's rags (though not the rag discussed below as an example of focal repetition) and serve to bring out sharply delimited thematic ideas, the "soft" rule (3) is typical of Schubert's *Waltzer* and serves to enhance a more amorphous harmonic flux despite the confining eight-measure groups.

I began this section with reference to the repetitions of two- and four-measure groups of Figure 2.2. In the same example there are also repetitions of single notes and of single-measure patterns; those are threefold: not formative but rather focal repetitions.

2.4. Focal Repetition

The structures I associate with the self-referential or focal type of repetition are a three- or fourfold immediate repetition of a musical unit or a twofold (i.e., single) repetition which crosses the boundary of a longer unit. The formative repetition is perceptually neutralized by fulfilling a syntactic role; the extra repetition or, in the second case, the displacement triggers a change of attention. Instead of focusing on the repeated material only, we focus on the repetition as a symbolic activity per se and seek an interpretation of it. In the aesthetic theory of Mukařovský (in Garvin 1964) this shift of attention is analyzed as reflecting "foregrounding" or "automatizing." I call the result "symbolic," because it is marked for

Figure 2.3. Joplin, *Magnetic Rag,* first strain.

interpretation and evokes expectations or associations. The associations, I would hazard, tend to rely on resemblance. Focal repetitions in music have a strong power to evoke the feelings of situations typified by repetition: activities that go on and on, rituals, compulsive actions, getting stuck "in a rut," emphatically accented speech, dancing, or laughing. (We can postulate that a sign is marked for interpretation without implying that listeners will agree in their associations.)

Figure 2.3 analyzes the first strain of Joplin's *Magnetic Rag* as an illustration of focal repetition. Notice that nothing repeats immediately more than once in the first eight measures, except at the level of single notes. These formative repetitions are confined to rhythm. The first three two-measure groups are transparent in respect to rhythm, that is to say, the one-measure rhythms repeat. The only completely literal repetition is the delayed repetition of m. 1 in m. 5. The second eight measures comprise a fourfold and focal repetition. Whereas the repetitions of the first eight bars are the faceless servants of syntax, the repetitions of the second eight measures capture our attention and demand a subjective interpretation. To me these repetitions seem at once mischievous and compulsive, sad and consoling; the music is "stuck in a rut" but makes the best of it.

Further Constraints on Focal Repetition

The principles suggested require one exclusion and two partial exclusions. First, Bartha's QSS again. Bartha points out that the third verse of the QSS often uses material of the first two. I quote his Example 2 (1971, p. 260) as Figure 2.4a. The letters above the staff are mine. Does AA'b'b'' constitute focal repetition? No, because, with respect to their common element, the first repetitions are delayed. Paying strict attention to length, we have either AA'B (two-measure units) or bcbc'b'b'' (units of five to seven eighth notes). In neither case are there threefold immediate repetitions. I would not deny that the density of repetition conditions the character of the theme or that the QSS itself has a connotative force here (it is folksy), but it would seem to me that the emphasis on repetition in itself is not comparable to the case considered in Joplin or the cases we will see later in Schubert.

In general, variation need not cancel the effect of repetition, but in a threefold repetition where two of the variants are much more like each other than like the third, the focal effect is strongly mitigated. Figure 2.4B shows another example from Bartha (1971, p. 263). Similarly, the potentially focal repetitions of the subject in a fugal exposition are restrained in their focal effect by the alternation of tonic and dominant (that is, two tonic statements resemble each other more than the others); however, a stretto, particularly an octave stretto, as in Bach's *Well-Tempered Clavier*, book 2, the fugue in F minor, has the focal character of an emphatic pronouncement.

Finally, does a threefold sequence comprise a focal repetition? Certainly, but it is *also* something else (e.g., a progression). The connotative power of sequences is easy to recognize, but we certainly cannot know, as a general rule, whether the repeating or changing aspects of different sequences will dominate. Traditionally, sequences are considered as rhetorically heightened moments if they are not excessively automated. This judgment is consonant with the relations we are considering.

2.5. Textural Repetition

Textural repetition occurs with the continuing repetition of an idea more than three or four times, which cancels out its own claim on our attention and thereby refers our focus elsewhere, to another voice or to a changing aspect. The figure maintains, nevertheless, a background influence on our musical consciousness. There must be an upper limit to the complexity of a unit that can be so used. I don't know what the limit is, but you may consult Satie's *Vexations* and Ravel's *Bolero* for clues. The tension in both pieces is our reluctance to transfer our atten-

Figure 2.4A. Haydn, *Symphony* No. 98, 4th movement, after Bartha (1971), p. 260.

Figure 2.4B. Beethoven, *Symphony* No. 4, 3rd movement, Trio, after Bartha (1971), p. 263.

Figure 2.4C. Mozart, K. 488, 4th movement.

tion in the way we usually do when notes or patterns repeat for a long time. We resist the change of reference. Textural repetition is familiar in Baroque, Classical, and Romantic accompaniments and developments, and it is the guiding principle of contemporary pattern music. This latter is sometimes described as ritualistic, which might seem to contradict the suggestion offered above that focal repetition might evoke ritual. There is no contradiction. Ritual uses both focal repetitions (the triple "Sanctus") and more extended and more hypnotic repetitions. The hypnotic quality of textural repetition is an essential point, though it may be very mild and subliminal. In the case of extended repetition we approach a threshold between systems of signs which convey information (or orientations or feelings) and physical stimuli which cause direct changes in physiological states of the brain. Eco suggests the category of "programmed stimuli" (1976, p. 241).

The distinction between focal and textural repetition is itself one that allows an ambiguous threshold which can be exploited expressively. As an example, I cite the Mozart Piano Concerto K. 488, the Presto and the theme which begins as shown in Figure 2.4C. These few bars must indicate a passage which ought to be considered in its context rather than excerpted at greater length. The theme, a kind of concluding theme, occurs three times, first in the dominant, then in the tonic, and finally in the subdominant area of the tonic key. The theme has both elements of prolonged (textural) repetition—the accompaniment, the motive in quarter notes reiterating the root and fifth of the main chord—and elements of quicker change. As it first occurs, its cleverness and sparkle, its changing patterns strike us most. As it recurs, each time more subdued in its tonality and with its novelty wearing off, its repetitious aspects gain more effect. Its recurrences evoke a change in our own attention state, a kind of increasing passivity through which the music expressively foreshadows its own departure.

One aspect of the quality of consciousness enhanced by textural repetition is heightened sensitivity to detail. Anticipating my final example, the Trio of the Scherzo of Schubert's Sonata in B-flat Major, D. 960, which is discussed in the next section, is an ideal example of textural repetition. Its relatively complex, syncopated, two-bar rhythm appears in fourteen consecutive versions (twenty-eight with repeats). The effect is that the repeating rhythm, acquiring a pervasive but subliminal presence, refers our attention to the tiniest nuances of voice leading, stress, articulation, and, of course, harmony, which become significant gestures imbued with evocative power. Notice that mm. 8–9 (Figure 2.5) would sound like filler in almost any more active context but sound rich in meaning here. The tiny difference between mm. 2 and 6 may go unnoticed the first time, but in the repeat it is elevated to a clear signal of the movement to III. Every change is magnified in import and effect.

2.6. Schubert, Piano Sonata in B-flat Major, D. 960, Scherzo

The Scherzo utilizes all types of repetition. Indeed, its elaborate play of so many repetitions belongs to a great tradition of Classical third movements which rely on a heightened rhythmic consciousness to lift us courteously out of the dreams of a slow movement and prepare us for the daylight of a finale.

The accompaniment figure (m. 1, etc.) looks more ordinary on the page than it is. The alternation of double notes on the beat with single notes off the beat requires a careful balancing act by the executant, which, when successful, creates a distinctive excitement. Though the repetition of this figure is textural and settles quickly into the background, the threefold repetition *within* this figure is focal and grabs our attention. We sense it immediately as a thematic force. The melody takes up this idea as a thrice-repeated quarter-note motive in the fourth measure.

Figure 2.5. Schubert, Piano Sonata in B-flat Major, Op. posth., Scherzo.

It is transformed into an octave leap, presented in four variants that complete the phrase. Here variation and repetition are opposed—the fluidity of melody versus the projective thrust of focal or self-referential repetition. The first half of the melody introduces this tension in mm. 2–3. These have the same rhythm, and because the rhythm repeats across a boundary of two-measure harmonic-metrical segments, it acquires focus. The focal repetition of rhythm must compete with a melodious curve that distracts attention from it. Perhaps the pat eight-measure repetition of this tune—purely formative—benefits from what magicians call misdirection; we are so absorbed in the focal structures of the small details that the cadence on IV can catch us unaware, like a rabbit out of a hat.

After the double bar, the conflicting structures which were entwined in the theme are separated into contrasting sections. For sixteen measures (mm. 17–32) repetition is essentially formative—by twos only and conformal with larger units. Then it becomes focal again. There follow thirty-five measures (mm. 33–67) with a minimum melodic content but a winning interplay of patterns. Threefold repetitions occur at both the measure level and the beat level, and, simple as the materials are, they generate overlapping two-, three-, and four-measure groups. Of course, these designs are coordinated with the harmony. The D-flat pedal finally terminates where it moves to the tonic of F-sharp minor (m. 51), so that the momentary interruption of its hypnotic, textural repetition (mm. 33–41, 44–50) lends urgency and an instant of seriousness to the minor key. The leading-tone major triad signals a turn toward the tonic (m. 56), but it is the compression of the phrase groups from six to five measures, achieved by closer overlapping of the focal and melodic units, which reveals its meaning. This Scherzo is a study in dominant avoidance. The dominant has no dramatic role; it only appears in lightweight conventional cadences. Thus, the master stroke of the Scherzo is the measure before the reprise (m. 67), where the reopening of the theme is doubly undercut: There is no dominant before it, and it is anticipated by a focal repetition, a repetition which at this point overlaps the most dramatic segmental boundary of the movement (between mm. 67 and 68). The final cadence is achieved by a focal repetition, the only one based on a two-measure figure.

3   The Allegretto of Beethoven's Seventh

I will try to demonstrate two points through my analysis of the Allegretto: that semiotic theory can enrich our appreciation of a musical composition, even one which is already well understood in terms of other musical theory, and that the study of music can contribute in turn to the formation of semiotic doctrine. Though reciprocal, these two propositions do not follow from each other. The hinge between them here is a method of describing the music (or any other text) in terms of the antithesis of *grammar* and *design,* a doctrine that I develop in the first half of the article, and a conception of *play* related to sign genesis that I describe later. In this frame of reference I can propose a particular philosophical interpretation of the Allegretto depending on principles which, I think can be readily seen, could find application in other media.

Some compelling semiotic relations, especially *denotation* and *logical truth,* have very little bearing on music, but the view of other basic principles is, therefore, less obstructed in musical research than elsewhere. Unfortunately, because many scholars of semiotics and structuralism are deficient in music-reading skills, the benefits of this happy circumstance are of no use to them. Probably this essay cannot be understood fully without some prior musical background, but the composition in question is well known, especially memorable, and widely recorded. For readers who might like to make the effort to use them, the examples in score notation show starting times in minutes and seconds that locate the excerpts in the Toscanini recording of 1936. (My reasons for choosing this version are discussed later. I do not think my analysis is inapplicable to other versions.)

3.1. Grammar (or Dialect) and Design (Idiolect)

The significance of the Allegretto is richest in the context of the full symphony, but the movement is substantially comprehensible as an excerpt. The case is similar with many Classical symphonic movements which may seem more or less self-contained, though rarely to the degree of the Allegretto. In fact, the movement succeeds much too well on its own; its independence and accessibility have been the basis of abuse. As Grove (1962, p. 255) and Tovey (1935, p. 59) report, early performances of the Eighth Symphony frequently substituted this slow movement for its own as a concession to audience taste. Hector Berlioz (1975, p. 35), whose

I am grateful to Ms. Shelagh Aitken for her assistance in the preparation of this paper, originally published in the *American Journal of Semiotics* 1, no. 12 (1981).

criticism contributed to the gradual acceptance of Beethoven's compositions in nineteenth-century France, complained that the Seventh Symphony was known only for the slow movement.

The wide popularity of the Allegretto must be due in part to the ease with which we can follow its shorter figures, particularly the recurrences of the main tune and the pervasive rhythms built from dactyl and dactyl-plus-spondee combinations. However, the more complicated longer-range relationships of themes, timbres, and tonalities which shape a form of great depth and beauty do not seem to be lost on the serious, untrained listener, even at first hearing. I regard the exceptional fusion of clarity and profundity in the Allegretto as depending largely on the coordination achieved in it between *grammar* and *design.*

Grammar and *design,* in the special technical sense given them here, denote two complementary organizational principles in syntax.[1] *Grammar* is order determined by a priori abstract rules. Grammar presumes a *dialect,* a system or language that furnishes those abstract rules in advance to the text that deploys them. *Design* determines an order, an *idiolect,* internally, within a single text, by concrete symmetries of all kinds, especially, for music, repetition and variation. I cannot understand a poem in a language I don't know, but I might notice some of the rhymes and alliterations and rhythmic constants. These latter are part of the design, constituting overall a probably unique idiolect for that poem. What I'm missing, collectively, is what I call grammar.

The form of the Allegretto is diagrammed in Figure 3.1 as a hierarchy of segments. I consider the entire form as a *design* because I regard the relations of design as best accounting for the plan at that level. I consider the versions of the theme to be *sentences,* my word for segments that are governed overall by principles of grammar—here, rules of metrical, harmonic phrase structure widely shared in a large musical dialect.

Usually music has both grammatical and design aspects. In the Allegretto, the structure as a whole mixes two conventional designs, both of which depend more on immediate symmetry than abstract models. In part, it is like a variation form with a repeating theme which, fixed in its essentials (phrase structure, chord sequence, and here melody, too), can support arbitrary changes of other kinds. In part, it is like a song form, ABA, in which recurrences of the principal section frame a juxtaposed, contrasting section that is not necessarily connected to the principal section by the grammatical contiguity of a sentence. In this movement the "B" section, which I call the Interlude, occurs twice; it is not quite a separate piece but like a "Trio" approaches that status.

The principal theme exemplifies the idea of a grammatical sentence. Its repeating rhythm and the recurring melodic motive form a design within it, but the framework is a conventional two-phrase formula (the second phrase repeated) with

---

1. My antithesis of grammar and design is related to but also substantially different from the frequently generalized antithesis of selection/combination, metaphor/metonomy, and paradigm/syntagm. This article does not undertake to compare semiotic doctrines. For a full explanation see my *Elements of Semiotics* (1999), Chapter 14.

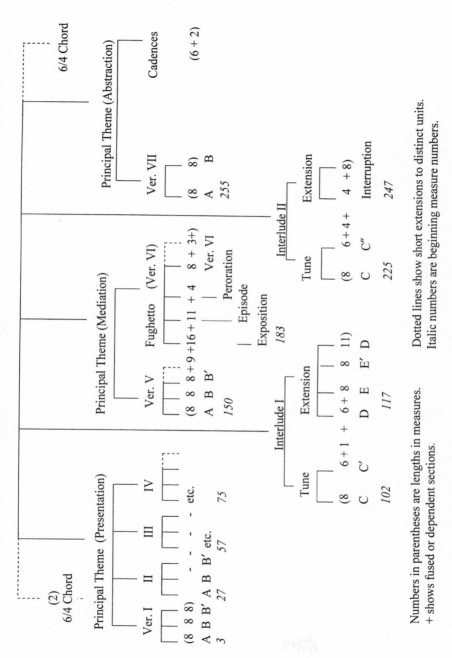

Figure 3.1. Segmental hierarchy of Beethoven, Symphony No. 7, 2nd movement (Allegretto).

Numbers in parentheses are lengths in measures.
+ shows fused or dependent sections.

Dotted lines show short extensions to distinct units.
Italic numbers are beginning measure numbers.

cadences in the semi-obligatory sequence of relative major (C major) and tonic minor (A minor). The eight-measure phrase lengths with their hierarchy of two- and four-measure parts can also be considered as realizing conventional abstract forms. (By the conventions of Chapter 2, the second phrase is [(4) 4].)

A premise of the doctrine of grammar and design is that understanding a text involves us in the act of classifying its parts. Our classifications might be multiple, overlapping, ambiguous, contradictory, and/or tentative, but we think of a text that makes sense as having *kinds* of parts. Grammar assigns parts of a text or repertoire of texts to a priori categories: "verbs," "silhouettes," and "syllogisms" are common categories in other media. Here triads, inversions, tonics, and dominants are applicable abstractions. Design groups parts together because of some inherent or contextual similarity without regard to a priori abstraction. For example, we note that the unit of mm. 13–14 is similar to mm. 1–2 and mm. 3–4 or that mm. 5–6 resemble mm. 9–10. We have not prior abstract categories to subsume these figures; however, in the process of listening, ad hoc abstractions are invoked, abstractions which may be freshly invented or borrowed from another context. The point is not that design always bypasses grammatical categories, but that when it employs, for example, triads, as a category, it is indifferent to their normal grammatical status and to grammatical constraints on their distribution. The power of design is to cause us to adduce categories and rules as a creative act of perception. The text is anterior to language.

Grammar and design are reciprocal in that a repertoire of related designs will serve to validate a grammar (a disputed example: the rules of "sonata form") and that a reiterated grammatical rule will produce symmetries of structure. In such cases the results of the two principles converge. This analysis will emphasize divergences: the role of design in providing logical coherence to a few key grammatical structures and differences of intention between grammar and design.

Figure 3.1 also diagrams a further interpretation of the Allegretto's structure. The analogy of the movement with variation forms and ternary forms is legitimate for an exposition of the design/grammar antithesis but otherwise very superficial. The thrust of my analysis is that the movement exhibits a species of progressive rhetorical development which justifies speaking of its design as a *discourse*. In respect to that argument, the first four versions of the principal theme comprise the presentation of the chief categories and oppositions of the design. The Interlude in its first occurrence prefigures the dissolution of these oppositions. In the remaining sections of music, earlier contrasts are blurred in a process of mediation and abstraction.

3.2. Berlioz's Appreciation of the Allegretto

Berlioz's critical appreciation of the Seventh Symphony, which I mentioned above, is one I find very sympathetic. No doubt his description of the Allegretto belongs to the tradition of appreciation which Barthes (1972, p. 179) must have had in mind when he challenged us to describe music without epithets and adjectives. Yet Berlioz's comments, which I will use as a foil or complement to my own, do not so readily reduce to adjectives. His description, if any genre subsumes it, is a dramatic narrative, and in consequence it paints the music as a drama as well. I do not agree that the Allegretto has the overall structure of drama, dramatic as much of it is, and we will find that Berlioz's is obliged to leave a gap. As for his adjectives, they are a pleasure, and if they prove unnecessary, we may keep them as souvenirs. I will quote a good number of Berlioz's comments twice, immediately below, the largest part given in full but with Berlioz's paragraphing eliminated and with section headings inserted to key his description to the segmentation of Figure 3.1. Then I will reprise bits of his prose for place markers as I work through the movement. I find it interesting in Berlioz's semantics that thematic elements of the music become either *objects* or active *agents* while the instruments of the orchestra may be *agents*, when the themes are not, or *places*.

	The rhythm consists exclusively of a dactyl followed by a spondee occurring without stopping, sometimes in three parts, sometimes in a single part, and sometimes in all parts in unison. Sometimes they serve as an accompaniment, often attracting a concentrated attention to themselves, or furnishing the first theme of a small episodic double fugue for the strings.
Version I	It first appears in the lower strings of the violas, cellos, and double basses, marked *piano*, with the intention of being repeated shortly thereafter in a *pianissimo* full of melancholy and mystery.
Version II	From there it passes to the second violins, while the cellos chant a kind of lamentation in the minor mode;
Version III	the rhythmical phrases rising continually from octave to octave, and thereby arriving at the pitch of the first violins.
Version IV	These by means of a crescendo, transmit it to the woodwinds in the upper region of the orchestra where it then explodes in all its force. Thereupon the melodious plaint, being stated with greater energy, takes on the character of a convulsive lamentation; irreconcilable rhythms agitate painfully one against another—these are the tears, the sobs, the supplications, in short, the expression of unlimited grief and of a devouring form of suffering.
Interlude I	But a gleam of hope has just appeared; these agonizing accents are followed by an airy melody: pure, simple, soft and resigned—patience smiling at grief. Only the basses continue their inexorable rhythm under this rainbow of melody, and it seems, if I may borrow a quotation from English poetry:

> One fatal remembrance, one sorrow that throws
> Its bleak shade alike o'er our joys and our woes.

| Version V ⎫
Fughetto ⎬
Version VI ⎭
Interlude II | The orchestra, after a few alternations reminiscent of anguish and resignation, as if fatigued by such a painful struggle, presents only fragments of the original theme and dies away exhausted. |
| Version VII | The flutes and oboes take up the theme with a murmuring voice, but they lack the strength to finish it: and the ending falls to the violins in a few |

barely perceptible *pizzicato* notes. After this with a flicker of fresh animation, reminding one of the flame of a lamp about to die out, the woodwinds exhale a profound sigh upon an indecisive harmony and all is silence. (pp. 35–36)

The paragraphing above reveals the gap in Berlioz's description. The final sections before the last are represented by a single sentence. Having regarded the first half of the movement quite close up, Berlioz is content to describe the second half from a distance. The elision shows where a narrative or dramatic description of the music falls short. The elided sections are recurrences. It is impossible to characterize them as contributing to an action, and the nuances of new feeling which they add are very difficult to describe. But these recurrences are not literal repetitions. They involve extensive changes of structure. Indeed, it seems to me, that if excerpted, this latter part of the piece would share little of the clarity and attractiveness of the music preceding it, except to a listener who already knew the earlier parts. Here it is not a story, but a discursive logic which advances.

Discourse is not a word for which a definition meriting consensus is ready to hand: usually it is taken to refer to a verbal text which is "about" something and which can be either true or false. Clearly my use of the word will be broader; yet it will not, I believe, stretch its usual sense unduly. In the following discussion, "discourse" refers to the type of design which embodies a sequence of *opposition* and *mediation,* the mediation being prefigured in a secondary substructure. Such a type of structure, for which the mythology of Lévi-Strauss furnishes the archexamples, and which he, himself, has applied to music, is familiar.[2] These two sets of criteria, one centering on "about," one on mediation, are not equivalent but are, I will argue, comparable. I hope to give a sense of how the Allegretto "talks" such that my way of using the word will not seem strained or unnatural. (A further variation of this principle is developed in Part III of this book.) The section of the movement which Berlioz has described in most detail is the one I call the *presentation;* it exposes the oppositional categories of the design. The first task in my analysis will be to portray these categories in terms of their relations of oppositions. The first interlude can then be described as a preliminary resolution. Like Berlioz, I shall give these first two sections preponderant attention and not be chary of metaphorical or adjectival interpretation. The remaining sections transfer the process of resolution or mediation to the principal theme itself and play with the features of the theme to develop a mode of abstraction. Perhaps, when the shaping and evolution of these sections is seen in its systematic aspect, the adjective may come to seem to have been unnecessary.

3.3. Measures 3–100 (Presentation)

It [the rhythm] first appears in the lower strings of the violas, cellos, and double basses.

---

2. The most celebrated and controversial example is Lévi-Strauss's own in *Mythologiques IV* of Ravel's *Bolero,* discussed in Hopkins (1977, pp. 253–57).

The full form of the theme is two eight-measure phrases (labeled A and B in Figures 3.1 and 3.2A) with the second of these repeated to make a twenty-four-measure strain. This form occurs in full five times and, in a shorter version, twice more. The first four versions comprise the first section of the piece (4 × 24 = 96 measures), to which a two-measure transition is added.

The theme is essentially homogeneous, but its very dark and deliberate character is defined most clearly in the first eight measures. The second, balancing phrase, which is more active and more pleasant, softens and departs from the theme's initial character. The three factors of the character which are most obvious as we hear it at first are the minor mode, the very original and nearly macabre three-voice sonority of violas, cellos, and double basses, and the march step, which, as Cooke points out (1959, p. 22), is distinctly funeral though in a quicker speed. It is a specialty of Beethoven to combine the greater energy of a moderate tempo with the emotional palette of a slower one, adding restlessness to disappointment or hope.[3]

The theme never recurs with the attributes of sonority which seem to determine its character at first. However, the second version of the theme establishes a new contrast to which the theme's other features seem, retrospectively, to have been subordinate, the opposition of ornamented and unornamented melody. This opposition is, in my view, the principal polarity in the movement's design:

> it passes to the second violins, while the cellos chant a kind of lamentation.

The lamentation (Version II, Figure 3.2B), actually chanted by cellos and violas in unison, is derived from the middle voice of the theme's three-part chords. This richly ornamented line takes a complicated and almost improvisatory rhythm, setting its spontaneity in relief against the constraining march beat of the first melody.

Ornamentation, especially in slow tempi, has a continuity of value in music from the Renaissance to Beethoven's time and after. Ornament represents eloquence of expression. It represents the freedom of the musical line to give voice to the passions which motivate it. In 1762, C. P. E. Bach wrote, "Expression is heightened by [ornaments]; let a piece be sad, joyful or otherwise, and they will lend a fitting assistance" (1974, p. 79).

The lament is continuous ornament. In retrospect, the most striking feature of the first version was its lack of ornament, most exaggerated at the beginning where the note E is repeated twelve times before the first melodic inflection. Less obvious than the meaning of ornament is the meaning of its opposite. From Renaissance music into the Classical Period it was generally understood that various types of musical scores allowed for, or required, the addition of ornament in performance. As an exception, ornament was written out, as in the case of the music Bach pub-

---

3. Technically, the double affect involves two rates of motion of nearly equal prominence, usually one identified with a figure or motive, and the other with changes in harmony. Two earlier examples are the contrasting sections of the middle movements of the piano sonatas Op. 7 and Op. 10, no. 2.

Figure 3.2A. Beethoven, Symphony No. 7, 2nd movement, principal theme.

Figure 3.2B. The "Lament."

Figure 3.2C. Beginning of the Interlude.

lished during his lifetime, but there was never a rationale for suppressing ornament or a method of indicating that a passage should be left bare. (General advice in favor of moderation is another issue.) The only precedents I can suggest would be early North German *Lieder*, where the subordination of melody to text gave fewer but more plain and honest tones a greater burden of signification, and the French heroic style now known to have been a major influence on Beethoven, where simple, bare chords contribute weight and force to rhythm.[4]

The suppression of melodic ornament occurs as a regular and early feature of Beethoven's style, often as a means of immediate contrast with its opposite. As an embodiment of grace or extravagance, rich ornamentation can sound very noble, but in Beethoven's style the removal of expressive ornament also contributes to the

---

4. For a detailed study of Beethoven's selection of ornaments, not directly orientated to the issue broached here, see Gal (1916). For evidence of French influences see Schmitz (1978, chapter X) on the heroic style of Beethoven.

representation of nobility, though it is not by itself a sufficient sign of noble character. What it contributes to that quality is the element of *sufferance,* in the sense opposite to expression: the capacity to experience a feeling without showing it outwardly. This quality has two links with a Romantic ideal of personality. First, it is conventionally aristocratic. From the courts of Austria to the salons of Paris, we find the paradox of social manners that the expressions of radical ideas were expected to be cool, elegant, and restrained. While C. P. E. Bach might advise the musical performer to show affects appropriate to the composition on his or her face, the suppression of spontaneous emotion in voice or gesture was a point of honor and duty. Second, sufferance is inherently aristocratic. To posit a dichotomy between inward feeling and outward show corroborates the sensibility for an ideal of feeling which is ineffable, exclusive to talent, and personal rather than social. The complementary ideal of a full, intimate, and ungoverned and passionate expression, a private confession to a friend, is contemporary with the other and is, as it were, its other side. The A-minor theme has two ways of signifying its misfortune. Its ornamented melody—elaborate, eloquent, confessional—laments. Its plain march, stoic and taciturn, intends to hold its tongue, to keep quiet.

In the Allegretto the dominant opposition of plain to ornamented melody is presented in a structurally unusual form whereby its values are placed in simultaneous conflict. The simultaneity is possible because both melodies, the plain and the embellished, are fully independent voices of the same theme. In Versions II, III, IV, and V of the theme, the greater prominence of one or the other is a function of orchestration, the only factor besides loudness which varies substantially from one version to the next. Within each version the orchestration is essentially constant, but from each version to the next, radically altered. In this framework it is easy to associate the alternating prominence of the stoic or the complaining melody with alternative ways of reacting to a loss. The presentation can be heard as an image of a soul in inner conflict:

> the rhythmical phrases rising continually . . . arriving at the pitch of the first violins. These by means of crescendo, transmit it to the woodwinds . . . where it then explodes in all its *force.* Thereupon the melodious plaint, being stated with greater energy, takes on the character of convulsive lamentation; irreconcilable rhythms agitate painfully one against another—these are the tears, the sobs, the supplications, in short, the *expression* of unlimited grief. (emphasis added)

(The irreconcilable rhythms are the crossed duplets and triplets which provide a slight link between Version IV and the Interlude that will follow.) The changes of orchestration in successive versions of the theme unfold systematically. As the orchestral forces build, each new sonority first presents the obstinate rhythmic line in one version of the theme and then takes up the expressive lamenting one in the succeeding version. This is the case by turns first for the violas and cellos in unison, next the second violins, then the first violins, and finally the woodwinds. (The woodwinds' turn at the lament, in Version V of the theme, is delayed until after the first Interlude.) These entering instrumental forces are quite unequal, so that the relative weight of the two melodies changes. The fourth version is climactic and decisive in effect both because it ends the presentation (saying the last word) and because the broad crescendo of seventy measures reaches and sustains its climax here before yielding to a diminuendo.

Here is the design of the orchestration of the theme in the presentation and in Version V after the Interlude:

	March	Lament
Version I	*viola, cellos*	—
Version II	second violins	*violas, cellos*
Version III	*first violins*	second violins
Version IV	winds	*first violin*
Interlude I	—	—
(Version V	basses	*winds*)

In each version my italics show the voice which is more prominent overall, though the competition between them is keen at several points. (The picture is always complicated in the chromatic measures of the theme which begin its second half, the characters of the two lines being slightly crossed there.)

One effect of these rearrangements and inequalities is that the presentation arrives by its end at a characterization of the orchestra which reinforces the categories I have already proposed. The sound of the winds, through prominent only at the end, is strongly identified with the stoic, rhythmic march theme; the sound of the string section, since the first violins dominate it, with the lyrical lament. This is a natural division of labor. Though strings can be forceful and winds—at least in solo lines—can be lyrical, the affinities exploited here are more ready to hand; the strings having an advantage in flexibility, the wind in power. Emerging at the end of a crescendo that began with the unusual, strained, *pianissimo* sonorities of Version I, the aligned polarities achieve a conclusive moment of clarity and definition in Version IV. We may summarize them thus:

> reserved + plain + winds vs. expressive + ornamental + strings

3.4. Measures 101–149 (Interlude, First Time)

> But a gleam of hope has just appeared; those agonizing accents are followed by an airy melody: pure, simple, soft and resigned— patience smiling at grief.

The alignments and categories of the presentation are not generalized rules like those of a grammar, though they may suggest a generalization just on the horizon, so to speak. When we have a new theme which does not obey these codes, there is no sense of violation or confusion. Rather, there is a change of context. Abstracted from their original context, the distinctions which were established in the presentation are each annulled in the Interlude.

The Interlude's tune, built in two phrases as the A-minor theme was, effects cancellation of all three oppositions (Figure 3.2C and CC' in Figure 3.1). *Strings vs. winds:* Here the winds are used soloistically, in unison with the strings; string sound and wind sound are blended and more equal in the flexibility they display. *Plain vs. ornamented:* The violins and the clarinet play the same melody. The clarinet plays it in a plain, legato form, and the violins double with a figured version, a chordal rather than melodic embellishment, which falls in the harmony and softens the melodic contour without engendering a conflict. *Expression vs. silence:* the tune itself is in no sense held back, but its slow legato motion and unemphatic syncopations leave it only minimally articulated, almost more a humming tune than a song—neither silent nor confessional—wordless.

In music a change of context which, as here, is primarily a harmonic or tonal change is phenomenologically a change of space. The mediation of these contrasts occurs in a new place foreign to the realm where the conflicts were first established, a new texture, a different theme, a distant key. The distance is immediately apparent as a change of sound when the Interlude begins, and the flightier melodic figures and fluctuating harmonies which extend the Interlude, from m. 117, further qualify it as an insubstantial space of ephemeral feeling.

The main tonal relationship of the Interlude to the sections based on the principal theme is the relation of parallel keys, A minor and A major. Relative major and minor scales are grammatically *contiguous.* Parallel major and minor are *selectionally* related. Movement between parallels is a common and established technique with certain conventional uses, but we should not therefore lose sight of the fact that the color of this relationship reflects its *agrammaticality.* An unmediated progression between major and minor does not constitute a grammatical sentence *within* movements, except for the borderline cases of dance and trio (which might be regarded as not one movement) and the *tierce de Picardy* plain or expanded. The employment of the parallel major for the Interlude makes it sound somewhat discontinuous with the main body of the movement.

My use of the notion of agrammaticality for music goes cross-current to the main drift of contemporary musical analysis. A signal achievement of this latter has been to develop an integrated sense of musical logic which echoes the compositional synthesis of harmony, counterpoint, motivic development, and sectional forms. The grammars and designs which I wish to separate are thereby integrated. I need to emphasize, therefore, that by agrammatical I do not mean illogical or unconventional. The notion of agrammaticality (or "degrees of grammaticalness," which appears briefly in Chomsky's *Aspects of the Theory of Syntax* [1956, pp. 148–53], where he considers metaphor) does not entail an abandonment of logic or even a transgression of prohibitions. A succession is agrammatical if its logic lies elsewhere than in its grammar. When we speak of a distant modulation, distant implies agrammatical. The art of modulation can patch the rift. Were there no rift, the patch would need no art. It is unfortunate that in teaching harmony we call every *succession* a *progression,* thereby failing to alert our students to what ought to be the main lesson of distinguishing chordal grammar from the other logics that rationalize chordal colors and tensions. When voice leading supplies the logic, it is a question of an alternative grammar. When motivic parallelism supplies the logic, the relation belongs to design, for outside of the raw biological tendencies of perception, motivic parallelism obeys no grammar.

In our present case, the full effect of the tonal conflict between the Interlude and the presentation is softened by the design context of the symphony's other movements, which changes the weight of the keys. The symphony as a whole is in A major. When the Interlude announces that same key, it has far less of the dreamy, unsubstantial quality that we would expect were it not so thoroughly prepared for by the preceding Vivace. While the Interlude established its distance with A major, it requires a third tonal axis, F major and C major, to compound distance with a magical and evanescent charm. These keys, F and C, are used similarly in the symphony's first movement introduction. Placed there in relation to A major, they are remote and enchanted. Furthermore, the themes of that introduction and the Interlude are strongly related, as Figure 3.3A shows. The paradox is that these "remote" keys are closer to A minor, the main key of the Allegretto, than A major is. In fact, C major had previously appeared as the first cadence point of the principal theme, where it sounds properly commonplace. By an extraordinary feat of compositional discipline, insulating the passages in question from mutual association, Beethoven succeeds in a double interpretation of C major within the Allegretto. At the end of the second Interlude it replaces F as a "remote" sound, while within the theme itself it functions as the close relative key. The dissociation of design bifurcates a grammatical identity.

Grammar is primarily social. The rules of a grammar, be they explicit or vaguely intuitive, are maintained by pedagogy and normative usage. Such rules serve with more or less force to regulate the intentions of a sign. Concrete pattern in symmetry and repetition, in itself, has the opposite tendency to liberate perception, allowing the receiver of the sign to define its meaning by personal and private associations. Even culturally foundational designs—myths—promote a dimension of private fantasy and individual interpretation. Ordinary prose requires a considerable defense against unnecessary repetition of words, rhythms, and other sound patterns, for its principle is to depend maximally on rules to clarify intention. In poetry, concrete patterning is amplified while syntactic, semantic, or pragmatic rules admit licenses. To the extent this happens, intention is diffused, and authority tends to shift from the social realm to personal experience; design patterns invite individuals to form their own abstractions. This is especially emphasized when design supports departures from grammar. Agrammaticality is a sign of subjectivity. In relation to the Allegretto as a whole, the Interlude is qualified as a dreamlike realm of subjectivity by its agrammatical events.

After the straightforward sentence of the main tune (its grammar just slightly muted by a pedal point), the extension following obeys no one formula in its overall shape, nor even all of its detail. The regular pace of eight-measure phrases is dislodged. A simple and lightweight cadence figure alternates inconclusively between clarinet and French horn without establishing a larger form. These figures are interrupted by the most propulsive harmonic pattern of the movement (Figure 3.3B), which leads nowhere in its first appearance but provokes a quick, remote modulation the second time. In the new key (F major), the same cadence fragments recur.

Figure 3.3A. Comparable melodic figures from Beethoven, Symphony No. 7, 1st movement and Interlude.

Figure 3.3B. Chromatic pattern from the Interlude.

Figure 3.3C. Motivic structure of Interlude bass.

Figure 3.3D. Dissonant chromatic pattern from the second Interlude.

Although one can reduce the whole Interlude to a grammatical harmonic skeleton, there is very little more than a skeleton on the side of grammar. In its movement from phrase to phrase, the music realizes no a priori construct. Its logic is mainly a matter of repetitions and contrasts.

We can facilely reduce the passage at m. 123, referred to above and indicated in Figure 3.3B, to a chromatic diminished-seventh neighbor embellishment of the dominant, but this terminology covers the breach we need to reveal. Up to this point the Interlude's harmonies obey a conspicuous grammar of functional diatonic root progressions. Here one stage of that logic is suddenly prolonged for a moment of unprecedented sensuousness and freedom; yet, for all that it is arbitrary, the passage seems unaccountably poignant and relevant.

Why, then, are these harmonies so right? Not because of the voice leading (neighbor relations), which is of too general a type to seem particularly significant. The logic is motivic. It develops slight residues of the A-minor principal theme that remain intact in the Interlude. In the Interlude, the bass line, which carries a steady dactyl rhythm, is, like the original theme it imitates, nearly immobile. When it finally moves, as Figure 3.3C shows, it moves through a variation of the same melodic motive that finally animated the theme itself. The figure, three notes ascending stepwise, would be too simple to merit notice, but Beethoven consistently places it where it will animate or contradict the harmony. What happens here then is that a recurrence (design relation) imposes a nuance of the woeful A-minor theme where the brightest textures of the Interlude are momentarily rent. The sense of recollection is intensified by a further parallel. The melody and the oboe echo the fourth measure of the first movement, a small but unforgettable gesture.

I will not dwell on all the other instances where repetitions or the three-note rising motive strain against chord grammar, but note the harmonization of the sixth degree as an accented upward passing tone in the fugue and in the movement's last four measures. Another case, mentioned below, is found at the end of the second Interlude.

The embellishment chord discussed in the preceding paragraphs is a high point of the Interlude but not an isolated event. After the main tune, the simple motivic repetitions, the recurrences of the special chord, and the eventual modulation which brings only a repetition (in F major) of the repeating figures are all design elements in a section of the movement where the role of grammar is skeletal and the music's "space" progressively more dreamlike. We are awakened with a cold shock. The delicate, repeating cadence motive in F is extended thunderously, arbitrarily into the bass register. The virtuality of the Interlude yields instantly to the harsh reality (grammar) of the A-minor theme. The mediation of contrasts prefigured in the first phrases of the Interlude does not count as a real solution; another mediation must be won on home territory.

3.5. Measures 150–221 (Mediation)

Here the mediations are transported to the context where they are truly critical; they are worked out within the materials of the main theme itself. Version

V is decisive. The winds en masse take up the lament. The wind band sound, much less flexible than that of the strings, brings that theme closer to the character of the more rigid march melody. The march tune for its part sounds in the basses and cellos, where its immobility, though dramatizing a prolonged six-four, is less of an imposition on the texture. The register allocation, with the slow melody two octaves lower than the quicker lament, decreases the conflict because bass lines don't need to move as much as melody lines do. The two melodies are welded together by a new sixteenth-note accompaniment and thereby achieve more unity of movement. Their differences are half settled here, and the lament will not be heard again. Listen to this version of the theme all by itself: It has a far more neutral sound than anything which precedes it; it mollifies the contrasts which had seemed so striking at the end of the presentation. While the sixteenth notes release tension in higher speed, the dynamic energies of the Allegretto are waning.

The cancellation of oppositions or blurring of categories, for which I use the general term *mediation,* renders a design discursive because it leaves the design unstable as a percept. To speak *about* some object implies (at least) two incompatible images—that of the object with its predicate and that of the object without its predicate or with a contradictory one. As C. S. Peirce requires us to observe, discourse is the agent of a fleeting transition that establishes one image as an actual signified idea and leaves its alternative or opposites as mere possibilities, glimpses, or recollections. When a composition suggests a certain perceptual structure on the one hand and dismantles it on the other, there is a comparable effect. We cannot keep it in mind except as an object in transition. At this stage of the Allegretto, it would not be natural to speak of contrast between a taciturn and an expressive melody. The two are unified. Yet these are those same melodies which had maintained a wide psychological distance before. The instability of the image is not simply a function of music's temporal embedding. Similar ambiguities of structure will keep our eyes on a painting; the perception of subject and composition in a painting generally involves some alternation of attention between them as well as synthesis, some regrouping of the spaces. When these shifts of image are compelling, a design seems to talk.

By positing them and at once canceling them, the design thematizes its categories, indicates them for attention, contemplation, and interpretation. The form, by vacillating, appears loquacious. Perceiving this, we can gradually wean the analysis from its adjectives. What I called "silent" and "expressive" might be more safely "X" and "Y." I had but the scantest authority for my labels. The argument, or pseudo-argument, referred to a social *grammar* (the rules of nobility as a musical ideal) which is half speculation. If the research is pursued, it will boomerang, taking the music right out of our hands. (We shall learn, with luck, what ornament meant—in certain circles—in Vienna—in 1813 . . . but not find its title to a region of our contemporary minds.) Design achieves precision and relevance by other means. All that is beyond doubt are the equivalences and differences we hear. We are shown exactly what to interpret, not exactly how, but this showing is active in the way discourse is active.

I won't pretend that I can put my finger on the sources of Toscanini's electricity, but one achievement I value highly in his performance of the Allegretto is that he lets the large-scale contrasts form and disappear. Perhaps his tempo is too quick, but it saves him from obscuring Beethoven's plan with extra detail as others do. For example, in Sir Thomas Beecham's version (which I nonetheless greatly admire), the tempo is much slower, and, to keep it alive, he adds an accent to the even-numbered measures of the theme. The accent makes a stunning gesture, but the extra, recurring inflection undermines the contrast between the bare march and the highly inflected lament. Where Beethoven is inexpressive by design, Toscanini follows trustingly. The winds are eloquent in their lament in Version V but only within natural constraints. They do not parody the infinitely plastic line of the violins in Version IV. The Fughetta follows, rhythmic, lively, without a hint of artificially exaggerated nuance. It is allowed the mediating role of neutrality essential for Beethoven's discourse.

The distinction between plain and ornamented melody is finally abrogated entirely by the Fughetta, where the melodic lines combine a bit of the march beat with the faster rhythms, previously reserved for embellishment, in a single contiguity. A more radical semiotic process than mediation occurs here. Despite the pawky syncopations, this is a very proper, even dry and academic, bit of fugue. No wonder that Berlioz should decline to mention it! Perhaps he may have felt it to be a lapse into mere learning, but that would miss the point. Though it rises to some vehemence in its peroration (m. 210ff.) the fugue neither suffers nor expresses. It plays. It *abstracts*. Its tone is neutral. Here, and in what follows, snatches of melody and even extensive recurrences of melodies will remind us of the qualities they formerly embodied but no longer do. Now the music, in the most exacting sense, becomes a sign. It stands for something which is absent. Through its appeal to memory, the neutral music serves as a symbol of a feeling that it in no way resembles and has no immediate connection with. At the end of the Fughetta is a fine *trompe l'oreille* which illustrates the point. Somewhat hesitantly, I have labeled it as principal theme Version VI. There is nothing to it but the theme's first four measures and last four. Eight measures stand for twenty-four. Joined together to make an imminently vacuous phrase, they are an eminently resonant reminder.

3.6. Measures 222–274 (Interlude, Second Time, through Coda)

Among Haydn's bequests to Beethoven, though I must wonder if Beethoven ever gave him credit for it, is the method of giving a philosophical tone to music. I do not mean by "philosophical tone" a philosophical message or content, for example, acceptance of death, humility, dedication to virtue, etc. Rather, by using the word "tone," I mean to point to objectification and distancing. This quality, evident in the mature styles of Beethoven and Haydn, is not mysterious. Its technical means are straightforward. If we do not speak more often and more inquiringly of the abstracted sound so prevalent in Beethoven, that is simply because the drama that operates side by side with it is so overbearing and masterful.

I have already noted the method. When musical forms and figures are subject to play, that is, freely varied so as to retain their identity while losing their character, they are abstracted from their content. To *play* with the theme is to set it partly free, free from one sound, one context, one definite arrangement. Beethoven is never more serious than when he reverses his themes. His readiness to be anti-dramatic, to deflate a theme (as in the Fughetta) which sometimes is almost dramatic in itself, manifests an intellectualizing and philosophical bent. It thematizes the *semiotic.* The music unfolds not as a representation of immediate experience but as a symbol of a representation or as a sign of thinking.

Two dissociations remain to be considered, the first nearly perverse in its simplicity, the second equally so in its surprise and originality.

The Interlude returns with the two phrases of its main tune almost unaltered but thoroughly denuded of their original spontaneity. The Interlude's characteristic undercurrent of triplets had been the crest of an accelerating tidal wave in the presentation. They act in their new location as a *ritardando,* for the preceding Fughetta and Version VI both featured a faster, continuous sixteenth-note motion. Also, the tune goes nowhere. Where the first Interlude finally unlocked its pent energies in a modulation to its dominant, there to be extended in flowing melodies and further tonal shifts, the second comes to a quiet halt on the tonic and veers straight back toward the minor. Whereas the harmonic contiguities of the first Interlude were of doubtful grammatical solidity, even the fiction of continuity is missing here. The axis of remote tonality reappears (C now substituting for F, the reverse of the order in the interludes of the introduction to the first movement), but it is not drawn in, connected by a flow of sensuous harmony. It is a bald interruption (m. 247ff.: Figure 3.3D). Again design overrides grammar. The only logic in these chords is that they repeat and what they recall. The brutalities of the passage have names (cross-relations between borrowed dominants, simultaneous neighbor tones) but no grammatical rights. The Interlude as a whole is dissociated from its qualities of fantasy and fulfillment; the brute gesture of three chords, coming from nowhere and going nowhere, stands as a sufficient if empty memento of the former promise of the movement's most alluring tonality. The first Interlude represented a vision. The second, only toying with its materials, a mere sign of the first, represents the frailty of that vision.

The final appearance of the principal theme (mm. 255–270) is complete except that eight measures of reiterated cadences substitute for the repetition of its second phrase. Berlioz's metaphorical description of Version VI, though apt, does not quite describe how it is played:

> The flute and oboes take up the theme with a murmuring voice, but
> they lack the strength to finish it: and the ending falls to the violins.

Specifically, the theme is broken into two-measure fragments which are presented by successively lower groups of instruments. This manipulation of the theme, a very ingenious way to play it, or play with it, is a further mediation, for the theme here is simply the original, stolid march, but in its progressive descent in register it has the effect of a lament. So fragmented, the theme's loss of continuity is the orchestra's integration. (At least in Toscanini's version; some others hiccough.) The previously contrasted sounds serve serially in a single syntagm. As play, this version is the furthest reach of abstraction in the movement. The broken theme is a shadow or an echo of its former effects. The distinctions of thematic type and orchestral function on which the movement's substantial categories rested have been erased, and only a manner remains. Whence those disembodied symbols? In music as in literature, there is always another, an author, a fiction (not Toscanini, not "the real Beethoven") who contacts me and addresses me. I pointed out in Berlioz's description that the instruments were agents of action, a natural feeling, but here they lose their differences and cannot be actors. When the orchestra becomes one voice, I hear the author.

3.7. Measures 1–2 and 276–278 (The Six-four Chord)

The woodwinds exhale a profound sigh upon an indecisive harmony

There is a hint of this harmony at m. 98, but that makes it no less remarkable that this one plain chord should be heard at the beginning of the movement and then recognized ten minutes later at its end. Berlioz gives a fair explanation of it as far as he goes:

> This plaintive [exhalation], commencing and concluding the Andante [Allegretto], is produced by a six-four chord, continually tending to resolve on some other; and its incomplete harmonic sense is the only one allowing its use for the purpose of finishing in a manner leaving the bearer with a vague impression and augmenting the feeling of dreamy sadness where all of the preceding must have plunged him. (p. 36)

What I would emphasize here is "incomplete harmonic sense." The chord is barely grammatical in its initial usage since it is isolated by its sonority from its completion in the following dominant. The final chord has an equally easy and totally irrelevant grammatical rationale in the principle of arpeggiation. The orchestral color isolates the chords from everything else but connects them, despite the ten-minute interval, to each other. Design displaces grammar. In the whole body of the movement the principal theme has kept its grammatical integrity. Only in the Interludes did the vagaries and personal willfulness of design take a momentary upper hand over the demands of grammar. But here the whole piece is framed by a relation in which solid compliance yields to weightless symmetry. It is as if the Allegretto as a whole were transposed to a more subjective sphere of abstract contemplation. The movement is a representation, and by framing it, Beethoven so labels it. The bliss of the first Interlude is never recaptured, but here at least is the one compensation we possess, the power of making signs, the possibility, mysteriously consoling, of representing our sense of loss by symbols.

4 Mediation as a Principle of
Musical Form: Three Examples

Mediation, in the sense developed in the last chapter and the preceding Introduction, is too general a structure to be subsumed in either dialect or idiolect; it is foundational for semiosis, foundational for thinking. This chapter describes three very different compositions as taking their form and import in patterns of mediation. The first example, from Debussy, is a miniature parallel of the Allegretto we have just considered. In the second, from Brahms, the moment of mediation functions climactically rather than as a resolution. In the third, from Liszt, mediation brings fluidity to a distributed matrix of interlocking oppositions.

4.1. Debussy's Formal Procedures in *Voiles*

It is still commonplace to associate Debussy with the whole-tone scale. The piece which is probably cited most often as an example is the second in book 1 of his *Préludes*, *Voiles*. The student who goes just a little further soon knows that Debussy's interest in the whole-tone scale fell quite short of an addiction and that *Voiles* is not typical at all, that it is in fact unique in its pure devotions to this rare harmonic geography. The whole-tone scale is very unrewarding. Who else has been able to make a whole piece of good music out of it? The astounding fact is that Debussy could always form a clear, subtle, coherent language from any harmonic materials whatsoever, however simple, however bizarre, however limited or however diverse. When we become aware of this aspect of his art, it is fascinating to return to *Voiles* to see how the master sets his course over strange and ungrateful waters. After surveying its harmonic plan, I will comment briefly on its phrase rhythm. In *Voiles*, Debussy created a form that is expressed independently by parallel and similar developments in the harmonic and rhythmic spheres.

Voiles has musical vocabularies of melodies, phrase shapes, registral assignments, and scale tones, which are grouped at first into contrasting functional categories. The categories of materials in one vocabulary (e.g., harmonic) are paired (coded) with categories of another (e.g., textural) by strict rules. Measures 1–41 of *Voiles* present these codes. In music, to present a system is, in a sense, to exhaust it. The pentatonic passage, mm. 42–47, prefigures a mediation. This brief passage transposes the categories to another domain and neutralizes their codes of opposition. The final section, mm. 47–63, which would certainly sound quite shapeless out of context, returns us to the original materials, which, free of previous constraints or codes, join in new harmonies and cadence in a relation of functional equality.

Paradigm A   Paradigm B$_1$ Paradigm B$_2$

$$\text{I} \left\{ \begin{array}{l} 1' - 3^\circ \\ 3' - 5^\circ, \; 5 - 6 \end{array} \right.$$

$$\text{II} \left\{ \begin{array}{l} 7 - 8 \\ 9 - 10, \; 11 - 14 \end{array} \right.$$

$$\text{I'} \left\{ \begin{array}{l} 10' - 11 \\ 12 - 13 \end{array} \right.$$

$$\text{I''} \left\{ \begin{array}{l} 15 - 16 \\ 17 - 18, \; 19 - 22 \end{array} \right. \qquad \text{II'} \left\{ \begin{array}{l} 15 - 16 \\ 17 - 18 \; [19 - \frac{21}{22}?] \end{array} \right.$$

$$\text{III} \left\{ \left\{ \begin{array}{l} 22' - 23^\circ \\ 23' - 24^\circ, \; 24' - 26^\circ \\ \qquad\qquad\qquad 26' - 28^\circ \end{array} \right. \right.$$

$$\text{III'} \left\{ \begin{array}{l} 28' - 29^\circ \\ 29' - 30^\circ, \; 30' - 32 \end{array} \right.$$

$$\text{II''} \left\{ 33 - 34, \; 35 - 37 \right.$$

$$\text{III''} \left\{ \begin{array}{l} 38 \\ 39 \end{array} \right. \qquad 40 - 41$$

Key: n = whole measure;

   n' = upbeat to measure n (♪ or ♩);

   n° = first part of measure n. (♩ or ♩.)

Vertically aligned segments are equivalent motivically and/or formally.

Figure 4.1. Segmental scheme of Debussy, *Voiles*, key to Figures 4.1A–4.1C.

It is easy to see the first marks of this tripart division of *Voiles*. Measures 1–40 adhere strictly to the six-note scale (except for ornaments in m. 29). At m. 42 Debussy notated a key signature change. With the common tones G♭, A♭, B♭, the music moves to a pentatonic mode. In m. 48 and to the end, the whole-tone scale is again employed exclusively. This is a very unequal division yielding sections of forty-one, six, and seventeen measures, respectively, but demarcated too sharply to be equivocal. Figure 4.1 divides the first forty-one measures.

   The functional categories of the first section distinguish the two triads of the whole-tone scale. The relations are patent if we lay out the materials in a chart of paradigms à la Ruwet. All of the largest melodic units defined by Figure 4.1A, with the exception of the last, begin and end on A♭ (G♯), E, or C. The priority of these tones is further reinforced by the melodic doublings of phrases of paradigms A and

Figure 4.1A. Paradigm A of Figure 4.1.

Figure 4.1B. Paradigm B₁ of Figure 4.1.

Phrase Forms in Figures 4.1A–C

* = "perfect"
? = ambiguous

I : 6 = ? (2, 2 (2)) = ? (2, 4)

*II: [8] = (4) [4] = (4) 2 (2)

I': 5?

II' = I": ?[8] = (4) 4

III: 6 = (2) 1 (2)

*III': [4] = (2) 2

II": 5 = . . . 2 2 1 . . .

Figure 4.1C. Paradigm B₂ of Figure 4.1 and summary of phrase forms.

B_1. These doublings occur only in the intervals of the octave, the major third or its compound, the augmented triad. Therefore, the melodies and their "doubles" all start and end within the same augmented triad (A♭, C, E). The other triad (B♭, D, F♯) is deployed with equal consistency in mm. 1–41 to orient the accompaniment materials, as Figure 4.2A illustrates. The permanent bass pedal point on B♭ is most obvious. This functional partition of the scale into two chords is expressed in another way which follows logically from the first and which resembles traditional tonic-dominant tonality. Each chord becomes the ornament or alternate for the other. The melody of Paradigm A has its "half-cadence" on B♭ (m. 2); those of group B_2, also on B♭; and melody B_1 has a similarly prominent, though rhythmically more ambiguous, midpoint on D. The accompaniment figures, on a smaller scale, reverse this logic. The dominating code for the harmonic world for mm. 1–37 is

$$\text{melody / accompaniment} = \{A♭, C, E\} / \{B♭, D, F♯\}.$$

Measures 38–41 are "modulatory." The principal motive of the B2 group (A♭, C, B♭, in sixteenths) is transposed down one step, reversing its harmonic affiliation with respect to the two triads, and leads to the pentatonic passage. In the new scale of this climactic episode the categories established in the first forty measures are obliterated. The five notes do not divide into a primary and a secondary chord. Though the B♭ pedal point is not relieved, the rest of the texture no longer allows for a clear separation of melody (and melodic doublings) from accompaniment. The arpeggio scale of mm. 42–43 is especially important in this respect; it is certainly neither melody nor accompaniment unless it is both.

When the whole-tone scale returns, as if after a sudden squall which clears the air, it is free from its former codes, and it presents relations which had previously been unavailable. In mm. 48–49, we have, for the first time, sequences at the interval of the second. The material which might be identified with the A♭, C, E chord in one version is therefore identified with the B♭, D, F♯ chord in the sequence. Furthermore, the intervals of doubling include the second and seventh, which effectively cancel any remaining affiliation of these doubled motives with either augmented triad. Since the partition of the texture into melody and accompaniment is no longer coded by a clear harmonic distinction, it, too, is weaker. For mm. 1–41, we could assert

$$\text{melody / accompaniment} = \text{active / static}.$$

From m. 48, this pairing is no longer clear. Indeed, the figure in mm. 48–49, derived from mm. 42–43, could seem ambiguous. Is it necessarily melody *or* accompaniment? The same question can be posed of the right-hand motive in mm. 53 and 55, the left hand of mm. 57–60.

If these brief remarks of the harmony of *Voiles* merely "elucidate the obvious," it is to provide a map for a somewhat more tentative exploration. The laws of musical phrase structure are not so clearly charted as the laws of musical scales. The categories I will propose next concern the constituent structures of phrases defined by the lengths and repetitions of their components. This is a subject which begs

Figure 4.2A. Debussy, *Voiles,* accompaniment orientation, mm. 1–43.

Figure 4.2B. Sources of phrase structure ambiguities in the Interlude.

questions from every side, and there is no hope of pursuing it in *Voiles* except by tacking. The purpose of my digressions is to arrive at a point of view from which it is possible to argue that this prelude establishes codes among functionally contrasted categories of phrase structure, which, like its harmonic codes, unfold their logic, unto satiation, in the first forty-one measures, then achieve a crisis in the pentatonic episode, and finally disappear in the freer-sounding textures of the final passage.

I don't want to use this slight and delicate prelude as the pretext for a complete rhythmic theory. Nevertheless, some of the "side issues" which tend in that direction are obligatory because our tradition is so incomplete and chaotic in this area. The categories of phrase structure which I perceive here beg both the question of symmetry—a concept of which has been called up frequently for phrase analysis without receiving the cross-examination which it deserves—and also the basic question of how we should measure and describe phrase components in terms of their length.

To begin with the second question, in *Voiles*, as in much metrical music, it seems reasonable to me to reckon phrase lengths on a scale of measures rather than by a finer scale of absolute durations. I think musicians do this casually most of the time, but a careful theorist might question it. I simply am asserting that the spontaneous habit is correct: The rationale for "rounding off" in this manner regards the phrase as a grouping of measures (sometimes half-measures) rather than as a length of melody. While the melody may start off the beat in the first or second half of the measure, the measure is a psychologically prominent unit, and the melody has the effect of linking these units into groups. I will use a symbol such as [2, 2, 4] to indicate a melodic phrase of two two-measure components followed by a four-measure component even though the melody itself may lack (or surpass) the exact length of eight measures by an eighth-note, dotted quarter, or so.

I will employ the notation suggested in Chapter 2 where parentheses mark a unit divided in half by repetition such that (8) indicates two parts of similar length and content. I explore here the hypothesis that phrases in the form [x (x)] or [(x) x] have a distinct structural role in Classical music and in some later styles, including Debussy's. This notion goes against the grain of much contemporary theory, but note that I single out this structure, that I call "perfect," because of its functional role, not its frequency. Perfect phrases may function as the kernels of a musical composition giving orientation and coherence to other less distinctly structured phrases.

Although this form, the perfect phrase, has a banal familiarity, especially in variants where the repetition is limited to the rhythm, rhythmic theorists do not describe its function. Riemann's passing observations do not do so. Cooper and Meyer have an elaborate means of analyzing such forms as what they call "fused," "pivoted," and "pyramidal" groupings, but the phenomenon they put a finger on leads to no functional interpretation. The perfect phrase coordinates two structural principles in one form by combining symmetrical division and asymmetrical content and frequently by coordinating a shift from hypermetrical accentuation to phrasal accentuation where weight falls on both the beginning and ending. Phrases in this form are perceptually salient, because structurally complex but highly unified. We find many sonata expositions in which perfect phrases occur only once or twice and at key moments.

These are also phrase forms which readily retain their identity under a certain range of transformations. The rhythmic plan of *Voiles* reaches its crisis when the transformations exceed that range. The kernel phrases which crystallize the others (prospectively or retrospectively) are

(from Figure 4.1B)   Unit II = [(4), 4]
(from Figure 4.1C)   Unit III′, which is similar but with halved
                       lengths, that is, [(2) 2].

Unit II is immediately succeeded by a more ambiguous variant (II′) that crosses paradigms, and Unit II″ lacks the first two and the last measure.

Unit III appears in retrospect to be like Unit III′ with a brief after-echo. Unit III′ has the proportions of the model, but further identities of material diffuse its formal definition. In sharp contrast with this material, Paradigm A shows no phraseo-metric regulation. Thus, with respect to metrical and phrase structure:

Paradigm A / Paradigms $B_{1 \text{ and } 2}$ :: amorphous / highly formed.

After m. 41 this logic collapses. Figure 4.2B shows that the pentatonic line establishes a reference to the materials of paradigm B2 but quite deforms the preceding phrase logic. An anacrusis becomes a downbeat. The six-measure length does not reduce to four plus two. Various suggestive repetitions do not coalesce in one scheme, and Debussy's dynamic markings further complicate the picture.

Then, for the remainder of the prelude an uninterrupted flow of two-measure groups is the salient organization. Even the material of Paradigm A, when it returns at the end with a metrical anchor, is absorbed in the same undifferentiated grouping pattern. Regularity has returned, but all oppositions have been dissolved. Even the pedal B♭ loses some distinctiveness as, after m. 48, it is not isolated by register.

Harmony and rhythm progress in step through the same logic of exposition, neutralization, and mediation though by entirely separate means. Considering the recent interest of many composers in deriving tonal and rhythmic procedures from a single structure, it is interesting that Debussy fulfilled this ideal in *Voiles*.

4.2. Brahms, a Folk-song Arrangement

This section is abridged from David Lidov and Gaynor Jones,
"A Comparison of Poeticity in Two Arrangements by Brahms of
'Erlaube mir, fein's Mädchen.'"

The Idea of the Poetic

Much of nineteenth-century art and criticism enjoyed what seems, at least in retrospect, a fairly broad consensus as to what constituted the "poetic," although the essence of the poetic lay in indefinite attributes which could not be readily defined or subjected to rigorous cross-examination. Critical writing approached the poetic by paraphrase more than by structural analysis. Toward the end of the nineteenth century, as new aesthetic positions took interest in the abrasive, the macabre, and the ironic, the time was ripe for a more critical view of the poetic.

This was the context in which scholars such as Roman Jakobson, members of the Prague Linguistic Circle in the 1930s, and later the anthropologist Claude Lévi-

Figure 4.3A. *Erlaube Mir* arranged for piano and voice by Brahms.

Strauss addressed themselves to fundamental questions about artistic experience and the nature of poetic communications. Insofar as their work is meticulous in separating features of artistic structure from features of artistic material, their theories apply as readily in music as elsewhere.

Brahms arranged the folk song "Erlaube mir, fein's Mädchen" twice, once with piano accompaniment and once as an *a cappella* four-part SATB setting. I shall explain the poeticity of the song with piano accompaniment (see Figure 4.3) as arising from its mediation structure.

At first view, the obvious refinements of the piano accompaniment—its chromaticism, cross-rhythms, and keyboard figuration—might be taken for conventional signs of poeticity; that is, the mere presence of these features might seem to reduce to triviality our question about the aesthetic difference between the setting. However, chromaticism and rhythmic and motivic complication are not always poetic, and more of the same would not be more poetic. To understand why Brahms's

B.

Figure 4.3B. Evolution of the bass.

elaborations are so uncannily effective it is necessary to compare the patterning of the poem and the patterning of the polyphony point by point.

Brahms's "Erlaube mir, fein's Mädchen" in either version is a slight document. But in the composer's folk-song settings, such as those in the collection *Deutsche Volkslieder,* we have one of the special repertoires of seemingly simple miniatures, like the preludes of Chopin or the chorales of Bach, which do not pale under intense scrutiny.

According to Max Friedlaender, the melody was written down by a friend of Brahms's on the Rhine about 1850. In the setting with piano accompaniment from the *Deutsche Volkslieder* of 1894, Friedlaender, sounding a theme close to the one we develop here, writes, "the modest folk-song melody is brought into the world of the art song" (1922, p. 166).[1]

The Folk Song

"Erlaube mir" has two stanzas of four lines with masculine rhymes *aabb.* Both stanzas are sung to the same sixteen-measure melody. The melody has a conventional period structure in which the first, second, and fourth four-measure phrases are identical. The third phrase is a modest variant which transposes the cadence of the third and fourth measures to the dominant while preserving intact the *Ländler*-like rhythm of the model. The translation below is arranged schematically. (See the score for the German.)

First stanza	*Second stanza*

(1) Allow me, fine maiden,
    to go into the garden
	(5) O maiden, o maiden,
	    you child so alone

(2) That I may there behold the roses so beautiful.	(6) Who has put thoughts into your head

(3) Allow me *to pick them*
    for it is *high time*
	(7) That I should not *see*
	    the roses in the garden?

(4) Their [her] beauty and youth
    have filled my heart with joy.
	(8) You are pleasing to my sight,
	    that I must say.

The imagery and syntax of the poem establish two planes of discourse—

---

1. die schlichte Volkstümlichkeit der Melodie ist hier allerdings in die Welt des Kunstliedes übertragen.

"horticultural" and "personal"—and two modes of assertion—"courtly" and "expressive." In *personal* discourse, the suitor speaks to the maiden about herself. In *horticultural* discourse, the suitor talks about the garden and the roses. Of course, we may understand this horticultural talk as metaphorical, with a deflected underlying purpose, but we emphasize the deflection. The second opposition cuts in a different direction. The poem's *courtly* statements attribute the suitor's motives for action to external conditions: the roses' beauty or ripeness, the maiden's thoughts. In *expressive* statements, the suitor confesses his own feelings without disguising them as attributes of external objects.

The first stanza is deflected; its nominal topic is horticultural. The second stanza is personal, with the maiden's supposed thoughts as its patent topic. This difference is clearest in the contrast between the opening pairs of lines in each stanza. The corresponding third lines blur the distinction, a fact we will return to presently. The fourth lines in each conform to the discourse plane of their opening lines but with a change of emphasis.

The opposition of courtly and expressive modes contrasts parallel sections within each stanza, dividing the first three lines from the fourth in both cases. Although first-person pronouns occur in earlier lines, they do not function there as the subject of expressed feelings. By contrast, in both fourth lines, the suitor expresses his own emotional state. Here "mein Herz" and "meinen Augen" are immediate metonyms of the suitor's feelings; they stand in an active, causative role.

In the melody the third phrase stands apart. This is the phrase that mediates between personal and horticultural discourse. In the first stanza, the third line presumes to speak of roses; but exaggerated diction renders their metaphoric status patent. Both "brechen" and "die höchste Zeit" (like "die Hochzeit," the wedding) suggest nuptials, casting a glow even on the fully deflected language of line four. In the second stanza, this structure is inverted. The first two lines are personal. Thoughts and feelings imputed to the maiden are their apparent topic. In the third line, the suitor suddenly deflects the reference, interpreting these suppositions as being her ideas about his own horticultural rather than amorous emotions. The fourth line is again frankly personal, softened, however, by an afterimage of roses from the third line. Thus, in both stanzas, but in opposite directions, the third lines transgress a boundary between the two distinct planes of discourse. This overstepping or blurring of a boundary mediates the alignment of stanzas with categories.

Mediation is pervasive. We must, therefore, distinguish between the common stock and special instances. Here are typical and quotidian examples. Rhythmic mediation occurs in each phrase of this song. The first two measures distinguish two hierarchical rhythmic levels, the motivic level and the groups level. The third and fourth measures identify or mediate these levels. Melodic mediation occurs in the third phrase. In mm. 2, 6, and 14 the first two motives oppose stepwise motion and leaps. Measures 9–10 emphasize the shared step progression A to G with similar weak beat descending skips (Figure 4.3A). These observations are trivial, but that is precisely the point. The instances we take up below, though not abstruse, are special because of their correlation with the text.

With his piano accompaniment to "Erlaube mir," but not in his chorale arrangement, Brahms created homologies between the musical structure and the poem. Where the poem mediates its two planes of discourse, the music mediates tonic and dominant tonalities. This pairing does not in any way imply any kind of translation between the *parts*. We are not asserting, for instance, that tonics stand for lovers or dominants for roses.

An unfortunate habit of music pedagogy is to talk about the "tonic-dominant relationship" as a fixed entity. Like an "employer-employee relationship," the character of the relationship depends on what is related or who is related to whom. In the folk melody and in its chorale arrangement, the dominant-tonic opposition of the third line to the three others is an unmediated contrast. Various unifying features link the third line to the others, but these constants, repeated but not reinterpreted, serve to sharpen harmonic contrast. The contrast is heightened further by the new features of the third phrase: its high first note, the melodic similarity of the first and second measures and their new contour, the new harmonies and new leading tone. All these features contribute to separating the tonic and dominant tonalities as completely distinct areas.

In the version with piano accompaniment, the tonic-dominant opposition is of quite a different stripe. Within the tiny temporal framework, the piano accompaniment brings to bear three different techniques of modulation, which mediate the two harmonic planes. First, there are chromatic alterations right from the start: D$\sharp$ in m. 2 and, with this passing tone as its precedent, the more significant passing C$\sharp$ in m. 6. When the melody reaches the leading tone of the dominant in m. 11, its harmony has already been accommodated within the principal key. Second, the accompaniment's rhythm changes. By moving the figuration of two quarter notes in the right hand from the second beat in the first line to the first beat in the second line, Brahms makes the fuller rhythm of the third line a motivic summation that refers back to or incorporates the earlier ones. Third, unlike the bass part of the choral setting of the third line, which sounds like a new, contrasting part, the corresponding bass part here is a gradually evolved variant (see Figure 4.3B).

The effect of the gradual preparation for the cadence of m. 12 is to make its ambiguity (new tonic/old dominant) more pregnant. Have we here, as the melody alone suggests, reached a contrasting cadence point, or have we, as the ensuing arpeggio suggests (m. 12, with C$\natural$), merely paused within the inflection prefigured in mm. 6 to 7? This particular ambiguity, familiar from sonata-form movement modulations, is used here in miniature scale with precise poetic effect.[2] Just where the text concludes its two lines of most patent double meaning, the harmony also says two things at once.

Both the textual and musical mediations established in line three exemplify the phenomenon of poeticity as it is represented in Jakobson's frequently quoted, apho-

---

2. Regarding the poetic force of miniaturization, see the introduction of Lévi-Strauss (1966), pp. 23–24.

ristic formulation: "The poetic function projects the principle of equivalence from the axis of selection into the axis of combination" (1960, p. 358). Where two distinct metaphoric levels of discourse or two distinct tonal levels of harmony are projected into the same sentence so that they sensually permeate and semantically pervade each other, the poetic function is at play, and here this relation occurs coordinately in words and music.

Continuous and Discontinuous

The music is also involved in mediating the poem's "courtly" and "expressive" modes of assertion. The alternation of courtly and expressive language coincides with a style change in the accompaniment, but in addition to the fact that they align with each other, the patterns which correspond here may themselves be understood as manifesting an archetypal theme identified in the anthropology of Lévi-Strauss as "the problem of the relation between continuous and discontinuous" (1966, p. 139).

According to Lévi-Strauss, intelligence imposes categories on experience at a heavy price. The loss of continuity is a deprivation and a rupture. The categories of culture—numbers, tones, concepts, personalities—are all acquired at the cost of emotional wounds and tensions (1970, p. 53). In compensation, culture exhibits its categories along with a continual production of mediations. In lines 1–3 of both stanzas, the suitor makes no direct attempt to cross the boundaries between separate subjectivities. He limits his communication to statements about things (roses, ideas) which are external to himself. In the fourth lines he gives vent to feeling. He asserts his subjective state. He acts to involve the maiden in a continuity of shared consciousness. To express is to press outward, to connect directly with another. Expression is a mediation of separate persons.

The changes of manner in the fourth lines of each stanza are climactic in the poem, but the tune is the same for the fourth phrase as for the first two. The folk melody miniaturizes the change of tone in the words. In the piano accompaniment, however, the poetics of fusion are enacted in coordination with the poem; verbal change of tone is enlarged. In the last phrase, mm. 13–16, dynamics, rhythm, and chromaticism all serve a transition from discreteness to continuity. For just an instant, where the suitor wants to deny the discreteness of "I" and "you," the accompaniment seems to lose articulation and to dissolve. In mm. 13 and 14, hemiola dissolves the discrete character of the measures, strongly marked before this point by motives coterminal with the bar and bass notes on every downbeat. In these same measures the sparse chromatic inflections of the previous phrases aggregate and extend in the accompaniment's upper voice, which dissolves the scale degrees into a continuity of pitch. With even the least use of the sustaining pedal, the new dynamic marking, *pp*, veils the discreteness of attack of the notes themselves, suggesting a more continuous sound. By invoking continuity, the accompaniment moves exactly in step with the poem; what was crystalline becomes a melting sound. The poem's conventional, stylized image of courtship swells with an immediate and sensual tonal image of fusion exactly where the verbal manner becomes expressive.

4.3. Liszt, *Tasso, Lamento e Trionfo*

In *Myth and Music,* Tarasti provides a narrative map of *Tasso, Lamento e Trionfo,* Liszt's second symphonic poem, first performed in Weimar in a version slightly different from the work we know today, with the composer conducting, as an overture to Goethe's *Torquato Tasso.* But Liszt wrote that he was even more deeply influenced by Byron's representation of Tasso than Goethe's, which establishes, as Tarasti rightly emphasizes, that for Liszt, the object of representation was neither Goethe's play nor Byron's poem but the *myth* of Tasso, which both those works elaborate. "Myth" also because the facts of the biography of the historical Tasso are not what count—Tasso, it now appears, was quite unstable and not blameless for his own fate—but as his age, desires, and paranoia were reimagined, he embodied the Romantic myth of genius.

Liszt's theory, which Tarasti discusses, was that the symphonic poem is a new form of epic and hence mythic where the action is psychological and where unity of theme establishes the subjectivity of the hero as a continuing presence. Tasso's story can be summarized in the type of paradigmatic-syntagmic matrix that Lévi-Strauss devised for myth:

A.	B.	(Romantic Archetype)
1. Tasso woos Princess, above his station; offends	5. Tasso presents *Gerusalemme Liberate* to Duke Alfonso	*Extroversion of yearning*
2. She is intrigued, but rejects him	6. The Duke is impressed, but does not pardon him	*Object of desire displayed, withheld*
3. Tasso imprisoned; he dies	7. Inquisition condemns Tasso	*Injury to hero*
4. Poetic madness; Tasso composes *G.L.*	8. Posthumous fame (union in death with Leonora)	*Apotheosis—Transfiguration*

> For I have battled with mine agony,
> And made me wings wherewith to overfly
> The narrow circus of my dungeon wall,
>
> . . .
>
> And pour'd my spirit over Palestine.

> Byron, *Tasso,* I.21–23, 26

The motive of the crusades and certain persistent musical ornaments both mark the work as orientalist, but age has surely made its orientalism innocuous (or even salutary if it reminds us that Palestine was then a reality). I must pass over that aspect and various other of its prejudices to emphasize the formalist preoccupations of this chapter.

It is of particular interest to me that Liszt does *not* speak of this symphonic poem as a narrative. His preface announces his intention of depicting the opposition or contradiction (*Gegensatz*) of the title and the "antithesis" of the poet's suffering in life and glory in death. The three scenes he mentions—Tasso's spirit hovering today over the lagoons of Venice, his life at court in Ferrara, his death in Rome—do not quite add up to a tale. Is Liszt telling a story or is he unfolding an idea? The preface suggests a philosophic point, not a narrative. I used to think it important to maintain this distinction, but I'm no longer sure I know the difference. For Lévi-Strauss (and for Greimas), to tell a story is to unfold an idea, and perhaps the converse is implied. I do not find the whole story in the music, and I cannot attach all of the musical episodes and reversals to particular events in the legend. It's easy enough, on the other hand, to locate the three scenes Liszt mentions in the first, middle, and final portions of the score. To deny the program any real presence in the sound would bleach it of color as surely as would a performance on the piano instead of in the orchestra. Yet, an episode-by-episode narrative translation would be beside the point.

The form of this twenty-minute work, with a Minuetto passage separating its initial slow sections from its rambunctious ending, faintly invokes a compression of conventional symphonic movements, but overall, the organization of *Tasso* is predominantly idiolectic. However, this is a design which contains an internal opposition between dialect and idiolect within it. Within the grand design, the opposition of theme to episode is prominent. I would suggest that this is where we see the crux of Liszt's technical innovation. In early Classical style, what we call a "theme" is either (a) an autonomous, complete unit, as in theme and variations or as in early rondos or (b) an incipit or a group of associated fragments integrated in a larger (developmental) grammatical form. In later Classical style and in early Romantic style we see more and more frequently that a theme of type *a* is inserted whole in a larger continuous form, as with rounded-out "second themes" in sonatas, but the framework is still necessarily conventional, dialectic. In Liszt's symphonic poems, the proportions can be inverted. A developmental texture, bounded by no emphatic grammatical unity, includes formed, closed themes as occasions in its flow, dialectic forms inside the idiolectic structure, like boats on the open sea. We might recognize this description as fitting some keyboard fantasies of the century previous but certainly not the symphonies. There was nothing new in beginning with a fragmentary fantasy or in ending with a coda that "liquefies" the themes. (I cannot use Schoenberg's term, generally given as "liquidate," because, as we shall see, thematic identity remains intact and critical.) The innovations enable a change in the scale, balance, and medium of *fantasia*. We do not hear the principal theme of *Tasso* until after an introductory, extended, and somewhat formless "developmental" episode. That theme, which Liszt claimed to have learned from gondoliers of Venice, who still sang the poet's verses, is substantially complete, closed, and rounded out in its first appearance. By the work's end, the theme has dissolved into sequences; it has become a raw material of the idiolect. On the other hand, the initial fantasy passage has proved unexpectedly stable. The theme has become episodic, but in exchange, the former episode emerges as a theme. This episode is internally modulatory, but its recurrences hold to the same absolute tonal level as the beginning, the Lento motto anchored by the diminished third, D♭–B♮, and the Strepitoso motto anchored by the dominant of C. The transformations we must study are not the transformations of the themes per se, not so very inventive, in my opinion, but the transformations of the oppositions, which, in total, suggest to me a very new feeling for how music signifies.

No symmetry of lengths guides the schema below, but I would say that the sections indicated balance each other in dramatic weight. The principal melodies are shown in Figure 4.4.

I. *Lament*
  Introduction
m.1.   Lento motto (I–VI–♭II–VII)
m. 27.   Strepitoso motto
m. 53.   Lento motto (to V^7 of C)

  Song
m. 62.   First strain of the principal theme in C minor, two phrases, cadencing on V, and then on I; both in bass clarinet first, then both repeated by violins.
m. 91.   Second strain of the theme, on VI, which cadences at m. 101. The repetition veers episodically and climaxes on V of E.

II. *Catastrophe*
m. 131.   Transformation of the first strain of the theme, now in E major, trumpet solo.
  G.P.
m. 145.   Reprise of the Lento motto, which moves to F-sharp major without any dominant.

III. *Interlude (Court of Ferrara)*
m. 165.   Transformation of the Strepitoso motto (but it may be read also as the Lento motto) into the Minuetto.
m. 270.   The principal theme floats over the Minuetto rhythm, the first strain in F-sharp, in the violins and then (m. 291) in B minor; the second strain, in G (or VI of B minor), in the woodwinds and brass but without oboe, then repeated in B-flat.

IV. *Agony and Triumph*
m. 348.   The Strepitoso motto returns at its original pitch, with the tag ending of the Lento motto, as at m. 53, but this time halting on an augmented sixth so as to reserve the dominant of C for
m. 383.   an Allegro con molto brio in C major, which vamps very energetically to a triumphal transformation of the Minuetto theme. Stable for a while, it eventually dissolves in fragments, sequences, and modula-

Figure 4.4. Liszt, *Tasso*, principal motives.

tions, precipitating a sort of chorale-march that is clearly triumphant but ex machina and which leads via a *doppio valore,* to a

m. 527.   Moderato pomposo for the final return of the principal theme, glorious and no longer fettered by grammatical form. It becomes fragmented and modulatory, giving way at last to a splendorous cadence in C major.

As the principal theme employs cadentially the same repeated descending third passing motion that marks the mottos, they all seem to be of the same substance, but what I call the mottos are merely motivic, while the principal theme, which will always be marked by distinct initial repeated tones, arrives at first in shapely periods. In addition to the material shown in Figure 4.4 there are descending chromatic scales and not very much else.

Mediation as a Principle of Musical Form 75

The opening section, suggesting an ABA, presents passages of maximally opposite tempi, a slow, abject melisma, and then a fast and violent outburst. The slow principal theme contrasts with that introduction by its broad period structure and conventional harmonic plan. The contrast between its unhappy first strain and visionary or desirous second strain is polarized by mode.

Nothing in Liszt's prefatory program note alerts us to the brief, loud, terrifying episode that I label the "Catastrophe," but the nerve center of *Tasso* is here. The expansive phrases of the theme, stretching what sounds like a four-measure frame to sixes and sevens, becomes a terse five-measure unit. The new key, E major, is at nearly maximum tonal distance from the original C minor. Instead of the quiet, vague syncopations that accompanied the theme before, we hear surging, diabolical scales in the bass. Of the several contrasts, the most awesome is in instrumentation. The retort to the soulful plaint of the bass clarinet in its upper register is a militant blare of unison trumpets in their lower range.

Tasso ends triumphantly in C major in a heavy, propulsive meter, with the principal theme returning in a manner that is the polar opposite of our first encounter, but all the oppositions I have mentioned are systematically dissolved. The key of the Minuetto, F-sharp, is remote from the C major-minor conflict. Here all the contrasts are mediated. It is metrically regular but not heavy. Its successive phrases, routinely alternating presentations on I and on III, shift between major and minor with minimal contrast of color or affect. Its form is periodic and grammatical but in such a glib manner as to prioritize its almost hypnotic repetitiousness. A graceful, nine-measure formula $(4) + 1 + [(2) + 2]$ is heard eight times; its harmonically functional cadences are tags without emphasis. When the theme returns over the Minuetto accompaniment, the formerly striking contrast between its two strains is overshadowed by internal contrasts within each since their repetitions are now in new keys. The whole theme, now beginning dreamily in the violins but eventually established in horns and oboe, closes the space between the original expressive orchestration, the trumpet episode, and the full wind choir that will dominate the finale. The Minuetto tempo is a mean between the extreme of speeds of the rest of the opus.

It remains for the finale episodes to flip the opposition of periodic (dialectal) and episodic (idiolectal) structure. If we follow Liszt literally, Tasso is a spirit in scene 1 and again in his triumph, where the tune is gradually reduced to its headmotive. At the end, the theme (Tasso, if you want to play that game) at the price of its own loss of form (death, if you are still in the game) acquires a euphoric force equal to its previous dysphoric transformation in E major, and still retains its home tonic in the brighter mode. But I cannot stay in the game for that moment that I identified before as the crux, the nerve center of the action. What were the trumpets in E major representing? Tasso's rejection by the Inquisition? His loss of Leonora? The Saracen condemning Sophonia in *Gerusalemme Liberate*? Tasso's discomfort in society? Could it be the opposite of these, his spiritual affirmation in composing the *Gerusalemme*? Not any one of these; perhaps all. Here Liszt is abstract, though not purely abstract: The brutality of the contrast is unmistakable and resonates with the antithesis of the subtitle.

We may be annoyed that the final triumph seems more a triumph of technology than a triumph of spirit, but we can look past the excesses. We should appreciate, in Liszt's pyro-technology of sequences, tremolos, arpeggios, and brass doublings, his solution to the problem of communicating genuinely new forms to an audience that would hear them once, in live performance, and not go home with a CD.

Part Two: *Semiotic Polemics*

Although many questions we encounter in semiotic research are old, perhaps permanent, and culturally ubiquitous, the flowering of semiotic research as an academic field identified as such by its own practitioners belongs to the twentieth century and, until recent decades, to the West. There are extensive writings on similar questions earlier and elsewhere, but always, as far as I can tell, these are excursions ultimately subordinated to another set of problems, such as those of theology or medicine or aesthetics. The twentieth century also saw the problem of the sign emerge as a central theme in academic philosophy. The extensive but by no means total isolation of these two streams of thought from each other, the philosophical analysis of "sign" and the semiotic construction of "sign," should probably embarrass us a bit more than it does. I have some idea why it had to be that way—owing to differences of heritage and discourse technology between scholars nourished in literary criticism and scholars nourished in abstract logic, for example—but to form a balanced picture might require a long investigation. A mutual point of departure that predates the isolation of semiotics from philosophy can be found in the work of Charles Peirce, of which I will say more below, but in fact, though most of his writings are earlier than Saussure's linguistics, they were simply unknown before the 1930s to any European semioticians, and their import is still unfolding. I can't say to what extent the recent fascination with Derrida's work mends a rift between semioticians and philosophers because philosophy itself is so divided—and why would it not be? We don't get into these matters to agree!

New disagreements about semiotics in musicology emerged in the 1960s and 1970s. Here, too, there is a more ancient history. A thoughtful, articulate, critical discourse about musical representation is part of Enlightenment thought. The nineteenth century had its quarrels about absolute and program music. More recently, Peirce's influence was absorbed indirectly by two American music theorists, Leonard B. Meyer (1956) and Wilson Coker (1972), who wrote on musical meaning before any Saussurian-style musicology crossed the ocean from France. What was new with them and with the structuralist writers was the reorientation of the debate on music's semiotic characteristics away from its previous participation in aesthetic value judgment and toward emulation or borrowing of theory from the natural sciences (especially in Meyer's work). In addition, they advanced methodology from a reformulated linguistics that had rapidly proved contagious for many branches of scholarship. In linguistics, Saussure's rationalism contributed to the framework for new empirical methods, including those of Zellig Harris, whose student Noam Chomsky effected another reverse turn toward more abstract rationalism again, but now with mathematical modeling. In the 1960s the study of language seemed to be among the domains of research best able to inform us how the mind works, and the possibility that musicology could define its work in relation to that project was inspiring.

Chapter 5 abridges my 1978 review of Jean-Jacques Nattiez's *Fondements d'une sémiologie de la musique.* Nattiez is now well known for his role in establishing an academic discourse on musical semiotics. A scholar of exceptional breadth and energy, he has done so much since *Fondements* that I believe I should say why I return here to his first major publication. Aside from the fact that he has moved prominently into ethnomusicology, that he has published ambitious and influential studies of Wagner and Proust, that he has assisted Pierre Boulez in publishing his writings, and that he has become well known as a public musical commentator to aficionados of Radio-Canada, he has also restated his semiotic principles in *Musicologie générale et sémologie* (1990a)—as well as the rather different English adaptation of that work, *Music and Discourse* (1990b)—and taken into account criticisms of his earlier work and greatly expanded its reach. I remain interested, however, in the early work for two reasons. First, in regards to fundamentals, he has remained loyal to his original principles. Second, given that constancy, the contests which his *prise de position* evoked are perhaps best understood in relation to the form his ideas took before they were further refined.

A portion of this review is given over to discussion of another book, a purely philosophical work, which I bring to bear on Nattiez's and which continues to influence our thought, Goodman's *Languages of Arts: A Contribution to the Study of Symbols* (1968). In relaxed parlance one might define notation as the representation of a concept. The philosopher, if not off duty, is obliged to ask what a concept is. But this is a question that has foiled every hypothesis since Plato's of "Ideas." Goodman makes no announcement that he is going after the dragon; yet, it might occur to us to note that he has, and that he is avoiding the fiery mouth by sneaking up on the tail. A *concept* (you won't find a definition of it in his book) might turn out to be exactly *that which can be notated.* The problem he tackles is to define notation operationally with no circular reference to concepts. Luckily for me, he chose to work this out with musical notation as his central example, affording the basic script upon which I constructed composition as "concept-like" and performance as "impulse-like" in *Elements of Semiotics* and elsewhere (see the introduction to Part III of this book).

The semiotic debates which are posed by Nattiez's initiative are chiefly about the methodological question of the place and limits of empiricism and about the semiotic question of the role of representation in constituting a sign. Although Nattiez had drawn on Nicolas Ruwet's analysis of the function of repetition in constructing his semiotics, Ruwet had, around that time, switched camps and had become for a time the chief spokesman for Chomskian rationalism in France and a critic of Harris's positivism, which he saw continued by Nattiez. Ruwet, who died in 2002, was himself an intellectual of wide range. He had intended as a youth to follow composition as his career and maintained personal ties with Luciano Berio for many years. His writings on music are exceptionally incisive though very conservative.

Chapter 6 expands on the plea of my first chapter that we attend to the tension between music's continuity and its crystallization as a chain of segments. The central criticism of Lehrdahl and Jackendoff's *A Generative Theory of Tonal Music* in this chapter is one that I broached to them when we met at the IRCAM Seminar on Music and Linguistics in 1975. They did not buy it; however, at that time I still relied on the insufficient analysis of the problem I had derived for my 1973 paper with Gabura. That paper, intending to structure Schenkerian logic as a "Chomskian" generative grammar producing tree structures (exactly what I now argue cannot be done), does not consider what I later came to regard as the crux of the problem, the principle of interruption, the main emphasis of the 1988 paper republished here with amendments.

My criticisms of Lehrdahl and Jackendoff are also criticisms of Nattiez's distributional taxonomy, as his method also produces a tree graph of music. The issues I raise overlap the concerns of E. Hantz in his review (1985) of this work and, less directly, those of J. Peel and W. Slawson (1983) and J. M. London (1997). Unlike any of those authors, my entry point is a critique of the analytic notation. It is not hair splitting; it deepens the issues. The lovely figure in the title is not mine. When I discussed these issues at a Princeton seminar in 1980, it was Peter Child who muttered about the "druids" who insisted that tree graphs were the foundation of the universe.

The discussion of the semiotics of Charles Peirce in Chapter 7 includes a brief appreciation of the work of a cherished Peircean musical semiotician, Naomi Cumming, whose early death I deeply lament. She was a brilliant young woman who brought to musical semiotics a disciplined analytical depth and a new engagement with humanism.

In this chapter there is a *pro,* but the *contra* is not fully specified. Until perhaps ten years ago, one often heard that semiotics was largely divided into two solitudes by the incompatible conceptions of the sign found in Saussure, who had provided the founding doctrine of European semiotics (sometimes *semiology*) and in Peirce, whose work oriented an American school. The formula which we repeated by rote was that Saussure's sign has two parts, *signified* and *signifier,* and Peirce's three, *sign, object,* and *interpretant.* But this is a bit wrong on both counts. Saussure does indeed characterize the sign that way, but it isn't as simple as it sounds because his signified and signifier are both positions in systems of "difference" (his term, not defined). Thus, the simplest possible sign system would be something like this:

{Zero, not one, means no, not yes. One, not zero, means yes, not no.}

Simple, but not too simple: two elements on each side of "means" make four elements that produce two signs. With more alternatives, larger messes would follow in the obvious way, but he is only concerned with the principle.

As for Peirce, who does not resolve facts and qualities to mere "differences," it is not entirely clear to me that he ever really meant to regard a sign as one whole with parts, though his language occasionally tends that way. What he says more often is that a sign is a *relate* with two *correlates;* that is, he prefers to speak of relations rather than parts. This is not very different but facilitates his understanding that the component relations can be immensely various, an advantage on which Cumming builds. For Saussure, the only relations are either *arbitrary significance* or *difference of value.* It also facilitates his principle that the interpretant of one sign becomes a sign correlated to a further interpretant in the next. "Next," because Peirce is more attentive to how signs develop thought over time than to how they form static systems. My reconciliation of these ideas in *Elements of Semiotics* retains Saussure's notion of system but ignores Saussure's concept of reference. For reference, I take my lead from Peirce. My standpoint in the interpretive studies in the remainder of this book is thus Peircean.

It is clear that with his triadic relations Peirce took account of a fact known to all careful observers at least since Kant that any reference reformulates its object. The object is seized in the raw, you might say, but transmitted in prejudice by its vestment. Saussure was not blind to this fact. He limited his analysis to contents already prejudiced by language, but he illustrates the difference of prejudice between different languages with great ingenuity.

5 Nattiez's *Foundations for Musical Semiotics*

Umberto Eco (1976) states, with regard to the status of musical research as a domain of semiotic inquiry, that

> the whole of musical science since the Pythagoreans has been an attempt to describe the field of musical communication as a "rigorously structured system." We note that until a few years ago contemporary musicology had scarcely been influenced by the current structuralist studies which are concerned with methods and themes that it had absorbed centuries ago. Nevertheless, in the last two or three years musical semiotics has been definitely established as a discipline aiming to find its "pedigree," and developing new perspectives. Among the pioneer works let us [cite] the bibliography elaborated by J. J. Nattiez in *Musique en jeu*, No. 5, 1971. (p. 10)

Nattiez's new book (1975), a fully elaborated study of nearly 450 pages, is a first for its discipline.[1] Most previous work purporting to treat musical semiotics—including a good deal which is scholarly, imaginative, and thoughtful and including the work of Nattiez himself—has been communicated through short papers or modest essays. Brevity may be the soul of wit, but it does not encourage stabilization of a technical vocabulary or construction of encompassing perspectives. We with an interest in such work have had no opportunity to appraise or contest an integrated problematic of musical semiotics as a whole. Nattiez's new book, which joins a thorough theoretical discussion to specific examples of musical analysis, invites us to raise the level of debate.

5.1. Musical Semiotics as Scientific Methodology

The first issue in such a debate might be whether or not semiotics does provide a new departure in musical research. The status of musical semiotics still carries an ambiguity of a special sort, in which, so far as I can see, no other semiotic domain is as deeply implicated, and Eco (*supra*) has not missed the point. Music has more than two millennia of intensive theoretical research to its account. The richness, diversity, height of abstraction, and insight in this tradition must be unrivaled by studies of any other semiotic medium save those of speech itself and—if we include it—mathematics. Is musical semiotics to be a revision of this tradition? A briefly fashionable addition to it? A new umbrella structure which includes it? A wholly different alternative to it? Eco seems to suggest that music's traditional theories already constitute a semiotic (even if an introverted one). Nattiez takes the

---

1. Except where noted, all citations of Nattiez in this chapter refer to Nattiez (1975).

ambitious position that semiotics represents an obligation to establish a new musicology on a new scientific footing. His option can draw support on two grounds: New formalisms and experimental methodologies have revolutionized the majority of intellectual studies in the last hundred years, and it is true that a good deal of traditional music theory is vague, incomplete, and inconsistent. Yet the music theorist may be well entitled to view Nattiez's onslaught with some skepticism and reserve or even a sense of affront: After all, in the Middle Ages it was theoretical musicology (with its honored position in the *quadrivium*) which defined scientific purity and not the converse. Since then musicology has been able to absorb initiatives from mathematics, physics, biology, and psychology without losing its identity as an integrated discipline. Now when a new science presumes to take music theory to task we are bound to ask if its inquiry is really broad enough and deep enough to illuminate the mysteries of our art and whether its claim to methodological sufficiency and intellectual certainty rests on a more secure pedestal than those of former doctrines.

Two chief sources of Nattiez's work are Molino's theory of symbolic function and Ruwet's proposals for a distributional taxonomy in music. I shall deal first with the direction he takes from Molino, which will involve us in a circuit of ideas about musical communication, and return later to the questions posed by Ruwet, which concern primarily the premises of analysis.

5.2. Objectivity and Communication: Some Semiotic Premises

The functional tripartition developed by Molino divides the symbolic relation into the *poïetique*, by which the sign refers to its conditions of production; the *esthésique* (*not esthétique*), by which a sign refers to its perception, interpretation, and appreciation; and the *niveau neutre*, the autonomous level of the sign as a structure embodied in material. Molino did not develop this scheme especially for music, but he has elaborated it in a recent essay devoted to musical problems (1975). The tripartition, intended to describe the human use of symbols with or without communication, is meant to encompass all relationships between the symbol and its users (producers and consumers), making no distinction like that of *noise* and *message* in communication theory:

> Nothing guarantees a direct correspondence between the effect produced by a work of art and the intentions of its creator. Every symbolic object presumes an exchange in which producer and consumer, sender and receiver are not interchangeable and have different perspectives on this object which they hardly conceive in the same way. (Molino 1975, p. 47)

The theme, stated thus, is plain enough. What disturbs me is the construction of a semiotics which discards so lightly the distinction between communicative and noncommunicative uses of symbols. Whatever its justification in theory, the tripartition has been utilized in practice to stage a retreat from the problems of meaning.

The central fact in Molino's exposition is music's actual diversity: historical, functional, material, and cultural. Seeking to embrace the whole of music, Molino argues that it cannot be wholly defined in structural or acoustic terms. It must be defined also in terms of its cultural functions as an object of production and perception. He would thus define music neutrally as an acoustic fact (the *niveau neutre*) and/or productively as an intentional deployment of sounds according to rules (the *poïetique*) and/or perceptually as a sequence of sounds "pleasing" (or otherwise effective) to the ear (the *esthésique*), any of these definitions being correct, *depending on the context* in which the definition functions. One type of definition—*poïetique, esthésique,* or *neutre*—cannot be reduced to another. Molino's tripartition is most persuasive insofar as he is engaged in a critical analysis of previous theories. The *poïetique* has preeminence before the eighteenth century (numerous counterpoint texts, for example, telling "how to do it"); the *esthésique* becomes more prominent in the age of Diderot (*Neveu de Rameau*) when "it became a concern to render an account of music not just to the experts, but also to [those who could not profit] by the multiplication of technical analyses" (Molino 1975, p. 51).

We encounter a serious fallacy where Molino takes the triad of articulatory, acoustic, and perceptual descriptions in phonetics as a case of his three symbolic dimensions:

> Contrary to what a certain number of amateurs or even linguists who are not phoneticians believe, there is no reason to think that the three approaches lead to the same units. On the one hand, sounds determining the same acoustical and auditory effects can be produced by different articulatory means; on the other hand, a single sound, as defined acoustically, can be interpreted differently according to the perceptual framework of the auditor. (Molino 1975, p. 48)

I thought this structural divergence of the perceptual and articulatory fields was one fact that even we non-phonetical laymen could be counted on to know well. But this divergence would hardly merit attention except for another salient truth, which Molino seems determined to ignore: The social fact of language has contrived a system of *agreement* between the two fields. The profundity of the distinctive feature theory lies in its proposal to sketch the contract between two parties, tongue and ear. In the agreement lies the possibility of communication, and in the actuality of communication, the raison d'être of our studies; in the agreement—the code—*poïetique* and *esthésique* are united, imposed upon in such a way that they need not always be distinguished either from each other or from the code itself. Molino formulates an empiricist slogan which holds, I fear, considerable dangers to the semiotic enterprise: "Let us then describe music, religion, or language before we ask ourselves [how] they participate in our thoughts" (Molino 1975, p. 52).

Controversy concerning Nattiez's adoption of Molino's tripartition has centered on the proposal of the *niveau neutre*. The objection runs thus: If all descriptions of music have their origin in the facts of production and perception, how is a neutral description possible except as a vacuous hypothesis? For Nattiez, it is not the origin (in a historical/psychological sense) of the analysis which is important, but rather the possibility of making it explicit. If an analytical procedure can be stated explicitly, it can be detached from its original motivation and followed uninterpreted; interpretation belongs to the other two spheres. The neutral description is conceived as a moment in the dialectical process of analysis. The configurations it identifies may be relevant to the *poïetique* or the *esthésique* or both or neither. As a *description* the neutral analysis testifies to the autonomous organization which might allow the neutral level of the sign to engender entirely new interpretations in unforeseen contexts. Translated to more conventional but, I think, perfectly fair terminology, the *niveau neutre* represents an ideal of empirical objectivity which takes the musical text as its sole object of observation.

Again we see that the problem of communication is excluded. Since the text as object is the only acknowledged link between production and perception, there are no criteria by which to judge whether the text has communicated anything besides the fact of its own existence. Nattiez attempts at one point to reconcile this schema of Molino's to the problems of communication by recourse to Peirce's theory of an infinite sequence of interpretants, but even this formulation fails to touch the structure of musical understanding. Nattiez's interpretants do not constitute a theory of semantic organization; their relationship to the musical sign is contingent and arbitrary. One may not say that a certain interpretation of a musical work is "true" and another is "false." Both Peirce, because of his interest in what I would call psychological logic, and Saussure, because of the web of value relationships which pervade the field of signifieds, invite us to foresee the universe of semantic interpretation as one with laws of organization (and as an organization, we should note, which has no a priori dependence on verbal concepts). Nattiez ignores the theoretical questions of a semantic *system* which are raised by the Saussurian and Peircean models. The semiotic tradition is characterized by the assumption that the meaning of signs is systematic—neither haphazard and isolated nor absolute. If music has a meaning, what kind of systematic basis for its meaning is possible?

5.3. Musical Meaning

Theories of music's function and content have a history at least as old as the history of its theory of structure and equally as diverse. In a worldwide perspective, Aristotle and Plato would have to share patriarchal claims with ancient Chinese and Indian sources and, no doubt, others (Nattiez, pp. 154–55). What is so striking in this history is the separation of structural and aesthetic interpretation. Usually we find the semantic description of music limited to the level of its genres and materials; only rarely is the specific text offered a special interpretation. When meanings are ascribed to specific works, it is usually at the price of abandoning the close structural scrutiny for which music theory is generally noted. Plato, for example, discusses the meanings of various musical scales. Apparently the meanings he specifies attach to these scales no matter how the scales are used. Or, to take a very different source, the illuminating and evocative analysis of the mazurkas which Liszt offers in his *Chopin* gives us few hints what technical means are responsible for the effects so persuasively described, nor does he suggest why certain techniques would produce particular results. On the other hand, the purely technical descriptions of authors such as Tovey, Reimann, or Schenker can provoke a feeling of illumination which matches the best hermeneutics in its power of clarification, but questions of extra-musical content are broached, if at all, only in the most general or peripheral contexts. There are exceptions. Among contemporary studies which attempt to link the structural and communicative domains, the most prominent is no doubt the pioneering book *Emotion and Meaning in Music* (1957), in which Leonard Meyer related music's expressive effects to the tensions of expectation associated with pattern perception in time.

I consider Meyer's book to belong to musical semiotics despite the disavowal in his Preface of any attempt "to deal with the general logical philosophical status of music—to decide whether music is a language or whether musical stimuli are signs or symbols" (p. viii), and have noted with interest both the author's acknowledgment of his helpful association with Charles Morris (p. x) and numerous references to works associated, via the Pragmatic Movement, with the semiotics of Peirce.[2] In Morris's pragmatism, the interpretant can be equated with physiological activity of the brain. This equation opens the door to a theory such as Meyer's in which cultural learning and affective response are physiologically linked at the level of gestalt perception. We need not agree 100 percent with Meyer about which aspects of music are arbitrary (i.e., socially defined; arbitrary in the Saussurian sense) and which are biologically determined to appreciate the ingenuity of the connection he has constructed between the two realms.

Meyer works from the psychological theory that affective states are a response to inhibition or delay of the fulfillment of a desire or a tendency. This mechanism of arousal can be observed and traced from the crudest level of biological function to the most refined activities of the cultural plane. In perception we tend to seek closed and balanced forms as defined by the general principles of gestalt organization and the particular principles of a culturally determined style. Music provides such good forms, but by deviation, attenuation, and delay, music frustrates the listener's expectations and evokes an affective response. The ultimate resolution of these tensions accounts for a clarified (and pleasant) emotional experience.

In his review of theories of musical meaning, Nattiez quotes Meyer and adopts a classificatory schema similar to his. Nattiez reviews, among others, the ideas of Ruwet, Lévi-Strauss, Meyer, Schloezer, Francis, Boiles, Schweitzer, and Imberty. Nattiez seems to favor those researchers like Imberty and Francis who are accumulating "hard data" in statistical form. His theoretical involvement with Molino's tripartition discourages the search for an explanatory theory of meaning.

I cite Meyer because he has shown us that there is at least one way to attack the problems of meaning in music on an explanatory level. Certainly we need not be content with Meyer's solution. At best it is incomplete. The only aspect of musical experience which it probes is tension. (Some music is very moving without being dramatic, but it is difficult to see how drama and expressivity are separable in his

---

2. Particularly works of Dewey and Mead. See in this connection Morris's *The Pragmatic Movement in American Philosophy.*

scheme.) The most telling fault of Meyer's theory, though, is a fault it shares with nearly all others. Meyer's theory, like most musical semantic theories, fails to distinguish the meaning of one piece from another. He talks about the meaning of "music," not "pieces." What we shall see now is that this failing is not limited to our descriptions of the *signified;* it is built into our traditional science of the *signifier.* In traditional music theory each piece is first an example of a system and only second (and ad hoc) an individual.

5.4. The Musical Signifier

Nattiez does not identify that problem in those terms, but I will contend in the end that he helps us to resolve it, at least on the side of the signifier. Nattiez's comparative study of linguistic theories and music proceeds from the *signified* to the *signifier.* The *signifier* is more accountable within the "neutral level" of the musical sign, and here Nattiez's discussion is more persuasive.

Nattiez asks whether the musical score is the musical signifier. Saussure worked out the framework for this question as it applies to linguistics. Linguists do not confuse the written and spoken word, but they are well able to take advantage of a degree of equivalence of the two which is well established. Does the score reveal the music? Once the question is broached we discover many grounds for doubt. The American composer Morton Feldman worked for years with numerous experimental notations and finally returned to conventional means. Summing up this wide experience, he has expressed the belief that no more than 10 percent of any music's intent can be conveyed by its written text.[3] Aside from the fact that the role of notation is challenged today by our increasing awareness of non-notated music—most jazz, Eastern music, folk music—and by the rebirth of improvisation as a compositional element in avant-garde music, we must all know how dull and meaningless a musical performance can sound when it is *merely* "faithful to the score." If we want to study the musical signifier, should we be content to study the score?

Nattiez, whose own work continues and extends the dialectic of score analysis, is sensitive to a theoretical need to justify score study and to assess its limitations. He notes that the score imposes an intermediate level which is *parole* vis-à-vis the *langue* of musical style but which is also *langue* to the *parole* of musical performance (pp. 109–17). Speaking of the material existence of music, he writes:

> We have alluded . . . to the fact that [the *niveau neutre*] is based on the score. In the western tradition, to be sure, and not in every case. . . . Well, music appears first of all as a phenomenon of sound. Is there not something scandalous in our proposal? (p. 109)

Nattiez makes several points in defense of analysis based on written texts. The score, the written text, is what the composer makes; it is his determination of "pertinent features" and "the trace which permits the work its identity" (p. 111). The

---

3. Lecture at York University, 1975.

particular execution of a work, a single recording, for example, could also be the object of an analysis, but the analysis, itself a static object, must work with some fixed thing (or with the invariants of a changing object). Since music *as* a sound object is in flux, the first step in an analysis of a performance could be to fix it by notation. As for oral traditions and the "open forms" of avant-garde composition, the progression of our analysis of these must be contingent on "the extent to which the object of analysis can be rendered in discrete parts."[4]

I suspect that Nattiez's concept of discrete elements may be limited to discrete segments and might exclude discrete *aspects* (e.g., loudness, timbre), the coordination of which might be subject to analysis without segmentation. Allowing this one reservation, his defense of score analysis is persuasive. It struck me that his brief argument touched on a number of points developed in a much more elaborated investigation of related problems in Goodman's *Languages of Art* (1968), and I think Goodman's investigations give us some sound advice about what we might fairly expect score analysis to accomplish and what is outside the score's signification.

5.5. Notation and Signification

Goodman's book is a study in stealth, like twelve months of whispering in the towers which erupts in a coup d'état. It hardly seems as though his unending refinements of categories of reference could ever touch on what musicians or their critics would recognize as artistic issues. To be sure, Goodman has ultimately kept himself at arm's length from many such issues, but his careful construction of the class of "notational systems" and his analysis of "metaphorical exemplification" reflect a strong light on the nature of musical conceptualization and the wisdom and pleasure it offers.

I must paraphrase some of Goodman's conclusions without trying to recapitulate their full rationales. There is a danger of distortion in excerpting his conclusions from the tapestry which supports them, but the finesse of Goodman's needlework is well known, and the risk is to the fabric of my argument, not his.

Goodman creates the class of notational systems by formal syntactic and semantic restrictions. It is an idealized class, but the ideal it defines is one which musical notation nearly achieves. Speaking in very general terms, the syntactic requirements have to do with the distinctness of each character in the system, and the semantic requirements provide for a clear determination whether or not a given performance "complies" with a given notational character. Goodman motivates his investigation of this abstract class with a proposal to learn why music can be notated, why painting cannot be, and whether dance notation may be expected to succeed. Behind these queries stands his distinction between "autographic" and "allographic" arts. An autographic work—a painting, a performance, or a calligraphic work—can be forged, and since it is never possible to prove that a copy is as good as the original, the original is uniquely valuable. An allographic work such

---

4. capacité, pour l'objet d'analyse, à se laisser discrétiser (p. 115).

as a poem or musical score cannot be forged: any correct copy of a poem or a composition is equivalent to the original. Goodman observes that choreography is allographic because a competent observer who sees two dance performances can judge reliably if they are performances of the same dance or not. (Just as a competent listener can judge whether two musical performances are performances of the same piece or not.) He contends that dance notation meets the same system requirements that music notation does (and notes that it requires comparable licenses to supplement its ideal scheme). Goodman foresees that dance notation could gain such conceptual authority that it would necessarily inspire the rebelliousness typified in music by John Cage's rejection of music's notational categories.[5]

Analysis and notation are mutually implicational. *Notating*, in Goodman's sense, which opposes it, for example, to *graphing*, presumes an analysis of a text into components. Analysis divides an artistic text into sets of parts, and the labels of the sets, taken in the right order and combination, become a notation of the work. Goodman does not discuss many examples of notational systems, but if I understand his definitions correctly, the symbols used in traditional harmonic analysis also constitute a notational system. A "compound inscription such as "IV^6-V^7" meets Goodman's requirements of syntactic and semantic unambiguity. This fact is not surprising (the chord symbols are notations of notations) but not inconsequential either.

To demonstrate the criteria, consider a harmonic analysis with chord symbols of some given score: (1) The given musical score may be only one of innumerable ways of complying with the notated harmonic progression, but, given any substitute text, we could quickly determine if it complied or not. (2) A harmonic analysis specifies the music in a way *conventionally* regarded as significant, even though a very similar passage could have a different harmonic progression and a very different passage could have an identical one. (3) The analysis notation system is very general and applies to a wide range of music.

On the other hand, we would not speak of notating a painting on the basis of some ad hoc analysis of it. In painting, as Goodman points out, a work is not made from antecedently classified materials. (Obviously it might use some such materials.) Any notation which we devise for painting would have a very limited scope. Arguing *ad absurdum*, we could "notate" a particular painting by dividing it into labeled parts, with the labels properly arranged and coordinated standing as a notation of the painting. The reason why this idea is silly or, at best, frustrating is that we have no reason to think that the kind of segmentation which works for one painting will work for another. In an autographic art, notation is an extraneous consideration.

The point of all this is that the limits of what we conventionally refer to as formal analysis in aesthetic theory are the same as or very similar to the limits of what Goodman calls a notational system. Goodman's investigation tells us something about what we can expect formal analysis—or notation—to accomplish and what

---

5. My *Elements of Semiotics*, p. 196, offers a refutation.

is outside its power. We can more easily see why all this matters and how it helps if we take his contrasting case, the category of aesthetic symptoms:

> Repeated failure to find a neat formula for sorting experiences into aesthetic and nonaesthetic, in rough conformity with rough usage, suggests the need for a less simple-minded approach. Perhaps we should . . . look for aspects or symptoms, rather than for a crisp criterion, of the aesthetic. A symptom is neither a necessary nor a sufficient condition for, but merely tends in conjunction with other such symptoms to be present in, aesthetic experience. (Goodman 1968, p. 252)

The symptoms which Goodman suggests are indicative of aesthetic experience ("syntactic density," "semantic density," "repleteness") all mark an aesthetic object as being unlike a notational character. "All three features call for maximum sensitivity of discrimination" (Goodman 1968, p. 252). Using again a much more informal explanation of these terms than Goodman's own, these symptomatic conditions provide that every shading and nuance of the sign will determine some shading and nuance of its meaning. Since a musical score is a notation, it does not matter just how round the heads of the quarter notes are or how neatly they sit on their line (convenience to the reader but not meaning is at stake in the variations). But when the quarter note is performed, everything counts, not merely the bare facts which ensure "compliance" with the notation. Intonation may be expressive as well as correct. The unnotated facts of vibrato, timbral nuance, and dynamic shape become all-important. In Goodman's analysis, the art work is important to us because of its power to exemplify metaphorically the qualities which we experience, but it appears that this specifically aesthetic power of art is symptomatically linked with modes of symbolic relations *excluded* from notational systems. This conclusion argues a pessimistic view of pure textural analysis. It suggests that score analysis (which is, I claim, equivalent to a renotation of the score) will not be able to reveal the artistic character of its object, and it suggests, moreover, that the score itself does not express the music's artistic character.

The fact is musical scores do not convey aesthetic qualities unless "interpreted" or, to use Goodman's preferred term, "supplemented" in the light of an external source of understanding. An interpretive theory of music must always appeal to some additional machinery outside of pure textual relations, as the Romantics did when they offered "programs" for their music and as Meyer does when he builds on gestalt psychology and the hypothesis relating tension to affect. But there is also a more encouraging hint that we might take from Goodman's analysis. Though score analysis, or more broadly, notational expression is insufficient to indicate the aesthetic *character* of an artwork, it is still possible for an analysis to define the *specificity* of the work. Musical notation is adequate to determine this specificity. We can *recognize* a reading of the Fifth Symphony even when the interpretation is completely awful. There is a real job to do which music theory until now has not done: to say what a given piece of music is as a unique entity without merely "reducing" it to an exemplification of some known formula of harmonic, rhythmic, or tonal organization.

The endless complication of systematic theory in music has developed and simultaneously obscured this prejudice of musical studies, which concentrate on systems at the expense of the individuating aspects of a single work. We place a given piece of music as in a harmonic system, a voice-leading system, a rhythmic system. Only the most difficult acrobatics allow these conventional methods to formulate a description of one piece that another piece would not fit as well. Nattiez's semiotics supplies an essential tool for this task in the form of his "distributional taxonomy," which, without reference to abstract rules or archetypal forms, displays the single work as an independent semiotic system of paradigms and syntagms.

5.6. The System of One Work

The third and longest part of Nattiez's book is devoted to what he terms a description of the *niveau neutre,* and the method of this description is the distributional taxonomy. The distributional taxonomy provides a hierarchical segmentation of a musical text on the basis of internal parallelisms so that like segments may be grouped as members of a paradigm while consecutive segments which form a single unit on a higher level may be recognized as a syntagm. The idea, first formalized by Ruwet, was heralded with considerable political fanfare on the theme of empirical methodology.

Ruwet's proposals for a distributional taxonomy, which take repetition as the primary determining formal mechanism of music, underlie all of Nattiez's techniques of score analysis. Ruwet has signaled severe reservations about his earlier work (Ruwet 1975), and yet it is surely among the more suggestive contemporary analytic initiatives in music. Ruwet's later modification—indeed, reversal—broaches broad questions about the status of musical abstractions (rules and universals) and the nature of music's signification; yet Nattiez has been wise to insist on the further elaboration of this work. I hope in what follows, besides illustrating and describing the basic proposal of the taxonomy, to rescue it from the cumbersome costume of scientific pretensions in which it was swaddled, to show how it complements and interacts with traditional theory (rather than replace it), and to suggest how it realizes a conception of methodological discipline more appropriate to our humanistic enterprise of music theory than the conceptions which we have seen marshaled previously to defend it.

Segmentation and Hierarchy in Music

> The verbal or musical sequence, if it is to be produced, followed and remembered, fulfils two fundamental requirements—it exhibits a consistently hierarchical structure and is resolvable into ultimate, discrete, strictly patterned components designed *ad hoc.*
>
> —Jakobson (1967), p. 341

Jakobson's assertion is generally true for music, but his rule is much more adequate for verbal than tonal art. Certain aspects of music can make its segmental and hierarchical relations very ambiguous.

The possibility of effecting gradual transitions between contrasting values allows for the suppression of boundaries between sections of a musical composition. Almost any values of music may be treated this way—loudness, tonality, texture, etc. Schumann is fond of a technique whereby one theme is gradually transformed into the accompaniment for another, and the Romantic masters could blend the colors of their orchestra so that we hardly know where the flute begins and the clarinet leaves off. The logical sense, which desires to hear distinct segments, is frustrated and delighted by these devices.

Music is a multidimensional art. Its rhythmic, melodic, harmonic, and timbral aspects may have independent though simultaneous structures. If rhythmic and pitch organization are clearly distinct in a passage, we can satisfy Jakobson's requirements by providing two hierarchical segmentations, one for the rhythmic and one for the tonal plane. More often, though, these will be interdependent in unpredictable ways, rendering the hierarchy ambiguous (see Nattiez's discussion of Boulez's analysis of the opening bassoon melody in *Le sacre du printemps* [pp. 279–85]).

Music thus enters a complex relationship of tensions and resistance with its own hierarchical and segmental structures, but the importance of its segmentation and hierarchy is not thereby diminished. We do listen for a segmental hierarchy. Traditional concepts like section, phrase, motive, chord, theme, bridge, and coda respond to our requirement for identified and oriented segments. Each of these concepts is potentially problematic and difficult to define. Probably the clearest in this list is "chord," but while the interpretation of a chord symbol is reasonably straightforward, the reverse path, division of a musical passage into a string of chords, can easily be ambiguous. (See, for example, Nattiez, p. 320. Here Nattiez does not wish to make an issue of problems in the traditional terminology, but he must still use two levels of analysis ["micro"/"macro"] to divide the music— Brahms, *Intermezzo,* Op. 119, no. 3—into separate chords.)

The segmentation of music conceived by traditional theory is based mainly on abstractions and archetypes. Consider a definition such as that of Hermann Keller in *Phrasing and Articulation:* "By a musical phrase shall be understood the equivalent of a line of verse in poetry, or of a simple unbroken sentence in prose" (1965, p. 13). I cite this definition as typical in the following way. It proposes we segment the musical text by recognizing *previously and abstractly conceived forms* (phrases, chords, cadences). It offers, as does all traditional theory, a function or mapping from the text onto some predefined set of abstract symbols, not a mapping of internal repetitions.

But the distributional analysis proposed by Ruwet and Nattiez is a mapping of segments of a musical text *onto each other* rather than onto preconceived abstractions. Ruwet's original concern was to find a method of segmentation for music which could meet a strong test of empirical objectivity, and he proposed that a segmentation strictly determined by repetition would meet this requirement. Music is highly repetitive. In the scheme of this analysis, longer repetitions determine higher levels, and shorter repetitions lower levels of the segmental hierarchy. In illustrating his analyses graphically, Ruwet's concern was to use only precisely defined symbols and relations; the format of the score is thus specified and deliberately simple. I give an example here which Nattiez (p. 245) quotes from Ruwet (1972, p. 116). The chart, Figure 5.1, is to be read two ways. Reading vertically, the musical figures which are aligned on top of each other constitute a paradigm.[6] Reading normally, the complete lines from left to right constitute a full copy of the song (a Medieval monophonic *Geisslerlied*) as sung. The example represents two hierarchical levels of analysis indicated by small and capital letters. Further levels can be shown on successive charts.

It has to be admitted right at the start that this particular diagram is not very informative. The usual printed transcriptions of this song use repetition marks anyway, which punctuate the text and tell nearly the same story about its structure as does this graph. Yet, as Nattiez explains, despite the simplicity of this example and the apparent obviousness of the analysis, Amrom (1969) demonstrated that several different, alternative segmentations of this song can result if different criteria of identity are used. One reason is that while music is highly repetitious, it usually repeats with some variation. We are not just looking for repetitions, then, but for variations or, as Ruwet termed them, transformations.

At this juncture we discover a limitation of distributional analysis which Ruwet came to acknowledge, though not Nattiez. The question whether or not two fragments of a musical text are equivalent as variations of each other is, in general, one that cannot be answered on a purely empirical basis. Its solution requires reference to abstract equivalence classes. For example, a strong measure of equivalence is established in eighteenth- and nineteenth-century music between any two versions of what we call the "same" chord. In Figure 5.2 all the chords are E-minor triads. In the twentieth century, Stravinsky was able to free his ear from the force of these family resemblances and to create in his *Symphony of Psalms* a masterful first movement which depends on one particular E-minor chord, the last in Figure 5.2, never being interchangeable with any other (Babbitt 1972a, p. 168). Thus, abstract equivalences are relative to style, and no objective and neutral reading of the text alone can uncover these equivalences, which we must learn either through special pedagogical materials or prescriptive compositional techniques. Inspection of a text for repetition and variation is no more objective a discovery procedure than inspection for phrases and cadences.

If methodological purity is the objective, we might contend then that nothing is gained by recourse to repetition as a foundational principle in analysis. If, more modestly, we simply seek a vantage point that doesn't subsume the specific heritage of tonal-metrical-phrase structure as a first principle, the distributional taxonomy has a strong basis in common sense. Despite, or perhaps because of, its pervasiveness, repetition has not been studied systematically in theoretical musicology: "The unique role of repetition in music is such that musicians and musicologists, when they reflect on their art, are liable to forget it while putting the accent on more

---

6. A figure and its replicate appear as distinct entries in the paradigm because their position is an attribute.

Figure 5.1. After Ruwet as cited by Nattiez.

Figure 5.2a–f. Members of abstract equivalence class of E-minor chords; f: from Stravinsky, *Symphony of Psalms*.

secondary characteristics" (Ruwet 1972, p. 135).[7] Typically an analytical essay begins with a statement to the effect that the work to be studied is in so-or-so many sections, which begin and end in such-and-such measures. If one looks for a rationale for this segmentation, it usually appears that repetition has been a key factor.

Ruwet's taxonomy is not a study of repetition in all its varieties and musical uses, but it puts repetition "on the table" as it were and gives musical analysis a more systematic access to important repetition functions. Establishing segmental hierarchy is one of the most important functions of repetition in music, and, looking at the same function from the opposite side, we can see that repetition defines the musical materials specific to a composition.

The only *concrete* elements in a particular piece of music which are defined in advance are its notes. As soon as any pattern is repeated, it becomes a defined component of its text, a quasi-lexical unit, or as musicians so often say, an "idea" of the music. Repetition is not the only relation which establishes units in music, but it is a preeminent factor. Music which avoids repetition (including varied repetition) stands out as stylistically extreme.

The Dictionary of a Musical Composition: Paradigm and Syntagm

The components of each musical composition, unlike the components of an English sentence, are the exclusive property of that composition. If they recur elsewhere, it is by accident. To study a musical composition as a combination of parts, to study their similarities, oppositions, sequences, and hierarchical arrangement, is to study that composition as an *individual* work. Repetition and variation are the most dependable tools by which music creates a new dictionary from a common vocabulary of notes. In a language dictionary, words define words. In the dictionary of a musical composition, units define each other through the complex web of their associations by similarity (repetition and variation).

When we represent a work on several hierarchical divisions as a combinatory system whose elements can be paradigmatically arranged, we have written the unique dictionary of that piece, the system (the idiolect) of the single work. I hesitate to demonstrate this point with reference to the *Geisslerlied* reproduced above. This simple tune, inevitably familiar to music students by its frequent citation, does not seem to beg for explication. Perhaps it may serve, though, to establish a model:

1. On an abstract plane (the dialect), we may describe the song as being in a certain mode (Lydian with B♭), having a certain meter (duple), or pertaining to a particular genre (*Geisslerlied*).
2. On a concrete plane (the idiolect), we can specify the materials of the

---

7. L'uniquité de la répétition en musique est telle que musiciens et musicologues, quand il réfléchissent sur la nature de leur art en viennent assez facilement à l'oublier, pour mettre l'accent sur de phénomènes de caractère plus dérivé.

piece at each syntagmic level. That there are other ways to slice the pie is not at issue, as long as we have at least one good one. Here are the syntagms, as determined by Ruwet's analysis and notated by the labels he gives them:

(*Highest-level unit*) Song = A A′ B B′
(*Second-highest-level units*) A = a b c b′; A = a b c b′; B = d_1 d_1 b′
The subdivisions of the lowest-level units are simply the tones themselves (as illustrated in Figure 5.1).

5.7. Nattiez's Analyses

In its more extended applications, the taxonomic analysis is craft as much as method. Nattiez and his co-workers at the University of Montreal have pursued the distributional model in different variations through studies in numerous styles and genres of music. The demonstrations which Nattiez has published are the fruit of this accumulating experience. They are detailed, thorough, and clear. Each raises distinct issues.

Brahms Intermezzo, *Op. 119, no. 3*

The *Intermezzo* analysis is not the most adventurous of Nattiez's presentations, for the music itself shows a self-conscious constructive technique which is not abstruse. Nevertheless, it is a very original little composition, and Nattiez has been able to bring its identity into immediate focus by showing how its thematic permutations result in two distinct segmental hierarchies. One design emerges when rhythmic repetitions determine the division of the material. This analysis proceeds naturally from longer to shorter units. The other design appears when repetitions of pitch sequences determine the divisions, an analysis which is generated by examining small units first and building larger blocks from these. Nattiez finds confirmation of this segmental ambiguity in a comparison of recorded interpretations by Julius Katchen and Walter Klein, the main differences being equivalent to opposite emphases on the alternative segmental schemes (p. 326). A key question then becomes whether or not the harmony determines which of the segmental schemes is more prominent. (The harmonic analysis is essentially a chord analysis which does not broach the matter of long-range voice leading.)

Debussy, Syrinx

Nattiez discusses the segmentation of *Syrinx* at three hierarchical strata: the formal level, where the music is divided into three or four sections; a middle or "macroscopic" level, where the elements are one or two measures long; and a level of minimal units, often one beat in length. (The total length of *Syrinx* is thirty-five measures.) His analysis demonstrates, as do Ruwet's analyses, the interpenetration of adjacent hierarchical strata which is so fundamental to musical construction (but for which we lack a standard descriptive terminology). The analysis allows Nattiez to compare the differing opinions of several authors from a single perspective, furnishing a concise critique of their results.

Nattiez presented his *Syrinx* analysis in a more detailed format (in 1974, as a mimeograph) which included a comparison of the repetition analysis with other approaches, particularly a voice-leading analysis in a Schenkerian vein. That quasi-Schenkerian voice-leading analysis is essentially syntactic. Nattiez's method here is a taxonomy of components; we could call it lexical. Ultimately we want to align the two conceptions, and in fact Nattiez comes quite close to that synthesis in the study to which we turn next.

Varèse, Density 21.5

This analysis, published separately (1973 and also in English in *Musical Analysis*) is the most elaborate and most rewarding. This time Nattiez has not shown us a segmental *procedure* in detail. He starts with a segmentation and proceeds to explore the relationships which justify it and to examine alternatives where they suggest themselves. This format allows him to emphasize the syntagmic axis more than he had in previous studies. It is an emphasis which the music demands, for there is no complete and literal repetition. Each paradigmatic group must accommodate such a degree of variation that the integrity of the paradigm cannot be explained without reference to its unfolding as a sequence in time.

The analysis proceeds via a meticulous accounting of every variable—pitch, duration, interval, direction, register, dynamic, and articulation—a kind of accounting which I confess to find usually a torturous tedium, the epitome in musicology of occupational hazards. Here it fits. The music may have a dominant hierarchical plan, but it suggests innumerable variants and contradictions to its dominant scheme. Every nuance of Varèse's text is revealed to weigh meaningfully in the dialectic of these patterns.

The distributional method is pushed to the point here of permitting significant abstractions. They are not the a priori abstractions of traditional theory, but they play an important role. They permit Nattiez to speak of the "assimilation" (1973, p. 18) of a unit to a paradigm so that it may seem to express slightly different features than it has (a modest encroachment of mentalism into the empirical world of Nattiez?). He also uses these abstract categories in searching for functions (implicational relations) between the different dimensions of variation (p. 75).

If we take a step back from this fine study and regard it at a distance, we see that Varèse's composition is stylistically characterized by the fact that such a method of analysis is suitable to it. Unlike Debussy, who belongs to two worlds, Varèse has left all the a priori implicational relations of metrical tonality behind. The unique system of the work is its *only* system. Instead of the tension between style (abstract) and example (concrete), the work takes its life and its energy from the complexity and ambiguity of its internally developed associations and contrasts. The taxonomy renders these explicit. This long study is an important complement to the *Fondements*.

5.8. Musical Semiotics: Status and Prospects

The distributional taxonomy is an important addition to our analytic techniques, but it does not provide a full semiotic perspective on music. Neither Ruwet's criticisms (1975) of his own earlier work and Nattiez's nor Nattiez's penultimate chapter, which purports to answer these criticisms, puts the problem in a satisfactory framework.

The Theory of Theory Construction

Nattiez proposes to extend analysis in the vein of distributional taxonomy to determine the general rules of different styles. This is the proposal which Ruwet (1975) criticizes most sharply. Ruwet grounds his criticisms in the philosophy of Popper, which holds a scientific law to be absolute in the sense that it admits of no contradiction. Such a law cannot be proven positively, but a single counterexample invalidates the theory. In biology or physics the idea has validity, but an artistic norm is not like a physical law. It may be as powerful when breached as when observed. The motivation for a phrase theory in music is the charm of "irregular" phrase structures. We could speak of disproof of a stylistic principle only if we knew: (1) exactly to what stylistic range a theory applied, and (2) our tolerance of "agrammaticality" in the given corpus. These are problems which the linguist will recognize. On a practical level, it does make sense (at least for a certain range of studies) to talk about standard languages and "ideal speakers" in linguistics. In musicology there are a few such plateaus in music, but only a few. One can speak of "common practice" harmony of the eighteenth century, but it is a far more amorphous entity than "standard English." That music evolves so quickly is not even the crux of the problem; the real difficulty is that in music we value differences above similarities. A theory which holds true for mediocre compositions but to which the great works are exceptions need not be without interest. Like the theory of sonata form, which seems to fit that mold, such theories can be tested only by their pedagogical utility and intuitive appeal. No counterexample can disprove them; neither can a hundred counterexamples. From time to time the theory is advanced or corrected, but progress is necessarily slow, not merely because our data and our categories are nebulous, but also because our test of validity is not Popper's.

Generalization about music is clearly possible, but it is inevitably bound up with the imprecision of all our notions of style. Nattiez's proposal is to use the results of the taxonomic method applied to a relatively homogeneous repertoire of works as the basis for generative models. I have not seen enough results from this program to have a sense of what it really means, but there is no *logical* path from componential studies to generative ones. I fear that Nattiez may be choosing a method which restricts his freedom of observation in exchange for the mere appearance of rigor. If we study Mozart's sonatas as a stylistic group, we will find each one an exception in some way to rules followed by the others. As Ruwet points out, the approach to stylistic study that Nattiez favors downplays contrastive studies. As he suggests, it is often more informative to compare a Haydn symphony with one of Mozart's than to compare several of Mozart's with each other. In comparative studies we wisely accept our intuitive capacity for hasty generalizations. We do not know what types of rules correspond to intuitive judgments about norms (statistical rules? generative procedures? implicational relations?). What is the point of formalizing methods in an area where our knowledge is so tentative? It is not really clear that the taxonomy of the series (the stylistic repertoire) has a definite question to answer. It may be in the essence of style that it remains a fuzzy concept.

The Quest for Discipline

I am not entirely sympathetic to an obsession with scientific purity in semiotics or musicology. Many an author wins our interest without earning our belief, and the converse is also true. Nevertheless, if it is methodological probity we want, I think Nattiez's taxonomy can meet both a test of theoretical relevance and a test of validation.

A test of validity which is appropriate to musical distributional analysis is not Popper's for scientific laws but Goodman's for notational systems. If there is no empirical proof that one analysis is better than another, at least we can test whether an analysis is clear. Are the paradigms distinct? (Syntactic distinctness.) Is it possible to tell, given a characterization of a certain paradigm, whether a given unit belongs to it? (Semantic distinctness: trivial if the paradigm is just a list of units; interesting if each group is described by economical abstractions!) We may predict with confidence that each existing analysis will fail one test: Goodman requires as a condition of semantic distinctness that compliance classes not overlap. What that means here is that no one musical unit can belong to two different paradigmatic groups nor to two different hierarchical levels. The most profound result of taxonomic research to date is to suggest that music does not allow this condition to be met. Music sets up categories, but it also determines material which mediates or liquidates its categories. A methodological challenge facing the taxonomy is to devise notations which will distinguish between oppositions (material conforming with categories) and mediations (materials not conforming). Nattiez's introduction of symbolism based on an information storage and retrieval model is a muscular reaction to this problem (pp. 341–54), but I think it generates a plethora of detail without clarifying the central issue.

Ruwet says of his (and Nattiez's) analytic procedures that it is "not easy to determine what theory underlies them" (1975, p. 26). The theory we want is not simply a theory about musical texts, but a theory (a semiotic theory) about how music makes sense.

Since Nattiez insists on the separation of the description of the neutral level of the text from the investigation of perception and understanding, he does not make any explicit theoretical statement about musical understanding, but I would argue that this kind of theory is implicit in his study. I would like to go one step further, though here it may well be that there is a fundamental divergence between Nattiez's understanding of his research and my view of it.

This further step depends on the opposition which I have stressed in this review between abstract musical systems and concrete, specific works. If we look at traditional theory as a theory of musical understanding, or even as a theory of competence, then that theory fails to explain how we can comprehend musical innovations or musical agrammaticality. Ruwet (1972, pp. 135–48) showed how a distributional view explained this difficulty in one case where Rameau's treatment of dissonance was problematic. Ruwet showed that where the stylistic syntax failed to hold, the paradigmatic relations in the single work took over. I would want to amplify the theory thus: *Music makes sense when it conforms to the abstract rules of a style and/or when we perceive it in some relation to a hierarchy of syntagms whose elements are grouped in paradigms.* This formulation expresses my chief difference with Nattiez. He has proposed that the taxonomic study can be elaborated to encompass all the problems of style. In my view its value is precisely the opposite. Traditional theory describes style. The taxonomy shows how the single sign complex of one work asserts its unique meaning despite the habits and constraints of style. Like the meteorologist, who is so notably poor at prediction but who can usually respond in good form to the fresh scientific challenge of explaining yesterday's actual weather, the music theorist will find plenty of work to do in reconciling the particular to the general, the concrete example to the abstract system. The weatherman may represent a more humble scientific ideal to us than the physicist does, but music changes as quickly and more unpredictably than do the skies.

6 Our Time with the Druids: What (and How) We Can Recuperate from Our Obsession with Segmental Hierarchies and Other "Tree Structures"

Both the first and fourth of Chopin's *Preludes,* Op. 28, begin with an oscillation of the fifth and sixth degrees in their principal melody lines, a common nineteenth-century gambit but still a suitable excuse for a comparison. Do these two melodic oscillations realize the same ornamental structure?

Figure 6.1 proposes that they do not. In the first prelude, I take the G and A as beginning an interrupted passing motion which is completed in the fourth measure. (In the examples, incomplete or interrupted motions are marked with slurs terminated by a double slash.) The following four measures roughly invert the figure. There are two ways to read the E to D motion as incomplete. We can think of the E as a locally unprepared upper neighbor, or we can be a bit more sophisticated and think of E as concluding the *Ansteig* in the first tonic chord, and regard the D as another interrupted passing tone, this time harmonized. Either way, the figure is locally incomplete.

Figure 6.1C shows the interpretations I reject, interpretations that deny the figures are incomplete. I am unwilling to regard the melody G of m. 2 as resolving a preceding upper neighbor A and unwilling to understand either the D or the E of m. 6 as completing a neighbor figure from m. 5. While I hope this seems correct, I am less concerned to argue the particular case than to develop the premise that the distinction advanced here between locally complete and incomplete motions is intuitively meaningful and pertinent to our ideas of musical structure. If it is, what data support the analytical decision? The voice-leading chart shows conclusions, not reasons.

In both mm. 1 and 5, the notes that would prepare or resolve the embellishments occur in the right order and in the right register. The evidence for denying that the resolution occurs is very straightforward, but necessarily suppressed on a voice-leading chart, even if we mark the chart *agitato.* The rhythmic and gestural shape

This chapter is a slightly revised version of the article of the same title in *Proceedings of the Third International Congress on Musical Semiotics, Contemporary Music Review,* vol. 16, part 4 (London: Harwood, 1997).

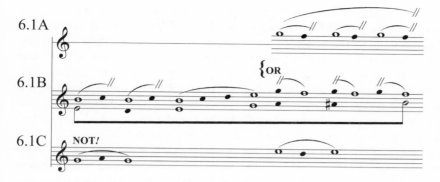

Figure 6.1A–C. Voice leading in Chopin, Prelude No. 1, mm. 1–7.

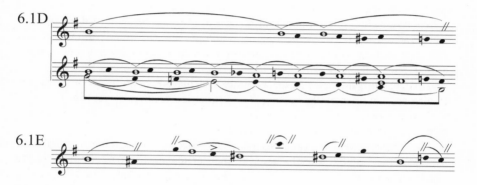

Figure 6.1D–E. Voice leading in Chopin, Prelude No. 4.

of the figures determines this interpretation. When the broken octaves of the tenor and soprano come together on the sixth sixteenth note, they make an accent followed by a syncopated rest. The figure, as Schumann's remark suggests, is "panting" (Schumann's appreciation of the *Preludes* is reprinted in Higgins [1973], p. 91). An analogue would be a person who is sputtering words, too excited to speak in sentences.

What is equally telling is that the passage of the climactic ascent in parallel tenths in mm. 17–20 of the prelude reverses these characteristics of the first phrase. The breathless, interrupted texture yields to a smooth web of complete chromatic passing tones, and the rests are eliminated by the quintuplets. At the very top we get a synthesis or a mediation of the contrast. The rests return, but the embellishments are resolved quite directly. Perhaps an analogue would be holding back speech despite great excitement, long enough to be able to say something intelligible.

When a salient characteristic is reversed in a musical composition, we may speak of that characteristic as an idea or topic of the piece. A topic, in general, is the matter at hand. We can use the word in that sense here, but topic also fits in the sense it takes in Hatten's writings and Monelle's of the conventional musical sign of a culturally determined idea. Interruptive articulation, especially incomplete and accented dissonance structures, has portrayed the mannerisms of passionate speech in vocal music since the early Baroque. The analogy with speaking suggested above has a historical grounding and is straightforward, provided only that we understand the analogy as referencing kinesthetic or haptic imagery of speaking, not a visual image. In the fullest sense, the articulations achieved by the interruption and connection of the figures function in the prelude as topical.

Figures 6.1D and 6.1E represent voice leading in the E-minor prelude. This prelude reverses construction of the same topic. The melody begins with complete neighbor figures. It does not move until the bass descends and then moves by complete passing motions to the tonic. At that point the melody continues with further complete figures. Comparing the opening phrases of the two preludes, we could say the first begins with an excess of articulation and the second with a deficit of articulation. This second manner also suggests a speech behavior. Taking into account the tension between the long melody notes and the quietly throbbing support, my analogy would be with a person in a state of quite passion who cannot, at first, release it into words.

Then, as with the first prelude, a climax is achieved via an inversion of the articulatory character of the texture. The dramatic exclamatory phrases interrupt their step progressions by arpeggiation and depend chiefly on locally unprepared upper neighbors for their affective character.

The comparative partial analyses which I've just run through focus on only one aspect of the preludes, the character of their articulations. Articulation is pretty much the same thing as segmentation. Therefore what I offered, be it correct or not, might be classified as segmental analysis.

6.1. Articulation and Segmentation in Music Analysis

Since the early seventies, musical semiotics has been very attentive to the problem of analytical segmentation for music but, so far as I know, has not given much attention to the type of distinctions I ventured in this sketch. One difference is, of course, that I suggested a figurative interpretation. If the only difference were a shift from structural to interpretive concerns, then we might say, "Good, one job is finished; let's move on to the next." That is not at all the case. The analytical sketch hinged on a distinction between complete and incomplete segments, that is, complete and incomplete ornamental motions. This is, for me, the tip of an iceberg which, if explored, shows that we will not so easily maintain a pat boundary between structure and significance in this domain, though I will try to do so for part of this essay.

At first view, the opposition of complete and incomplete structures seems related to our experience of musical continuity. In the case of the music we were just thinking about, one might sense a one-to-one correspondence. The passages which utilized more locally complete structures could be described as projecting more continuity. I think there is some correspondence between experienced continuity and structural completeness, but the relationship needs examination. We know continuity by acquaintance, but as a concept it is not easily tractable. The elaboration of the idea in topology and physics may not fit our needs here. What we feel to be continuous is not so from the viewpoint of neurophysiology. Current neurophysiology, if I understand correctly, is inclined to depict all of our consciousness as flickering the way pictures do in the cinema, a phenomenon invisible to introspection. Experiential continuity or phenomenological continuity, which is something else, would seem to be a characteristic of attention as much as it is a characteristic of the music or any other thing we give our attention to.

The problems motivating this essay concern the relation between musical structures with their variable appearance of continuity and the aesthetic role of that variation and our means of notating that variation in musical analysis. My method takes an extended detour that regards the structural features of logical connection and articulation. Connection and continuity are not the same thing, but afterwards I will offer my best guess as to how they are related.

In the last two decades some of our most interesting theorizing has centered on linguistic models for musical structure. I think this work encouraged some blind spots which we should now endeavor to correct. For my part, this is not entirely a matter of being born again, but I think the issue merits further attention.[1]

6.2. Conjunct and Disjunct Segments

To investigate the structural question, I will contrast conjunct and disjunct segmentation. Two *adjacent* segments are either conjunct or disjunct. They are conjunct if the last element of one is the first of the next.[2]

Figure 6.2A is the familiar chant fragment, the *Benedicamus Domino*. This tune occurs in different rhythmic and segmental schema in various Medieval *clausulae*. Figure 6.2A is quoted with the phrasing slurs shown in the *Historical Anthology of Music*. These slurs provide a disjunct segmentation. I presume that they reflect syllabification and ligature groups. Whatever their raison d'être, the tune has some significant identity independently of those groupings. As it is arranged in various two-part modal rhythmic *clausulae* (see Figure 6.2B for examples), each of the clausula tenors imposes its own schema of disjunct segments, but *in some sense* we hear the same melody through the variations. I suggest that an underlying tonal hierarchy (taking tonal in a broad sense) remains intact.

Shorn of any particular rhythm, the *Benedicamus Domino* fragment is still interpretable as a tonal hierarchy. I imagine it was precisely because it projects an unusually self-sufficient tonal shape that it was favored by clausula composers for

---

1. Lidov (1973, 1975a, b).
2. For a larger scheme including adjacent and non-adjacent segments, see Rahn (1983), p. 59.

A.

Be - ne - di - ca - mus Do_____ - _____ mi - no_____

Figure 6.2A. *Benedicamus Domino,* chant.

B.

Do_____

Figure 6.2B. *Benedicamus Domino,* as clausula tenor.

C.

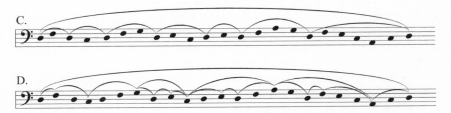

D.

Figure 6.2C and D. *Benedicamus Domino,* with conjunct segmentations.

their experiments. That shape is a continuous series of inflections most naturally described as a series of *conjunct* segments.

Figure 6.2 represents the melody as conjunct segments in two different ways. Figure 6.2C shows conjoined excursions from and to D. The melisma is represented here as a succession of increasingly elaborate excursions from the tonic culminating at the upper dominant. Each of these excursions is an individual unit of motion, but the units don't separate; the recurring D's belong both to the excursions which they terminate and to the excursions which they initiate. Figure 6.2D shows increasingly wide unidirectional segments. Considered just as a tonal shape, the melisma does not determine one dominant segmental scheme, but surely, conjunct segments offer a more natural model than disjunct segments.

Benedicamus Domino is peculiar. We can analyze its various rhythmic manifestations and its tonal structure independently because historical compositional practice separated them. More often, rhythm and tonality interact to produce structures that, like those of the Chopin *Preludes,* lose their identity if we analyze their factors separately.

The problematics of segmentation has a long history. The primary source of our conception of segmental hierarchy in music has always been language. Powers's historical review in *Ethnomusicology* (1980) demonstrated the continuity of language models in music theory since antiquity. In the twentieth century, linguistic theory itself undertook a sweeping critical reformulation of its methods. In the

1970s, we very appropriately imported that critical vision into musicology; however, there was no basic change in the type of segmental hierarchy proposed. The hierarchy, whether arising in Medieval musicology, in Koch's system, in Riemann's, in Cooper and Meyer, in Ruwet and Nattiez, or in James Tenney's adaptation of visual gestalt theory, was the type of hierarchy that correlates with a tree graph.

A tree graph models the least ambiguous type of hierarchy of disjunct segments. I mentioned in Chapter 1 the strong correlation between linguistic and visual hierarchies in this regard (see Jackendoff 1987). To import this graphic metaphor for music risks prejudice. Analytic notation is not always a critical factor. Newton proved his theory of gravity with geometric notations, heroically more difficult than later algebraic paraphrases. Mathematics stands out as a semiotic domain where exact translation is possible. Newton's signifier did not distort his signified, but translation is rarely so perfect.

6.3. Analytical Graphs for Music

Tree structure hierarchy is not the only type of hierarchy. To see what choices we are making or omitting to make, it behooves us to give some attention to the metaphors, in this case graph diagrams, that we exploit to formulate and convey our notion of hierarchical arrangement.

Graphs can be regarded as mathematical objects. In this conception, a graph is a collection of *branches* and *vertices* or *nodes*. Every branch connects two nodes; two or more branches can be connected at one node. A succession of branches, each connected to the next, forms a *path* between the extreme vertices of the succession. If a graph has one and only one path between any two nodes, the graph is a *tree graph* (as in Figures 6.3C, D, and E). If there is ever more than one path, the graph is a type of *net graph* (Figure 6.3B). If there are *always* at least two paths to every node, the graph is a *cyclic* net (as in our rare example, Figure 6.2). Even if we imagine that we employ these diagrams casually, their inherent properties are likely to color our thinking in specific ways.

The grouping rules in Lerdahl and Jackendoff's *Generative Theory of Tonal Music* (1983) guarantee that a segmental hierarchy ascribed to music in accordance with them will be isomorphic with a tree graph. The rule that if one segment is included in another, it must be included in its entirety, prevents overlapping. Of course, the authors are not blind to the obvious fact that music projects overlapping segments, but they treat these cases as secondary, as transformations, just as Riemann did and just as all linguistic theories do. Disjunct segmentation is the only kind of segmentation considered in linguistics. (Saussure's description of the syllable in the *Course in General Linguistics* in terms of vocalic peak suggests an exception, but so far as I know, no one has had any use for that angle.) A tree graph can also be used, given certain ground rules of interpretation, as an awkward but logically consistent metaphor for conjunct segmentation. What you cannot reasonably do is use a tree graph to show a mixed case of disjunct and conjunct segments such as we considered (before I introduced the terms) in the Chopin *Preludes*. For that purpose, the natural choice is a net graph.

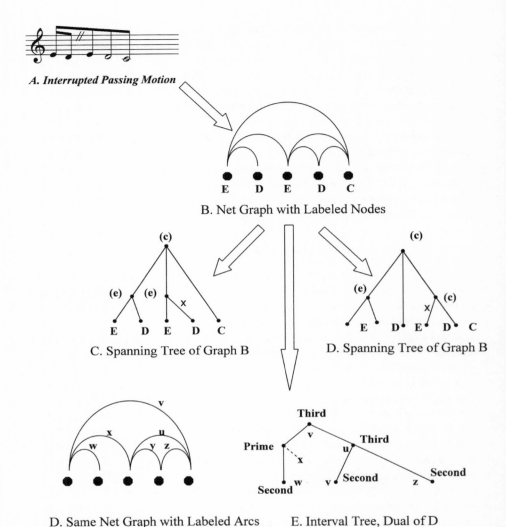

A. Interrupted Passing Motion

B. Net Graph with Labeled Nodes

C. Spanning Tree of Graph B

D. Spanning Tree of Graph B

D. Same Net Graph with Labeled Arcs

E. Interval Tree, Dual of D

Figure 6.3. Various graphs of an interrupted passing motion.

This is hardly a new proposal. If you take one of Schenker's graphs and erase the staff lines, the more or less pure diagram which remains is, essentially, a net graph. It should be no surprise: Schenker was very concerned to distinguish complete and interrupted segments. Schenker's primary metaphor was organic structure, not linguistic. Indeed, we might push the point a bit further and say that Schenker's work extends the Romantics' devaluation of language as logic.

The historical line of segmental models in musicology derived from language, all corresponding to tree graphs—those, for example, that are reviewed in the Powers article (1980) which I mentioned before—did not include any models for tonality except for contemporary studies. They were, essentially, models of *phrase structure* only. To cast tonal motion in the same graphic mold may be quite misleading. While the logical study of graphic models readily opens onto a quicksand of infinite regressions and unlimited digressions, I offer some short variations on graphs of complete and interrupted passing tones to spell out this point.

Figure 6.3A shows an interrupted passing motion using a notation in Schenker's style. The next figure, a net graph (Figure 6.3B), is a paraphrase based on the rule that two notes connected by a slur or a beam in Figure 6.3A are regarded as musically connected on some level. The notes and slurs and beams of 6.3A thus correspond to the nodes and branches of this net. This graph shows six connections, and it expresses one disconnection, or interruption, between the second and third note. This one interruption makes the graph noncyclic, a mixed case. Figures 6.3C and 6.3D show two tree graphs approximating the methods of Lerdahl and Jackendoff but in a simpler manner, without certain subtleties of their system. These two tree graphs differ only in that one has a right branch while the other has a left branch (to the fourth note). Notice that neither of them conveys the information we have been highlighting. The distinction between the complete and incomplete passing motion is not retained. Furthermore, the possibility of creating two different tree graphs means that we have to make a choice between symbols that, so far, mean the same thing. What is the difference signified by the right or left branching? Since culture abhors a vacuum, we will want to attribute some meaning to this extra choice which is thrust upon us by bad notation. Lerdahl and Jackendoff exploit the difference in a very interesting way (1983, pp. 186–91 and elsewhere), but in the end it muddies the water. Their distinction between progression and delay seems, especially in comparison with the distinction between complete and incomplete motions, a red herring. (By the way, it would not be reasonable to use right and left branching to mark complete and incomplete motions because some are incomplete on the left and some, like ours, are incomplete on the right.)

The two tree graphs (6.3C and D) are called spanning trees in relation to the net graph of Figure 6.3B. They are derived by erasing branches of the net graph. They would have worked if the net had been fully cyclic, that is, were there no interruption (see Lerdahl and Jackendoff 1983, pp. 114–16).[3]

(There is another way to derive a tree graph from a net graph which is a bit more excruciating mathematically but very straightforward musically and, therefore, worth a moment's attention. This method *exchanges* nodes and branches. The graph of Figure 6.3E relates to the net graph in this way. Every branch of Figure 6.3B is a vertex of Figure 6.3E.[4] The branches of the net graph, 6.3B, can each

---

3. Keiler's (1983) very limited claim for tree graphs as formalized language yields exemplary results. He uses triple branching as well as double, and in the context of his own examples it might seem as though he had thereby resolved the difficulty of distinguishing complete and interrupted structures in a treegraph notation. That this is not so is easily evident if one tries to graph $\hat{5}$–$\hat{4}$–$\hat{3}$–$\hat{2}$–$\hat{1}$ as an embellishment of $\hat{5}$–$\hat{3}$–$\hat{1}$ following his model.

4. The converse fact that the five nodes of the first have been replaced by just five branches is an accident of this particular example; in my paper with Gabura (1973), this point is misunderstood.

be interpreted as a foreground or background interval. The musical interpretation of graph 6.3E is a tree of intervals instead of notes. It says, in effect: our descent of a third is prolonged, first by an extension of the first note to become a prime plus a third. Then the second third is divided into two steps while the prime is also elaborated by a descending step which goes nowhere. The dotted branch, which has nothing to do with the mathematical derivation, is an easy way to add a symbol for the disjunction. The interval tree is not better than the other graphs; it is a mess. I include it only to emphasize the duality of notes and intervals, which is a duality of tonal *positions* and tonal *motions*. This graph might suggest another view of segmentation. Instead of taking the ultimate constituents of a melody to be notes, we could say the ultimate constituents are intervals. In this view, we take conjunct units as primary because the intervals are conjunct. Each interval overlaps another one. Perhaps we are already dealing with continuity when we take this view.)

6.4. Primary and Complex Structures: On the Limits of Rules

With regard to tonal structure, taking the idea in the broadest sense to mean movement from and/or to a remembered or anticipated pitch, it seems to me that the primary form is conjunct, like that we observed in the melisma of the *Benedicamus Domino*. The conceptions developed by theorists since the Renaissance which deal with what we now call prolongation are consistent in this regard insofar as I am acquainted with them. A dissonance which lacks either a preparation or a resolution is regarded as incomplete, that is as a license, and the resolution of one dissonance can be the preparation of the next. The idea of modulation, which had a slow historical transformation, described at first the deflection of the continuous motion between cadences and retains the implication of a movement from one point to another, any goal being potentially another starting point. When C. P. E. Bach describes the construction of basses from one cadence to the next, his logic entails a conception of these cadences as formal articulations within a continuum, that is, a focus on the harmonies which are both a point of arrival and a point of departure.

The identity of tonality with connectedness would not need to be represented at all if it were constant. It isn't. It varies. There are a number of ways in which disjunct structures appear as certain stages of tonal prolongation. Arpeggiations may give rise to disjunct segments. Locally incomplete or registrally transferred voices create disjunctions. Simple rearticulation, in certain rhythmic contexts, effects a division. Most crucially, there is that formation which Schenker called the "interruption technique"—the passing motion articulated by repetition of the first two tones.

The interruption technique achieved by repetition is the most clear-cut kind of interruption, whether it occurs on a large scale, as with the repetition of an exposition, on a medium scale, as at the end of the first phrases of both the Chopin

Preludes, or on a small scale, as with the first motive of the first prelude. In all these cases we are not dealing with a pure tonal structure but with an interaction. We have tonal motion *plus* the formal mechanism of repetition *plus* whatever support is provided by textural details—dynamics, rests, timbre, etc. The principles which inform a hierarchical analysis of articulated tonality are not simply principles of tonality. These different types of structure continuously interact. It is tempting to think of prolongation as a domain of conjunction, surface grouping as a domain of disjunction, and metrical hierarchy as *hors de combat,* but to do so is to downplay the interactions. The remainder of this chapter continues to resist such a clean division of functions, though one might possibly be able to recast the same analyses in language which preserved a more orthogonal scheme. The interactions of form, meter, and tonality provide a complexity which may not always be well illuminated by grammatical rules. Of course, we must keep looking for rules and trying them out, but with tempered expectations. One potential limitation on the scope of useful rules is the reliance of music on idiolectal structure. It is symptomatic of art that individual productions develop singular solutions to singular problems. Poetry is less fully described by rules than ordinary speech. Another potential limitation is the role of idioms, particular solutions to particular problems that recur throughout a dialect but without the range of variation that justifies an abstract representation. In fact, Schenker's treatment of interruption tends to be limited that way, though I think it merits more generalization. He restricts the application of the idea to descents from the third degree.

6.5. Conjunct and Disjunct Segmentation of the Musical Surface

A stunning positive result of the musicological critique inspired by modern structuralism was the demonstration that to a considerable extent we can display a segmental hierarchy for music on the basis of surface features with minimal recourse to abstract categories. This demonstration has two principal versions. I adopt the term "form" for the kind of hierarchy Ruwet and Nattiez have explicated, and Lerdahl and Jackendoff's term "grouping" for the kind that they (1983) and Tenney (1964) demonstrate. The difference is that form involves correlations of similar segments which are not adjacent and thereby establishes a systematic basis, in parallelism, for the hierarchical strata which emerge in pure grouping only as an artifact of calculation. Perhaps it is tendentious to retain the loaded term "form," but the choice is not arbitrary. The nineteenth-century category of form included tonal and metrical features, but a focus on surface pattern is what distinguished it from harmony and meter. "Form" here is the hierarchy of part-to-whole relationships established by surface discontinuities and by a given composition's content of repetition and variation.

Unlike tonal and metrical hierarchies, which organize features abstracted from music, the formal hierarchy concerns segments of the piece of music as it immediately appears (see the discussion of the relation between musical data, structure, and conscious appearance in Jackendoff 1987). I explain it to my students as the analysis you can notate with scissors and Scotch tape.

My own first criticisms of Ruwet and Nattiez (1973, 1980), who put the issue on the table in a clear fashion, argued that it was impossible to establish a segmental hierarchy for fairly ordinary melodies purely on the basis of surface features alone. Ruwet himself came to the same conclusion (1975). However, the idea of a segmental hierarchy established by relations between parts of the concrete musical surface is, at the very least, important as a limiting case, and it ties together lots of data.[5]

The hierarchy of form and the somewhat simpler hierarchy of groupings which it subsumes, are, as I have noted, disjunct segmentations isomorphic to a tree graph. A straightforward interpretation of this correspondence is that form creates musical objects: motives, themes, etc. Objects are disjunct. That is what we mean by objects, and that is also the tie-in with visual perception. Nevertheless, the assumption that there is a Platonic heaven for music theory where all melodies will reveal their primary, essential disjunct segmentation is out to lunch.

Phenomenologically, the musical surface is not always object-like. Music offers objects as well as spaces, streams, and other configurations, like textures, which lie somewhere in between the perceptual poles. Moderately extended melodic passages which do not determine a unique segmental scheme are not at all rare. The following three arbitrary examples may indicate something of the range of complications. The first (Figure 6.4A) is from de Lassus. Any disjunct segmentation of it is musically arbitrary. The long notes exploit opposed gestalt principles to function equally as beginnings and endings. Figure 6.4B is the fugal subject of the last movement of Bach's Sonata for Violin and Keyboard in B Major, BWV 1016. Here the density of possible articulations and their monotony cause ambiguity. You can segment it quite a number of ways. If you stop changing your mind, the movement, which repeats the tune over and over, becomes a bore. At least that's my experience playing it. Figure 6.4C, from another Chopin prelude, the G minor, pits suspensions against gestalt relations, causing a perceptual strain which is aesthetically crucial. These are mixed cases, but essentially conjunct patterns have some role in each of them. Figure 6.5 is a visual ornament, the less common case of a visual non-object (but consider also haze, ocean waves, and mountain ranges). I believe it is called the Greek key. I leave it to unlock what it may.

6.6. Conjunct and Disjunct Time Spans
(or *Satz* vs. *Ursatz*)

Compared to poets or to musicians in a number of non-Western traditions, we've accustomed ourselves to a very impoverished notion of meter which is really hardly more than a concept of metrical notation. Surely we have recourse to ab-

---

5. I provide an overview of the viewpoint and the analytical technique of distributional analysis in Lidov (1992).

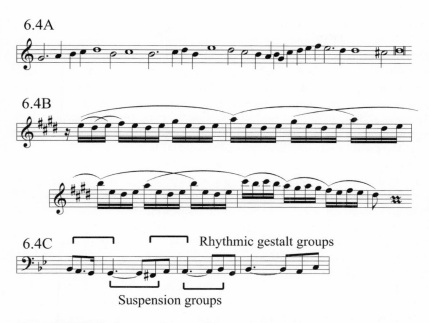

Figure 6.4. Melodic phrases resistant to disjunct segmentation.

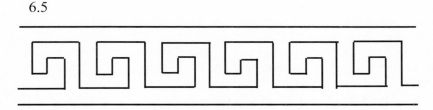

Figure 6.5. A visual design.

stract templates which stand midway between rhythm as a concrete surface pattern and meter in the most skeletal sense of a bare hierarchy of time points. Obvious examples are dance patterns, which I personally would rather call dance meters than rhythms, such as the anacrustic grouping of the gavotte and the repressed third beat of the sarabande. These templates inform our hearing of passages which do not express them. As an alternative to bare time points, recall the scheme in Chomsky and Halle (1968) where meter is a cyclic pattern of abstract variables plus a system (which can be very localized in repertory) of realization rules. For a brief and hypothetical example, a realization rule that recognized a special function for the initial anacrusis in Lutheran chorale phrases would avoid both the error that Peel and Slawson (1984) object to at the beginning of Lehrdahl and Jackendoff's span reduction of "O Haupt voll Blut und Wunden" and their own equally silly contrivance, in an otherwise admirable analysis, of pretending the first chord isn't there.

The intuition which stands behind the following remarks is that phrase structure can appeal to templates which are metrical in character. My argument does not hinge on a particular definition of meter but may lend some support for a richer notion of meter than just layered, ungrouped points in time.

As many authors have reminded us, we have in meter the same duality, with beats and durations, as we have in tonality, with notes and intervals. Beats are disjunct to start with. Durations are conjunct to start with.

Various patterns of *metrical* organization typically emerge in music as conflict between hypermeter and phrase. With some risk of paradox perhaps, I suggest that we can profitably regard metrical components in phrase patterns as conjunct and disjunct time spans. In all the radical effort to rethink phrase structure in the light of the conceptual tools impressed on us by modern analysis—I'm thinking, for example, of Komar's suspension theory, Yeston's work, that of Westergaard—I don't think anyone has fully escaped Riemann's error of expecting hypermeter and symmetrical phrasing to fall under one system of description. But they must not; they conflict. Joel Lester's book *The Rhythms of Tonal Music* (1986) is perhaps the exception. He does separate these structures in principle, but I don't think he adequately acknowledges that they conflict. It is the play of their antitheses that gives topicality to symmetrical measure groups in Classical style. And let us be clear, the question is topicality, not prevalence. The mechanism of the conflict is typically that conjunct harmonic spans support hypermeters. Typically—this is not a law— disjunct (that is interrupted) harmonic spans correlate with stronger phrasing and weakened hypermeter.

There—I did it. I wrote the magic word "phrase," a concept effectively banished both in Nattiez's analytical technique (in favor of "units") and in Lehrdahl and Jackendoff's (in favor of "spans"). Phrase is not just a loose-size category for spans or units. Phrase invokes a richer field of relations. Phrasing concerns the strata in the hierarchy of form where meter and tonality conflict. Meter wants to go on. Tonality wants to conclude. In Classical style the phrase hosts a constellation of relations involving motivic interplay, repetition, meter, and harmony.

One way of looking at phrase structure is to regard it in terms of groupings of beats, conjunct and disjunct, and patterns of accent, hypermetrical and contrahypermetrical. To get a sense of the role of the antithesis between conjunct and disjunct spans in establishing phrase and hypermeter as opposed principles, consider three opening themes from Mozart's piano sonatas shown in Figures 6.6–6.8 in terms of this conflict. The charts use crosses to show accents contrary to hypermeter, degree circles at beats where a hypermetrical accent could be projected but is not realized, and accent marks where hypermeter is restored after its previous suppression.

K. 279 seems to me not to have quite emerged from the Rococo. Its elaborate articulations of phrasing are dominated by the continuity of hypermetrical units. Using slurs (as a fragment of a net graph) the example shows conjunct one-measure spans in mm. 1–4 and conjunct two-measure spans throughout. The overlapping

Figure 6.6. Mozart, K. 279, mm. 1–12.

of the treble and bass figures in the first four measures is not an elision but a simple decoration of conjunct two-measure groups set by the alternating tonic and dominant. In mm. 6–12 there are various hints of disjunct groups projected by harmonies syncopated against the measure and simple articulations on the beat highlighted by melodic fragmentation. These groups suggest stronger phrasing and contest the hypermetrical spans without really dislodging the two-measure beat. The strongest contrametrical event is the arrival of the tonic chord in the middle of mm. 6 and 8, but these harmonies that disjoin groups of four half notes conform fully to the two-measure units.

The second example, K. 284, illustrates a more decisive suppression of a hyper-downbeat. The first four measures are a disjunct group, a forceful $\hat{1}$–$\hat{5}$ motion which is left dangling. The fourth bar's downbeat dominant makes a contra-hypermetrical accent. The surface continuity of the pedal tremolo suppresses the

Figure 6.7. Mozart, K. 284, mm. 1–9.

following hyper-downbeat in m. 5, despite the forte-piano accent. The texture change at m. 7 recalls hypermetrical grouping and the D of m. 9 restores hyper-metrical accent. Overall, the speechlike forms of disjunction assert a much more vigorous competition with the underlying regular and connected tonal and metrical space here than they did in the previous example. Neither hypermeter nor phrasing dominates the other.

The third example, K. 311, shows real elision. The four downbeats of mm. 1–4 are strong-weak-weak-strong on the basis of chordal inversions:

| I | I$_6$ | I$_6$–II–V | I | I |

This pattern, in itself, *because* it is contra-hypermetrical, establishes a distinct phrase. The phrase is not thoroughly ametrical. The bass alternations of register promote a hypermetrical interpretation. The conflict, in which tonality scores the winning point, makes the span or unit stand out as a phrase. The repetition of the phrase includes the downbeat of m. 4 only retrospectively. Note that the pitches of that beat are not the same as the first chord of m. 1. You simply have to hear the first four downbeats as a phrase group. There is no choice about mm. 4–7 either; the pattern having been established, you have to hear those four downbeats as a phrase group too. The structural feature of four downbeats comprising both a strong beginning and a strong ending has nothing do with "feminine cadences" which occur inside one measure and never disrupt its meter. Our pattern here occurs when a strong disjunct phrase shape *cancels* hypermeter. The first ten downbeats of the piece project three groups of four as elided, disjunct units. The resultant is also a simple pattern of conjunct three-measure groups, but that simplicity

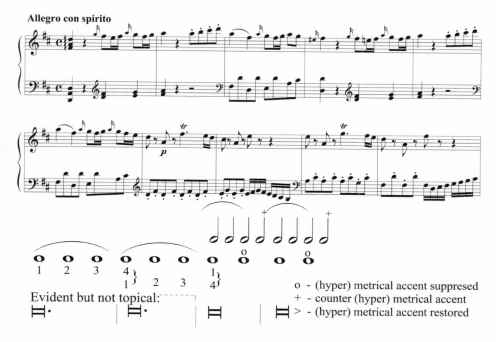

Figure 6.8. Mozart, K. 311, mm. 1–10.

is irrelevant to the culture which framed the pertinent rhythmic topics. Mozart is playing language games.

We have something in common with the generations of Koch and Riepel in our fascination with linguistic models and tree diagrams or equivalent notions of segmentation of transformation. Linguistics has been the last word in science for us. For music in the eighteenth century, catching the last long wave of the French Enlightenment, language had a similar significance. Classical style makes a topic out of phrase structure, displaying that era's enthusiasm for verbal language, its faith that the logic of language was capable of representing reality. Historically, this attraction to *langue,* language-like phrase structure, contrasts with earlier and later generations' fascination for *parole,* reflected by interest in rhetoric and (as in the Chopin examples) resonance with the kinesthesia of personal utterance.

When four-measure groups become routine, they lose topicality and do not invoke interpretation. By way of contrast, it is interesting to study the first-movement exposition of Beethoven's *Pastoral* Symphony in terms of the same variables we attended to in Mozart. I give some results in summary:

The exposition is 138 measures. It can be read as an unbroken series of thirty-five four-measure units, though there are ambiguities, with elisions at mm. 100 and 115. Measures 16 to 96 can be read as eighty measures of unbroken conjunct parts. There are many subtle modulations of the force and placements of hypermetrical accents, but, in that whole span, nothing to establish a disjunct phrase group. This is music of continuity. It does not take linguistic articulation as a model of truth. It projects a radical turn from the articulation of culture to the continuity of nature, and that is, in part, why the music really does sound like how a walk in the country feels, a rather different way to appreciate trees.

6.7. Continuity in Music

What is continuity in music? Musical continuity is not physical continuity of sound. Staccato needn't interrupt the flow of melody. Certainly the lyricism of a guitar or piano is in some fundamental sense uncompromised though very different from the fuller physical continuity offered by a voice or violin. We hear continuity that almost contradicts the physics of sound. Pitch changes in music are physically discontinuous but are heard as continuous movement in melody. Even unaccompanied drumming can convey a seemingly palpable flow. The continuity of music is in the nature of a sign constructed in perception, a form added to the data by the intelligence—as Charles Peirce would say, a hypothesis. It is useful to recollect that Peirce also suggested that sensations are hypotheses or essentially like them in that they substitute one image for a multitude of data. Continuity is encountered as an aspect of sensation.

The experience of continuity in music is open to investigation as a distinct phenomenon. Alexandra and Roger Pierce's work seems to me to deal with this very issue. It suggests that musical continuity represents music as a correlate of the kinetic motion of the body itself (Pierce and Pierce 1989, 1991). Whatever else it may be, continuity is a sensual experience. Our question here is how continuity as a sensation is determined by logical arrangements of segmental conjunctions and disjunctions. I suggest a figure-ground solution.

Continuity may be regarded as the normal, primary, unmarked state for music perception and, in a sense, for all aesthetic absorption. It is the condition which permits identification of the artwork with the proprioceptive sphere and thereby with feeling generally. All the arts offer sensual and/or imaginative continuity of some sort. The ability to create continuity is a central focus in the artist's craft and craft training: the steady tone of the musician, the relaxed flow of the draughtsman's hand, the implacable poise and balance of the dancer, the integrity of the surface in painting, the persuasive unrolling of sound and image in poetry. In music a continuous flow is particularly palpable and penetrating, even in language-like styles that chop it up. Isn't this the reason why the combination of music with poetry or cinema so deeply transforms their appearance, and why both song and cinema favor less articulated styles as their accompaniment except when they need to depict special stress?

On the other hand, disjunction is special—marked, and all of the structures and features which convey logical disconnection are its signs. In the first Chopin prelude a sense of flow is engendered from the beginning which extends right to the end, but at the beginning the *agitato* motives resist that continuity. The difference between the agitated opening and the freer continuity of the middle is not due to the introduction of a new ingredient. A positive factor, the articulation, is withdrawn.

In a Schopenhaueresque figure, it is the interruption which requires artistic will, the continuity already being felt in the will of the tones.

But if continuity enthralls the body, it is certainly the case that articulations are arresting to conscious ratiocination. It may be that our intelligence is so constructed that highly articulate tree-type structures are more intelligible than densely connected cyclic-net types. Thus, when articulation is withdrawn we become more immersed in sensation and in somatic-kinetic imagery. When articulation is emphatic and topical, we are more sensitive to images of arrangement and argument. Our emphasis on these trees, to which our thinking is so strongly drawn, is surely not wholly misplaced, as long as we also see the forest.

7   Why We Still Need Peirce

In his "Essay before a Sonata," Ives asks, "What has sound to do with music?"

Partly as rhetorical question, partly in the manner of a Zen koan, Ives made a plea for content in opposition to expression.

For language, Saussure proposes that sound as such is entirely supplanted by structure and that sound has no significance. Sound is an arbitrary carrier of structure. We all know the truth is not so simple. In Peirce's semiotics, the place of sound is as well marked out as the place of structure.

It is possible to get rid of sound and still use language. We do just that in written communication. The sound of music is more difficult to dispose of, but its operation as part of musical semiosis is not easily integrated into music theory. Some musical semiotics has broached issues which approach the consideration of music's sound as a sign, for example, Hatten in his discussions of resonance in Schubert (1993), and Monelle (1997) in his analysis of timbre as a topic in Debussy. More persistent than either of these, in her intimate contact with the grain of timbre, was Naomi Cumming's construction of musical tone quality as an immediate icon of the human voice and, consequently and more importantly, as a component sign of the musical subject: the "speaker" of the music we hear.

7.1. *The Sonic Self*

Cumming's book *The Sonic Self: Musical Subjectivity and Signification* (2000) provides a development of Peirce's semiotics categories that makes a big difference for musical epistemology. The writings and thought of the American philosopher Charles S. Peirce (1839–1914) continue to attract a widening circle of musicologists who are interested in semiotics, although the case for musicologists to attend to Peirce's writing is not obvious. Peirce himself had little to say about the arts, and his few remarks on music are not sophisticated. Peirce was not indifferent to the arts—he was an amateur thespian—but his primary intellectual stimulus was practical science. Also, musicologists might have the impression that Peirce is out of date and unfocused in some ways. He continued to believe that the appropriate goal of a philosopher was to find the true foundation of all knowledge at a time when others were becoming suspicious of such grand schemes. And, as if fate were determined to punish his hubris, he did not complete a consistent, coherent treatise expounding a unified system.

Science was Peirce's principal orientation, and science provided the grounds of

This chapter combines papers read to the meetings of Semiotic Society of America (Pittsburgh, 2000) and the International Musicological Society (Leuven, 2000).

the question that was, I believe, most central to his thought. It is a fairly familiar question. I will state it my own way. Given that the number of wrong ideas we can have appears to be infinite, our chance of guessing the truth should be infinitesimal—virtually impossible. Nevertheless, it appears that a community of scientists who persistently and critically investigate their best guesses do slowly progress toward true knowledge. How can that be? How can it be that in practice the wrong guesses are merely a manageable, *finite* majority but not *infinitely* preponderant?

This question, venerable and profound as it may be, is not on first view suggestive for musical research. However, Peirce's further development of it provides our motivation for joining in. It led him to examine all knowledge as mediated representations. In his view, our consciousness must always be a consciousness of the *interpretation* of a sign.

Theoretically, music should have no special privilege in this perspective, but in practice it does, because we are highly aware how ephemeral sounds are. A famous question: if a tree falls in a forest and no one is nearby to hear it, does it make a sound? The philosopher *could* have asked, especially in October, do the leaves in the middle of the forest turn red if nobody is there to see them? It's quite the same question, but that would be a less popular version of it. Sound puzzles us more than color does, and that is the first reason why musicologists might feel a special kinship with Peirce. We already know that merely to hear music as music, not just as sound, is already an act of interpretation.

The totality of Peirce's achievement is probably still hidden from us because we do not yet have a chronological edition of his complete work. In this circumstance, different musicologists have been drawn to emphasize very different aspects. Bill Dougherty has published a series of studies of song that adopt Peirce's conception of the interpretant as a synthesis (1993, 1994, 1996, 1999). This model enables Dougherty to articulate the absorption of words and sounds in a signifying unity. José Luiz Martinez (1997) ingeniously explicates the aesthetics of raga in relation to Peirce's foundational categories of phenomenology. Leonard Meyer and Wilson Coker, whom we might regard as the founders of American musical semiotics, both have indirect debts to Peirce because of their reliance on philosophers who formed part of the philosophical movement to which Peirce gave much direction—George Mead in the case of Coker and John Dewey for Meyer.

My own book on general semiotics, *Elements of Semiotics* (1999), also has extensive debts to Peirce. Peirce's concepts make it possible to separate the problem of representation from the problem of structural elaboration. Also, in that book and elsewhere, my understanding of musical gesture depends on the broad compass of Peirce's description of signs. An intelligible theory of gesture requires that we acknowledge interrelations among conceptual interpretations, causal interpretations, and qualitative interpretations. Peirce brings all three together because he focuses on the mind, on the act of interpretation, rather than regarding the sign and its object as mindless facts.

Naomi Cumming's book *The Sonic Self* is the most thorough and careful of all the Peircean musical studies that I know. This book owes much to that question which I said at the start did not sound promising for musicology—How do good guesses happen in a world with infinite possibilities for error? She develops this question in retrograde, as it were. She asks, When should we believe our musical intuitions? Her book argues, in opposition to many other philosophers of music, that we can and should respect our intuitions regarding particular aspects of music though not equally for all aspects. Although we cannot be certain about our intuitions, they are not arbitrary.

The central topic of her book is the construction of a musical self or *persona*. Her analysis is enormously enriched by Peirce's analysis of the interpreting subject. As the structuralists would do later, Peirce formulated a semiotics abstracted from persons, but unlike the European structuralists, he did not eliminate the subject. Peirce identifies the subject with a continuity of interpretation.

Peirce's focus on interpretation is encapsulated in his concept of the *interpretant*, an idea he developed throughout his life, but he did not leave us a clear and consistent explanation of it. Before I explain my construal of this idea, the one point where I find Cumming in error, I must say what I mean by a correct construal of an idea whose own author has used it inconsistently. My standard is not philological: I don't propose an inventory of all of Peirce's pronouncements on the interpretant. It is also not biographical. I'm not tracing Peirce's development. Nor is it psychological. I won't argue what Peirce "really meant." What I mean by a correct construal is one that refers to Peirce, but that is ultimately decided by what produces sense for us. This is a solution loyal to the principles that Peirce called "pragmatism" and later "pragmaticism."

Although for a sign to function as such Peirce requires its present co-relation with an object and an interpretant, there is nevertheless an implication of temporal priority among the correlates in that the interpretant is a *consequence* of the sign relation. This is no paradox. You can't be a mother or father until you have a child, but there is a sense in which the mother and father, not in that role, come along earlier. Peirce seems to me quite consistent in describing the interpretant as consequent upon sign relations as well as consistent in describing the object, even if it's not yet identified or determined as such, as manifesting some kind of existence a priori to the sign, something already in your experience that the sign can refer to, in the case of the *immediate object*, or something already in the external world in the case of a *dynamic object*.

It is sometimes appropriate to think of the interpretant as the conception of an object induced by a sign of it. By this way of understanding the idea, the interpretant seems the most ephemeral of the trio of sign, object, and interpretant. In artistic perception this need not be the case, a point that I think Cumming missed and that I also do not find clearly and consistently worked out in my *Elements*.[1] Consider sculpture before we turn to music. If we understand what is represented by Michelangelo's *Pietàs* on first view, then it must be the case that we already had

---

1. Cumming's exposition confuses the interpretant with context and syntax, ignoring Peirce's consistent principle that the sign determines or gives rise to the interpretant, not the other way around. These errors do no damage to her main arguments.

some notion, before seeing them, what a pietà is, the notion of the moment when Mary receives the body of Christ. This is a cultural notion; our private version might be a slight variant. But private or public, here is one immediate object to which the three statues all refer. What stands before us is a block of marble. The marble is not invisible to us as marble. Seeing stone is part of the experience. The shaped stone is the *sign* and our prior conception of a pietà is the *object*. The *interpretant* is no more ephemeral than these. Rather, it is what we see most vividly, the stone come to life: We *see* Mary weeping over the body of Jesus. The image that arises, what Langer calls a *virtual* entity, is the interpretant. It is a consequent of stone connecting to a concept.

When a flute plays the Gigue from Bach's B Minor Suite, we have before us an *aural* image of dancing, swaying movement. We recognize flute sounds as such, which, like the marble, constitute the sign. We have some prior, partly social, partly private notion of dance kinesthetics that constitutes one immediate object. (Not the only one. It may be troped by references to social or private notions of grace and sadness, for example.) Our prior understanding of expressive dance is referenced in various ways by the flute melody, and a language-defying musical image of sad, gracious movement is conjured up. That image, at once the most seemingly immediate yet impalpable thing, the virtual entity, is the interpretant. Cumming is persistent and insightful in arguing that we don't contact raw sound in music. We always interpret. In this perspective, what we perceive as music is not simply the qualities of sound but an interpretation arising from all the qualities, effects, and conventions embodied in the sound.

The best-known aspect of Peirce's semiotics is his classification of the relations between a sign and its object. His categories depend on his phenomenology, which distinguishes (1) the apprehension of relations or rules or regularities, such as a tonality, giving rise to *symbols;* (2) the apprehension of events and facts, like an accent or a group of notes or a gesture, giving rise to *indices;* and (3) the apprehension of possible qualities, like ironic or *gemütlich* or Wagnerian, giving rise to *icons.*

Cumming's analysis of music takes advantage of these foundational categories to develop the questions, What degrees of definiteness, and what degrees of privacy, and what degrees of certainty ought we to anticipate in explaining different aspects of music? Without any simple-minded claim of a one-to-one correspondence, she takes tone quality or timbre as emblematic of iconic signs, gestural imaging as emblematic of indexical signs, and tonal regularity as emblematic of symbolic signs.

As I mentioned, she is especially interested in timbre as an icon of the "speaking subject" in instrumental music. Metaphorically, the violin, her instrument and in the book the *leitmotif,* can be and often must be the "voice" of its music in the fullest sense of "voice"—the expression of a human agent. But she recognizes that the possibility of a sign of that general type immediately guarantees the possibility of alternatives to or variants of that normal representation. Pursuing this corollary, I would ask, What does the recognition of this metaphor leave out? Why should I play the violin instead of sing?

For an example, for one very incomplete answer, I would suggest that it leaves out technology. When we listen to a violin, or for that matter a highly trained vocalist, we are immediately confronted with the replacement of a natural subject by a machine, with all the excitement and anxiety such a replacement conjures. I would suggest that this may be historically and geographically a universal component of musical experience and one that inheres in the phenomenon of sound in music from the first moment that two stones are struck together to make a rhythm which incites our identification. It is interesting to observe the commanding role of musical instruments that reflect the most exciting and threatening technologies of their own societies, be it a laboriously, painstakingly engineered pod rattle with magic properties, the new metallurgical fluidity exhibited in the brilliance of the nineteenth-century orchestra and piano, or the digital synthesis that surrounds us.

Though there is no level of musical perception more simple than hearing a tone musically, the moment of hearing a tone musically is not too simple to evoke a dialectic of the enlargement and the annihilation of the voice, which is the relation also of technology to the human subject.

Cumming does not explore the further possibility of the utter disruption of the sign function of timbre. Not only does the instrument compete with the voice it represents, but there is a reason why the notion of an *uninterpreted,* pure sensation is posed for us both on the side of Husserlian philosophy and on the side of musical projects, such as those of Pierre Schaeffer and some American experimentalist composers. Indeed, I would guess that every composer who is not a hack has, at some point in his or her work, looked for a strategy that would confront the hearer with the sheer beauty or terror of sound-in-itself. The contest between material and representation is part of semiosis, not anterior to it.

7.2. Developing Interpretation

Peirce's attention to representation as continuously developing (in contrast to the Saussurian tradition of reference to a fixed system) and his attention to phenomenology might help us to integrate our ideas about final state analysis and analysis of musical understanding as a process in time. David Lewin (1986) examines this problem with reference to a tradition of phenomenology from Husserl that was contemporary with Peirce in its origin. I shall not compare methods here. (And as for his punishing satire on musical semiotics in that article—well, I will just pretend I didn't read it!)

I propose to reflect on listening to Morton Feldman in a Peircean perspective, the third composition, for viola and piano, from Feldman's cycle *The Viola in My Life.* My reason for suggesting Feldman is to focus on an example, unlike Lewin's of Schubert, that is recalcitrant to structural analysis. Like Lewin, I will imagine—just briefly—that we can inspect the development of interpretation step by step.

The opening figure is a brief chord in the piano attacked simultaneously with a long note in the viola. The pitches of the piano chord are indistinct, though not totally obscure. Peirce points out we begin with conceptions that we already know. Thus, we might hover between two interpretations corresponding to known categories: (1) Perhaps the chord is a cluster and identified with a pitch range rather

Figure 7.1. Feldman, *The Viola in My Life,* first phrase group, schematic score.

than specific pitches. (2) Or perhaps it is part of a contrapuntal complex with details that will assume further identity as its context unfolds—a structure that promises some kind of cognitive if not harmonious resolution. If we peek at the score (see Figure 7.1), or if we have very quick ears, we might note that the first interpretation is supported by the presence of three semitones inside the compact span of a major sixth, but the competing interpretation has preliminary evidence in the perfect fifth between the piano's highest note and the viola, a fifth with further consonant support from the bass.

The second figure, again in the form of a brief piano chord and held viola tone, confirms the idea or the hypothesis (3) that we are confronting a motive. But the notes, alas, are sufficient to discourage both preceding interpretations (1 and 2). We perceive more of the pitch, for the bottom five tones of the piano belong to one whole-tone scale, a color a bit too distinct to regard merely as a cluster, but as far as making sense out of what we might remember from the first chord, no relationships have been introduced that contribute any logic, least of all the arbitrary common tones and the viola's move to a new pitch that sounds like a random choice. Perhaps we will wonder (4) if a special role lies ahead for whole-tone scales.

I forbear comments on the next three things that happen, except that they are motives or figures of the same type and do not change the story. Then the viola plays a phrase alone and more quickly. The aural intellect is now refueled, for here is what the structuralist in each of us has been determined to discover, an indisputable contrast. A whole battery of interpretive search engines might go on alert. One of those engines may be disappointed to discover (5) that this little twelve-note aria does not avoid octave duplications. On the other hand, even though the phrase doesn't conform to a whole-tone hexachord, most of the note-to-note intervals larger than minor seconds do. Perhaps we are not to discard the whole-tone hunch (4) just yet.

So far, nothing that makes a musical logic. But wait! The next figure is a duplication. The viola returns to its very first tone, and the piano repeats its very first chord in octave transposition, higher and also now longer.

The limitation on hearing pitch identities when notes are close together is called the critical band, and it varies with register. I don't know precisely what to understand regarding piano tones with respect to that theory, based so far as I know on sine-tone research. But clearly we get more pitch and less vagueness when this group of minor seconds sounds an octave higher and sounds longer—more but not enough to resolve any issues. Even if we notice the repetition, and it is easy to miss, the ambiguities aren't resolved; they are restated. The duplication of harmony we just observed is the beginning of a more extended repetition. The ensuing figures are variations on the series we first heard. But careful—the tenth and eleventh figures correspond to the fourth and fifth, as we might predict, but in reverse order. Before the viola restates its aria, another solo figure will intervene, isolated notes that blunt the contrast of melody and chord. Surely these little changes invite us to look for another level of planning. But to no avail: I don't think we find any.

What is it adding up to? The notes are not random. The music is patterned with accessible similarities and differences. Do the differences make a difference?

The composition displays a refined craft, a music meticulously constructed to foil interpretation by categories and rules. There is enough form and enough promise of form and sufficient challenge to memory to keep the aural intellect engaged, but our usual interpretive habits garner only trivia (such as the AABA form of the whole)[2] and confusion.

What might help us is Peirce's fascination with hunches and his understanding that interpretation cannot simply be equated with conceptual diagrams. The false promises of similarities and differences are a technique that focuses our attention, but as we go on, our attention must shift from structures to qualities. In fact, we noted a quality at the very beginning, but we haven't followed it up: the quality of indistinctness. The indistinctness we hear is not an artifact of perception. As Peirce would certainly be quick to insist, it is a quality of the music itself. Let's take it seriously (Feldman obviously did) as well as other qualities—fragility, sadness, passivity, and other fragrances we cannot name.

My pathway has a precedent in the work of José Luiz Martinez's Peircean study of raga and rasa (1997). We are not bereft of orientation when we shift from structure to quality. Peirce alerts us to the play of indicators that orient qualities. One pointer here is the dynamic, marked "extremely quiet" throughout. The slow, vaguely irregular, and harmonically indistinct music develops an image closely matching perception near the edge of sleep. Forty-three slow musical figures, slightly irregular in spacing, occupy six minutes. The pace and the rhythm is of quiet breathing. Another index is tempo. Feldman himself commented a number of times on his identification of music with breath. Now, this in itself is not very distinctive. We are ever after performance students to get the sound of natural breathing into their phrasing, but whereas most music sings with exhalation, the image here may be of inhalation—not only because it is so soft, but because the whole opus (as he notes) is focused on the viola crescendos (from *pp*) and because in this number, the piano is used to create a viola tone with no attack:

> In my own music I am . . . involved with the decay of each sound, and try to make its attack sourceless. The attack of sound is not its character. Actually, what we hear is the attack and not the sound. Decay, however, this departing landscape, *this* expresses

---

2. I am grateful to Mauro Savo for pointing out this and many other technical details of the music in the course of a study he undertook of this work modeled on the Lewin article mentioned above.

where the sound exists in our hearing—leaving us rather than coming toward us. (Feldman in Zimmerman 1985, p. 89)

Comparison of musical speed with the heartbeat or with the breath, though not mechanical, as a physical measurement belonging to what Peirce calls indexical relations, invokes a category generally maltreated in contemporary aesthetics. Here the *index* is only a preliminary sign. Getting to know this music means learning to hear it as an *icon,* the sign of a *general* quality of particular states of consciousness.

I emphasize "general." We are *not* listening to a musical description of Morton Feldman's well-known chronic insomnia, *nor* does the music refer to the penumbra that follows the last glass of a fine port. Also, the drowsiness that comes on with a bit too much time in the sun is certainly *not* the musical object. It is of interest that any of these particular experiences might have contributed to our image, but none of them are represented. The music induces an *abstraction,* a *generalization,* a pure *qualitative possibility.* We must not seek a familiar name for this precise quality; the music itself is the name. Perhaps this music will be the first name we ever knew for this previously unnamed feeling.

For a sound to *possess* a particular quality and for music to function as a *sign* of that quality are not the same thing. In the irritating, technical language of Peirce, which I counsel nobody to adopt, as we develop knowledge of the music, we progress from knowledge of its individual figures as "Iconic Sinsigns"—"object[s] of experience . . . [that] determine the idea . . . by likeness purely" (I quote with severe abbreviation) to a memory of the whole composition as an "Iconic Legisign . . . governing iconic Sinsigns of a peculiar kind" (Peirce 1955, pp. 115–16).

This strenuous language all revolves around the center focus of generalizing. Vincent Colapietro cites a rhetorical question by Peirce: "What is man's proper function if it not be to embody general ideas in art-creation, utilities and . . . in theoretical cognition?" (1989, p. 25).

It is peculiar, old-fashioned, biased language, but that is no reason to dismiss Peirce's post-structuralist insights. Peirce's idea of what a sign *is* is not the idea of an inert correspondence. Peirce's idea is that the sign is a charged moment of interpretation. If we care about interpretation, we may still need Peirce.

I recommend Peirce because his problems remain current. They are relevant to our understanding of the construction of the subject in music, to our idea of the identity of the subject who constructs, to determining a standpoint to account for significance, and to understanding representation as active agency. Peirce is a resource if we do not want to become locked to the intellectual fashions of the moment.

Part Three:

From Gestures to Discourses

The theory underlying the chapters which follow is that somatic imagery in music anchors the semantics of musical discourses that are very elaborate in their scope of reference. In expounding my position over several years and in developing my own understanding, I have frequently cited the work of the pianist, inventor, and neuropsychologist Manfred Clynes (1989, for a fairly comprehensive summary and further bibliography), who until his retirement was research professor at the University of Melbourne. I review his work once again here but with a partial change of mood, emphasizing the interrogative and hoping, thereby, to draw attention to the problematics that his theory constructs rather than just to his proposals. In my opinion, the questions constitute a powerful agenda. One must expect, of course, that different answers would adjust or displace the questions—we know what happened when Christopher Columbus looked for the shortcut to India, but without the question of a westward route, he would not have set sail. (Not that I *endorse* the results, but they were decisive!)

My personal relation with Clynes's work was cemented in the early 1980s at a semiotics convention where I read a paper leaning on his ideas. A famous, senior scholar offered me a hushed warning afterwards that I could endanger my career by depending on such controversial theories. The very suggestion of trading in career politics with new ideas or even the suggestion that truth was secondary to consensus was all I needed to hear at that time to form an unbreakable attachment to the theories I was advised to regard cautiously. However, if my would-be mentor's advice lacked intellectual integrity, his skepticism was not without a basis. The proposals rest on laboratory experiments, which, still today, thirty years later, have not been duplicated by independent, professional researchers. I need the qualifier "professional" because I, a total amateur in that domain, finally got so fed up with waiting that I bought the equipment and tried some lab work myself. My results, more or less positive, were the basis of a paper I read to a 1993 meeting of the American Association for the Advancement of Science in Boston. When I managed to get sober advice from other members of the master's fan club—although controversial, Clynes's experiments win high adulation from some leading scientists—it confirmed my impression that my work was too skimpy to publish. There were also some anomalies. Certain durations predicted as nearly constant appeared in my results, although stable, to be twice what they should have been. (Two-bit computing errors? I will never know.)

One barrier to experiments is the complexity of Clynes's ideas. I have several times (for example, in *Elements of Semiotics*) referred to my synthesis of Clynes's work as a "gesture hypothesis," but several very interdependent and yet quite separate hypotheses are involved. The consequence for experimental studies is that you cannot try out the paradigm one piece at a time. Another difficulty was cultural. When Clynes first reported his work on biological universals in emotion expression, cultural difference held sway in new psychological and anthropological thought. The crucial concept of a temporal shape, which we must look at in a moment, has also proven difficult to convey, but musicians who know what an "envelope" is in acoustics understand at once. A further obstacle to understanding is the notion that an innate behavior might require practice or (I go beyond him here) that even though innate, it might require social triggers, as sexual behavior seems to require for certain primates. (In my little experiments I tried to teach subjects the "wrong" expressive gesture, but they went back to the "right" one.)

We employ the word "gesture" with considerable metaphorical range. I take "They gave him a big office as a gesture of respect" to be metaphorical and "They bowed their heads in respect" to be literal.[1] You might imagine someone bowing when you hear the assignment of the big office so described, but I don't think you need to imagine a big office as the meaning of a curtsey. As for the musical representation of a curtsey (an example follows later), we ought not to give it the same name as we apply to the corporal enactment. I used to avoid "musical gesture" as confusing the model and the representation, but I have been convinced at last, by Robert Hatten's work, that it is a perfectly good term so long as we think of "musical gesture" as *one* compound term, not a noun with a contingent adjective.

A bodily gesture, literally, is a molar unit of motion, initiated by a single impulse, and accomplishing nothing other than expression or communication. I will never speak of gesture as compound in the sense of being divisible into parts or of a hierarchy

---

1. As protested in *Elements of Semiology* (Lidov 1999), pp. 178–79, I refuse to abolish the distinction between metaphorical and literal usage.

in which one gesture includes another. While a corporal gesture is an unbroken unit, the musical representation of a gesture might involve several notes. We have no rule of translation between such musical forms and the somatic patterns which they represent. To speak of gesture as a basis of musical reference is theoretically vacuous unless we are aware of the questions this idea puts on the table. How is somatic gesture expressive and of what is it expressive? How do distinctions among musical representations of gesture correspond to distinctions among gestures of the body? What is the place and function of these representations in music?

The word "gesture" is not a key term or a technical term in Clynes's theory, so there is an element of adaptation in my summary. Below are some questions which Clynes's work develops (and in parentheses some questions that he does *not* address). I think it is evident that precise, experimentally validated answers to these questions would have a bearing on our understanding of music. If one doesn't want to adopt Clynes's conclusions as a hypothesis, it is still the case that they put before us a more concrete notion than we would otherwise have of the ground that a good theory of musical gesture needs to cover.

1. What are the universal (or innate) characteristics of gesture (as against culturally determined), and how do these relate to an emotion feeling?

What Clynes calls a *sentic form* is a neural activation envelope, that is, a pattern for growth and decay, which has a set duration (ranging from half a second to a few seconds). Expressive gestures are gestures which realize innately determined sentic forms. These distinct patterns of acceleration and decay are the universal element and have fixed relations with emotion states. The emotion *state* which has the expressive gesture as physical correlate also has a feeling as a mental correlate. (The emotion state is typically of relatively long duration, and the growth and decay of an emotion state—during an hour or a month or whatever—is not what is at issue when he talks about the acceleration and deceleration of a brief expression.) Clynes does not give any systematic attention to cultural differences such as attitudes and practices which facilitate or repress expression or which channel it or which might favor, for example, a head nod rather than a hand gesture or a vocal inflection in executing the same activation curve.

2. Are emotions of distinct types or do they belong to a continuum? (What is the place of emotion within the total of what we call "feelings," including, for example, moods?)

The significance of this question to a theory of music representation is due to the linked question, whether musical gestures would fall into semantically distinct categories. In psychology the question is very controversial. Clynes understands his evidence as demonstrating a finite number of distinct emotions, each correlated with a distinct sentic form (anger has the shortest sentic form, grief and reverence have the longest). There is no continuum between the distinct types, but there are composite states which are expressed by hybrid forms. Other than emotion, Clynes does not deal with a larger range of feelings that would include moods and other states of being.

3. How do expressive corporal motions become vehicles of communication?

Any group of muscles can be activated under the influence of a given sentic form. Therefore, there is an equivalence of dynamic form that you can observe between an angrily shaken fist and an angrily stamped foot, an angrily spoken word, or even an angry glare. When we perceive these expressions we are inclined to respond mimetically (empathetically) and thus to feel what is expressed. As the theory takes neural patterns, not their muscular realizations, as the ultimate basis of expression, sonic forms are considered as immediate realizations of sentic shapes, not as translations of the corresponding muscle patterns.

4. To what extent can expressive behavior be faked?

The question might seem silly at first, but recall Eco's suggestion that a sign is anything you can employ to lie. At stake is the status of gesture as automatic or voluntary. According to Clynes, only to the extent that the corresponding feeling can be fantasized and dwelt in can an expressive gesture be faked. You cannot put on a convincing show of anger or grief without vividly imagining the feeling. This position implies that musical performance, to be emotionally expressive, requires a fantasized image of feeling to guide execution.

5. How do brief expressive gestures relate to the longer-term growth and decay of an emotional state?

The corresponding musical question would concern the relation between the expressivity of a short figure and the tone of an extended passage. It will be clear in the chapters that follow that I don't pursue any simple analogy of this sort. Unlike expressive gestures, musical figures are extended and concatenated by an elaborate syntax. But Clynes offers a provocative observation. According to his research, when gestural expressions are repeated in a regular rhythm, they tend to discharge the corresponding emotion state rapidly, but if they are induced as responses to rhythmically irregular stimuli, they tend for a while to amplify the feeling up to some point of saturation. This proposal is relevant to the gestural interpretation of metrically recurrent figures.

6. What parameters of gestural expression correlate with intensity of feeling?

Clynes's development of this question makes the intensity of expression completely distinct from dynamic intensity or the excitement of speed. Precision is the key. The more accurately the innate sentic forms are realized, the more intense a feeling they communicate.

7. How can music convey expressive gesture? (Is that the whole basis of musical meaning?)

Clynes's work supports the conclusion that the determining features of a gestural representation in music are too subtle to be captured by notation. They depend on what he calls "musical microstructure," that is, subtle differences between nominally equivalent durations and subtle dynamic shading. Clynes's measurements are in thousandths of a second for time and in less than a tenth of 1 percent for the range of force. Performance nuance responds to this level of detail; composition does not (but see Chapter 14 regarding a possible exception). All of Clynes's experimental studies of emotional communication in music depend on specific performances. His numerous conjectures about the relationship of sentic communication to music, including sonic analyses of the emotional content of musical themes (though not the most rigorously argued aspect of his work), are suggestive. Although piano music uses tones that, once struck, are of a constant shape, combinations of factors such as dynamic nuance, rhythmic nuance (and, of course, the complexities of composition like harmony) can contribute to a virtual image of continuous motion that reproduces the continuous energy curve of a sentic form, even in piano music. (See the first example in the following chapter.) As for the place of all this in a full-fledged musical discourse, Clynes discusses many aspects of musical communication, but I find no response by him to this question.

The experimental apparatus that Clynes developed in the 1960s to study gestural expression and, later, musical beats included a pressure transducer that measured impulses from the finger tip, his "sentograph," and his then very novel computer of average transients (CAT), which was widely adapted for other purposes. In Figure III.1 I have redrawn the sentic forms that Clynes reports as the average toward which expressive forms approach as they are practiced without guidance. He measures both a horizontal, outward pressure and a vertical, downward

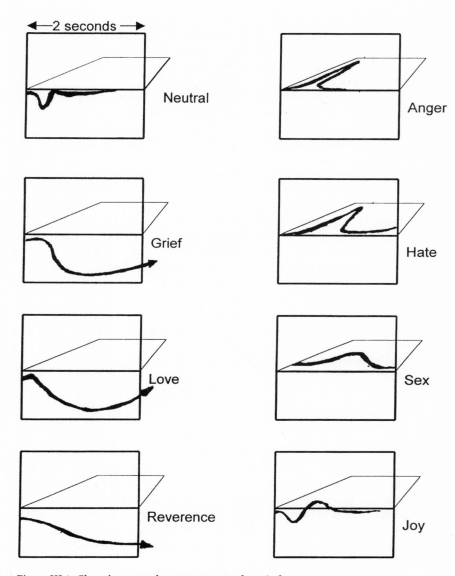

Figure III.1. Clynes's averaged measurements of sentic forms.

pressure. I have drawn only the more prominent of the two, turning the curve sideward to show the horizontal pressure. The sentic forms vary in length from about 0.2 seconds (anger and hate generate the shortest forms) to around 5 seconds (grief and reverence have the longest expression). This means that they correspond, very roughly, to the typical timescale of musical motives. The attractive feature of the results is that they hold no surprises. They seem, rather, to confirm an intuition. Anger, the shortest sentic form, flashes. Hate is similar but slightly more prolonged and seems to "drive home" its blow. Grief droops. Maternal love caresses. Eros pants. Joy rebounds (the upward tail is vertical here). It takes no great leap of the intellect to think up critical questions about the research paradigm or the results, but I would like to insist that it requires only a few hours over a couple of weeks to get a feel for the data, not just by reading the relevant chapters of his book on sentics (1989) but also by practicing his "sentic cycles" with the click tracks he has made available. In this case, a bit of hands-on experience makes the theory more interesting to talk about. Today, with our ubiquitous desktop computers and with new recording technologies, it would be possible to explore the phenomena from many other angles. If one takes the inquiry seriously—never mind the answers—then we consider the possibility that gesture in music is not a "mere" metaphor but some kind of determinate mapping. The very idea waves two red flags.

One flag is a signal that we may have a reason to rely on intuition more than our academic training suggests we should. The other flag alerts us to the possible presence of the dreaded "stimulus-response" relation in musical representation. I hope that the next three chapters make a good case that the opportunity is greater than the danger.

Gestural expression is indexical, obeying a stimulus-response pattern, but music is an art, not mere expression. Its forms and materials comprise systems. Our problem is to bring system and expression into relation, to understand gesture as an element, not an end. What composition, in contrast to performance, provides in relation to expression is never completely specific. What is specific is the identity of the expressive figure, not its "meaning." The figure is an intellectual property, available for storage, retrieval, combination, and analysis—available, in other words, for composing. It remains for us to consider how composition contextualizes these figures in a cultural discourse. This problem is the most central issue in the viewpoint I have been describing, but it requires a new analysis in every instance. It does not permit a systematic general solution. We deal here with a synthesis which compositional style continually renews. The widely felt intuition that music conveys philosophical values reflects the capacity of music to mirror every nuance of conflict and interplay between somatically and mentally controlled experience and between individual impulse and social constraint. I am reluctant to adopt Edward Said's term "transgressive" (1991) for these relations because the word seems to me too strong for such a ubiquitous and eminently musical feature of music, but it is obvious that Said has pinpointed the principle. He credits Wagner with an explicit presentation of the idea in *Die Meistersinger*. The relations between somatic representation and culture encompass a potentially unlimited number of perspectives which are as varied as the musics of history and of the world.

The interplay between the representation of gesture and its formal contextualization creates discourse—a representation of think*ing* as action. Before I attempt to further specify what I intend with this term, which was not used casually in Chapter 3, I offer three tiny examples as a warm-up.

Eine Kleine Nachtmusik

Suppose the opening four-measure phrase is taken as gesture of self-presentation: Enter and bow. Can we then make sense of the answering phrase, which is clearly the same but reversed in direction? Bowing to stage rear won't do. We can immediately see that artifice is resisting spontaneous impulse. That is of course what eighteenth-century elegance is all about. There is, according to a fascinating paper I once heard but cannot cite, a satisfactory possibility of gestural translation. The commedia dell'arte audience sat in two rows and instigated a style of double presentations, first to one side, then the other. However, this balletic interpretation is still a matter of artifice. The balletic gestures, like Mozart's musical gestures, are gestures transformed to become signs of a concept, losing their character of natural expression but gaining other affiliations. In the marked context of this artistic discourse we immediately access issues of culture—questions of symmetry, the place of reason, taste, and so on.

Schubert, Sonata in A Major, Op. Posth.

Robert Hatten has published a superb analysis of this sonata (1993) which is developed further in his book on musical gesture (2004). My comments, again reflections on just one single phrase, are a footnote to that analysis. (For clarity, I should mention that what he calls a "gesture" is specified as a compound signifier, not a unitary signified, a slightly more abstract sense of the term than mine, but I have no quarrel with that.)

Figure III.2A shows the beginning of the second theme of the first movement. Its gestures seem to me to center in the two rising fourths, the first perhaps like a dazzled glance, the second,

A.

Figure III.2A. Schubert, Sonata for Piano in A Major, D. 959, mm. 55–59.

B.

Figure III.2B. Perfunctory answer without tonic cadence.

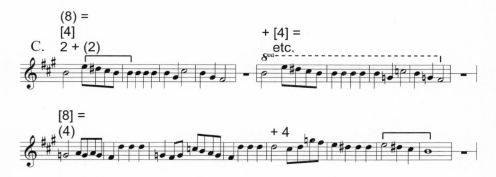

Figure III.2C. Theme reduced to formulaic period.

more like a caress, the whole overflowing with love and consolation and tinged with regret. It does not matter a whit to my argument if you prefer a different name for the feeling or even a different feeling, but my contentions will have no substance for you if you don't find the phrase expressive, much in the way gesture is expressive.

What Schubert does next is really dangerous. I must give two different accounts. First, the front-page story: After the phrase cited, Schubert provides no filler. He pauses, then repeats. We listen for a balancing, answering phrase that never arrives. Up to this point in the sonata, Schubert has demanded only very minor concessions from the rationalism and artificiality of his eighteenth-century predecessors. Like Mozart, he has responded to each gesture with a formal, motivic resolution, if not a harmonic one. Here he takes a chance on letting the representation of gesture stand on its own. The absence of the tonic is not critical. If you supply one in the fifth measure, the gesture is still unresolved, though softened. Furthermore, as my invented extension (Figure III.2B) shows, an answering phrase can equilibrate the gesture without arriving at the tonic. (The phrase is so gesturally rich that it is hard to calm it down in a four-measure answer.) When a further thematic idea (a balanced "perfect phrase" in the sense of Chapter 4) follows the repetition of this first one, we might think for a moment that the initial phrase was just an introduction, but, no, it comes back again, still searching for a complement, and then again once more to round out the exposition without ever being rounded out itself. (The quick tip of the hat to the tonic in this last does not tip the balance!) The unresolved charge of this phrase is exploited as a fund of motivation for the ensuing development, and it is never fully neutralized.

But there is another story on the editorial page: No problem—Schubert is gradually unfolding a longer period, and Figure III.2C shows the underlying normal form. The notation of the sketch and the model proposed conform to those of Chapters 3 (with Beethoven) and 4 (with Debussy). But this rationale will not do. The sketch is reductive, and gesture does not submit to reduction as docilely as tonality and metrical forms do. The fifth measures excised from the sketch are not motivic extensions but freeze-frames. It is possible and relevant to hear the new nine measures as completing the first ten but only as complementary signs of a distant and unavailable unity. The rhythmic impulse of the second eight-bar phrase, which would, in a more formulaic solution, flow unimpeded to a conclusion in its eighth measure, is exhausted by the seventh and continues via a slow motion reprise of a fragment (bracketed in the sketch) that neither resolves nor answers the opening motion but instead problematizes it. This period can not contain its overspilling gestures. Schubert pulls the conventional period apart so that it is more a rhetorical ploy than a container. The reduction is valid as a technical history, but Schubert's technique is closer to parody (in the Renaissance sense) than to prolongation. The reduction may help explain how he did it, but the first account tells correctly what he achieved.

Leaving the gesture nearly bare the way he does here, Schubert moves, as his later works often do, almost into viewing distance of expressionism. The phrase evokes a different ratio of reason to feeling, one in which emotion intervenes in social order. The figure itself is hardly so exceptional as its treatment in form.

J. S. Bach, Prelude and Fugue for Organ in B Minor, BWV 544

Figure III.3 is the opening section of a work, as I read it, of deeply tragic tone and monumental grandeur. Its tragedy and grandeur are *not*, however, simply expressions of feeling. The music conceptualizes complexes of feeling and attitude which depend on the enactment of culturally evaluated tropes. Our historical knowledge of musical thought in the time of the music's composition immediately alerts us to the possibility that we will find a key to its relations of expression and system in the tradition of rhetorical categories, but I do not claim to meet the exigencies of thorough historicism in this sketch.

In Figure III.3, A, B, and C mark three fragments in which the voices presenting melodic figures have the same composite rhythm (shown separately). In the first and third fragments, A and C, the rhythm carries harmonic tensions and syncopations suggesting a strong affective expression. The second fragment, B, is composed of a four-square formula which is essentially neutral in affect, though it may well seem to pick up the mood of its context because moods are pervasive.

To deal with expression first, the primary figure of this passage evokes grief. We could draw support from the conventions of Baroque ornament which recognize here the "sigh motive," but beyond that vague cliché we can be more specific on biological grounds. Intense grief has, in conjunction with the dropping, drooping gesture of the sigh, the characteristics of a minute pause between a slow exhalation and a rapid inhalation and of the tendency of the body to twist. These gestural shapes are all suggested in the *contrapposto* syncopations of the melody and bass and in the upward skips from the twin figures.

The expressive figures are embedded in large, symmetrically planned phrases and presented in the sonic texture of the full organ, a performance medium that embodies power. Fragment A combines an ascent based on a systematic process of repetition and variation—similar to the sequential type sometimes referred to as "climax" in the musical-rhetorical theory of the period— with a descent in declamatory style. Both these cultural forms, the ascending sequence and the declamation, *resist* the passive

Figure III.3. J. S. Bach, Prelude for Organ in B Minor, BWV 544, mm. 1–17.

character of grief, and, enlarged as they are by the echoing lamentations of the first measures and the massive pedestal of the bass ostinato, may be understood here as heroic.

Fragments B and C are both parts of the phrase answering phrase A. Fragment B, built on an emotionally neutralized version of the same rhythm, emphasizes its powerful sound material. The identity of rhythms is not prominent immediately: we are distracted from this identity by the intervening recitative (mm. 8–10), by contour and voicing changes, and by the new bass pattern in the pedals. We discover the identity at C, where the bass syncopation returns and the rhythm is reinvested with expressive content. In terms of the formula familiar for tragedy, fragment C provides recognition and reversal. The identity of the rhythm is recognized, and the motivic fragment, heroic when it had climbed, becomes piteous in its inexorable descent. Of course, I don't mean to suggest that Bach is recalling Sophocles or Aristotle, but rather that he invokes a narrative archetype. The structure of tragedy which we may observe in this passage and which recurs later is not the design of the work as a whole. The prelude progresses toward a fugue of deep repose and consolation.

The point is that the action of this passage does not simply express a natural feeling but presents a pattern of cultural significance achieved through the synthesis of composed relations and performed expression and which is not reducible to either.

Discourse in Music

Is it an exaggeration to speak of the complex representations I attribute to music in these three examples as "discourse"? Suzanne Langer's distinction between discursive and presentational forms in *Feeling and Form* (1953) appears to me to shortchange the capacities of music. The differences for her hinge on the capacity of predicative discourse to express truth and aboutness, but her analysis of "about" does not settle the issue.[2] If one sign modifies our sense of another, we might say the second is about the first.

Music is not congenitally disbarred from being about. Therefore, I would rather speak of different types of discourse. Music realizes a type of discourse that I call *transformative*. Corporal actions, not necessarily gestures, are transformed by a state of feeling that makes them a vehicle of sentic expression. I might

---

2. This point is discussed further in Lidov (1999), pp. 147–52.

wash the dishes joyously or set the table angrily. If the dishes are not plastic, considerable restraint is required, but a good actor could convey the emotion without words. A structure of notes is similarly transformed when performance imposes expressive shapes on them. The reverse also holds. When a spontaneous expression is resisted or framed or manipulated by cultural models, it is transformed, becoming less impulsive and more like a representation of a concept. The materials of Classical music are very neutral in expressive content: bland scales, bland chords, metrically balanced rhythms, symmetrical forms. When groups of notes are performed in a manner that brings out their gestural characters, that is, performed expressively, the entire musical structure is transformed from a merely rational construction into an expressive construction. At the same time, the rational construction of the music parlays the representations of gesture into an elaborate discourse. Although its aesthetic function belongs to a different universe, the music discussed above puts in play a recurrent movement of thought: attention to immediate experience alternates with reflective conceptualization. That the *activity* of thought is represented is what motivates the term "discourse." In our first example, self-presentation is evoked in the cultural perspective of formal courtesies; in the second, love is evoked as an intervention; and in the third, grief as heroic. It is not a horrible exaggeration to say the first is "about" presentation, the second "about" love, or the third "about" grief so long as we acknowledge that these are potential, not regulated, meanings.

8   Mind and Body in Music

Associations of somatic experience and music are so prevalent as hardly to require demonstration. The most common tempo indication in Classical music, *Allegro*, means walking, and the comparably common jazz term, *swing*, is also kinesthetic in reference. The connection of the body to music is direct and immediate. A skilled conductor can convey what he or she requires of an orchestra by silent movements of the hands, even though a minimal part of the message conveyed is codified by conscious rules. The conviction that music has a direct effect on the body arises among disparate cultures, and music has been used to promote trance and exorcise illness throughout history. All around the globe, music commands and directs the dance. Anterior to its status as sign, music is an action on and of the body.

If music is (among other things) a transmutation of physiological impulses, it is not merely this, to be sure. Music is a part and a product of mental life. Still, unlike mathematics or speech, much more distinctly than in painting (even abstract expressionist painting), and for much less obvious reasons than in ballet or acting, a sense persists of strong and precise and intimate correspondences between the details of music and bodily properties: gestures, tensions, and postures as well as such psychosomatic (or neurochemical) properties as states of consciousness, mood, and emotions. Those correspondences which involve kinesthesia in a direct and simple way appear ubiquitous.

One might suppose that the problem of elucidating referential aspects of music could start with an analysis of its references to the body. We might interpret Rousseau's mimetic theory of music as starting with this tack. (For a review of Rousseau's elaborated conception of music as a system of signs see Blum 1985.) Rousseau focuses on the larynx: "Melody in imitating the inflection of the voice expresses plaints, cries of pain or joy. . . . All the vocal signs of passion are at its disposal" (1970, p. 159). This view was popular, but with the compelling dialectic of absolute and descriptive music that arose in the nineteenth century, it seems to have been overshadowed. Controversy about musical meaning since then has tended to bypass somatic reference, suggesting a paradox: Stravinsky, who once claimed that music can express nothing outside itself, was the century's greatest composer for ballet. Similarly, Chopin, who did not share the taste of some of his contemporaries for explicitly descriptive programs and titles, wrote many more dances than Schumann, Liszt, or Berlioz. (In some measure this also holds true for Schubert and

This chapter was originally published as an article in *Semiotica* 66, no. 1/3 (1987). It included some material that now appears in the preceding Introduction.

even for Brahms.) On the other side, if we examine records of the interests of composers more fully committed to descriptive music, we find relatively little that bears directly on the body or its behavior as a subject. In the titles and texts of works by Schumann, Berlioz, Liszt, Wagner, and Debussy there are, of course, references to dancing and entrancement, sometimes to floating or flying, but relatively few. Where the body or its actions appear, they tend either to be reduced to symbols of something else or to form a contextual background. "Les Valses" and "A Walk in the Country" are not primarily intended to represent dancing or walking. It might seem that somatic reference in music is on the one hand too obvious to command the interest of descriptive musicians, and on the other hand too innocuous to earn the proscription of the "absolute" musicians.

One answer is that this is no paradox at all because movement is not a "meaning" of music but rather an intrinsic property. Aesthetic theories as diverse as, for example, Coker (1972), who regards all music as a form of gesture, Gurney (1967), who describes music as "ideal motion," or Goodman (1968), who regards the qualities of artworks as irreducible, would vitiate the paradox by attributing motion to the signifier, not the signified. Motion is one of the essential illusions of music, like the closely related one of reappearance. (We do not say that a theme "recurs" but that it "returns"—as if it had been staying somewhere else in the meantime.) I would deny that anyone hears musically who does not hear change as motion and repetition as persistence. Nevertheless, if these illusions are properties of music, they are still not properties of sound, and if perception of these illusions is essential to musicality, that is because we require them, not to perceive the structure of its sound (which would be clearer without them!), but to perceive its significance. Music is significant only if we identify perceived sonorous motion with somatic experience. To call this complex chain of signification an intrinsic property of sound is simply to refuse to attempt its analysis. It is as if we were to say the virtual image of Mona Lisa is not a representation; it is simply a property of the color patches.

A cliché of music appreciation held that the original sources of music, song, and dance (however they might eventually be cultivated) arose as the natural acts of the primitive body in an emotionally heightened state. The expressive force of music is linked with kinesthesia by linguistic idiom; music "moves" us and "stirs" our passions. What does this actually mean?

The primary and predominant basis of reference in the graphic arts is *similarity:* visual isomorphism. The corresponding point of departure for music is *causation:* interaction with the body. I emphasize "point of departure" for music alienates its somatic transactions in achieving formal structure. The exploration of any of that abstractive process will show us what is entailed when a reaction of the body becomes a property of the mind. The body becomes or acquires mind to the extent that it identifies with or, to use Polanyi's felicitous description, "dwells in" abstract formal systems of articulation such as those of music. In speech we see predominantly the final extreme of the abstractive process. In music we can observe every part of the spectrum from immediate physiological expression to the purest play of form.

8.1. Semiotic Transcendence in Music

The abstractive, transformational, and compositional process by which sound takes shape and motivation from the body but transcends it to become music is representative of a general semiotic phenomenon. In acquiring signs, sensations and impulses formed in and of the body transcend it to become mind.

To survey the distance between mind and body we may contrast "freedom of composition" and "freedom of performance." Freedom of performance is the uninhibited effect of a cause, the freedom to follow an impulse or to obey a force. Freedom of performance is essential to art but not specific to mentality. In fact, it may seem to display the subjugation of intellect to passion, instinct, or other powers. This is the freedom exemplified by *rubato* or by spontaneous performance of a memorized piece of music but also by downhill skiing or any purely emotional spontaneity. Freedom of composition is specific to semiosis and occurs nowhere else. Freedom of composition resides in the possibility of choice among alternatives and in a capacity of the relationship between an articulated formal system and its users. It is neither the user nor the system which enjoys this freedom, but the semiotic act itself, which comprises decisions irreducible to real causes or real randomness. To illustrate this, consider a profound and monumental instance: the volcanic eruption of the recapitulation in the first movement of Beethoven's Ninth Symphony, where the empty fifths of the opening return over a bass of the major third. Here the convention of repetition becomes a locus of reversal. Such freedom expresses no necessary cause. Obviously, Beethoven did not have to write what he did, but we have no trouble finding reasons why he should have. (Interpretations of this passage are discussed in the Postscript of Chapter 14.) Reasons—which are interminable networks of logically associated signs—are the hallmark of compositional freedom. They show a decision not to be random, yet they are not its necessary causes. In supplying the harmony with a third while reversing mode and dynamics and inverting the chord, the recapitulation permutes polarities which were already foregrounded in the theme and latent in its stylistic system. There is a logic within its spontaneity.

Signs are not all equal in their power to transcend biological determination. The criterion of transcendence, exemplified by freedom in composition, induces a hierarchy in sign typology. At one end we have signs which belong to independently articulated systems, and at the other, those signs which are most strongly determined. It may seem that I have put the cart before the horse in separating composition from performance when many of the world's musical traditions which lack notation seem not to make this distinction. But if notated music had not provided the clue, semiotics would still require this division, and for the reason given here. Composition is articulate; it concerns the aspect of music established by articulatory elements whether notated or not. Performance is particular; it concerns variables outside the system.

A system of articulation is a vocabulary of individual and distinct sign types (equivalence classes) from which more complex structures can be assembled: phonemes, embroidery stitches, types of wearing apparel, scales of pitches, and so on. Articulation has both a negative and a complement. The negative, the *inarticulate,* is not without bearing in music or in semiosis generally, and we shall see that loss of articulation can be a profound sign of surrender to the body. The complement of the articulate is the *particular.* Unlike articulation, semiotic particulars permit no allophonic equivalences. They are not tokens of types. Musical signs encompass both the articulate and the particular as well as the inarticulate. *Rubato* is particular. Timbre is particular in the voice and articulate in the orchestral score. Notes themselves are variable in their articulatory status. Normally distinct at moderate speeds, they may seem to lose articulation in rapid or very plastic performance, in vocal ornament, or in thick orchestral passages.

Where the concept of articulation is most fully developed in semiotics, as in Saussure, Hjelmslev, or Lévi-Strauss, it is usually assumed that articulation is a prerequisite of semiosis. This view of articulation is impoverishing. Articulation stands at one end of an axis. Articulation is the condition and result of formal sign systems. In music we study the interrelation of performance signs barely removed from unarticulated somatic experience, compositional structures formed by the free play of pure articulation, and the full spectrum of musical imagery that lies between these poles.

I adapt the Peircean triad of icon, index, and symbol to categorize signs according to the hierarchy outlined above. My borrowing does not follow Peirce strictly. The standard, formulaic definitions—icon, a sign by similarity; index, a sign by cause; symbol, a sign by convention—are too abbreviated to be true to Peirce and do not capture my intentions. I reject (as he does) any sharp, unqualified opposition between relations of similarity and relations of real connection. The general rule (so very well illustrated by photographs and seismographs) is that significant similarities have real causes and that real connections transfer features of similarity. (An example from aesthetics: Catharsis, a caused effect, depends on mimesis, a similarity.) The central distinction between the index and icon for Peirce is that the icon is *independent* of its object, whereas the index and its object are *dependent.* The symbol for Peirce is the sign which bears conventional meaning. I shall retain only the negative aspect. The symbol is a sign loosened from its natural meaning (cause or similarity), a sign which is thus available for a conventional assignment but which—and this is more important in the arts—stands as the antipode to natural reference whether a secondary meaning is assigned (e.g., a word) or not (a nonsense word). We thus arrive at the following scheme.

The *index* is the most particular and least articulate sign. In music, tempo, *rubato,* nuance of intonation, and dynamic level are usually unarticulated signs, indices. They are directly expressive, representing an immediate mutual influence of body and sound.

The *icon* is a particular arrangement of articulated materials, an arrangement which may be interpreted as the isomorph or trace of some object or force not immediately in contact with it. In composition, the shapes of melody, chord progressions, and rhythmic patterns may be icons. These shapes are understood as images of movement or of somatic states governing movement, but they are not immediate copies, causes, or consequences of these. They require interpretation. Performances which reconnect them to (or index them to) the body reveal their force.

The *symbol* is an articulate arrangement of articulated material, that is, the relation of arrangement as well as the materials are abstract types. In music, symmetries of structure give rise to symbols, abstract patterns with the most indeterminate somatic content.

The transformation of body to mind in music appears as a transcendent process of articulation. The immediate expression of physiological values in sound as performed nuance is indexical. Where these values are translated into arrangements of formal units, for example, melodic contours, harmonic modulations, and so on, we have iconic signs. The further substitution of formal relations for physiological values (the developmental calculi of fragmentation, inversion, transposition, and so on, which can be but need not be subordinated to images of feeling) carries us toward the symbol.

8.2. The Body as Semantic Context

In order to acquire as good a foundation as possible, and to ascertain, independently of common opinion, how far particular movements of the features and gestures are really expressive of certain states of the mind, I have found the following means the most serviceable. In the first place, to observe infants. . . . In the second place, it occurred to me that the insane ought to be studied. . . . Thirdly, Dr. Duchene galvanized . . . certain muscles in the face. . . . Fourthly, I had hoped to derive much aid from the great masters in painting and sculpture, who are such close observers. Accordingly, I have looked at photographs and engravings of many well-known works; but with a few exceptions, have not thus profited. The reason no doubt is, that in works of art, beauty is the chief object; and strongly contracted facial muscles destroy beauty. The story of the composition is generally told with wonderful force and truth by skillfully given accessories.

—Darwin (1873), pp. 13–15

The referent of a reference is double. It is both a second sign, the internal semiotic object (Eco's "cultural unit," "form" in Hjelmslev, "immediate object" in Peirce, or Frege's *Sinn*—these being only very rough, yet arguable equivalents) and is a "real" or external object (Peirce's "dynamic object," Frege's *Bedeutung*, Hjelmslev's "substance"). We can hardly separate these objects, for we wear thick mittens made of a cloth of other signs when we work. Yet, when it comes to comparisons of media, comparisons which the student of musical semiotics can hardly avoid, it will not do to confine our view to the formal relations of a strictly internal semantics. A sign translates the external object into a semiotic unit by its act of misrepresentation; part of our job, ultimately, is to compare translations.

To regard the body as a privileged context of external reference divides the total universe of our discourses into mutually inclusive objective and subjective realms.

The objective, exosemantic realm, with its coherent three-dimensional geometry and ordered locations, certainly contains the body as an object in its space. But the body perceived subjectively is an infinite space, not in its inner representation of its own substance, a palpably finite volume, but in its inner representation of its condition. Vigor and anxiety, boredom, or curiosity have no spatial boundaries and no location. Whatever is excluded from the neatly ordered arrangements of the exosomatic realm finds accommodation in this inner space.

The body itself appears in both spaces. Feeling feverish is endosomatic; taking one's temperature, exosomatic. The dance has both a visual and a kinesic appearance. We learn to understand each in terms of the other, but they are separate at first. The dancing child does not know how he or she looks, and an adult who has danced little is rarely quick to grasp the *feeling* of ballet.

We must guard against thinking of the endosomatic realm as insubstantial, ephemeral, ineffable, and unaccountable. Language—perhaps for reasons which we explore below—adds vagueness to the reality of our inner space by an unnecessary duplication of concepts. Ockham's razor can improve our grip on the observable. I will assume that all states of feeling (taking that word in its full range of references from sensation to emotion) are the appearance of states of the body. The feeling of an object, event, artwork, or even idea is then the subjective appearance of the somatic states which it (and/or its referents) induce. The principle I adopt here, influenced by Darwin, James, Kohler, and others, is that of thorough psychosomatic isomorphism. It is a rational principle, not an experimental one, and independent of measurements of adrenaline, perspiration, or brain waves. This postulate will permit us to work back toward the problem I have labeled above as "comparing translations"—eventually comparing verbal and musical images of the body—with the least extra metaphysics.

The endosomatic world is one that we feel; the exosomatic world, one we see. The exosomatic realm is preeminently visual, stabilized and articulated by the physiology of gestalt perception. Its objects commute without apparent distortion; that is, we can move ourselves and many other things around in it without altering them. The endosomatic realm is largely unarticulated. To be sure, it has its distinctive entities just as the other space has its fogs and clouds. Hunger is as definite a thing as a tea cup. But as a general rule the conditions of the body shade into each other and affect each other, and there is only a little room to maneuver when it comes to reordering them. The endosomatic space is chiefly a realm of flux and influence. Its chief contents are changing states rather than fixed objects.

Language, a commutative system of fixed elements, is allied principally to exosomatic space. Most words attach to visual objects or to visible relations or have meanings which derive from such attachments. Even the majority of words for sounds conceive them in terms of visible sources. (For example, "barking" is the sound of a dog; a note is the sound corresponding to a mark on paper.) Visual appearances, since they so readily commute, can be replicated. The visual sign is, therefore, in the first instance, the real or imaginary replication of an appearance. The primary basis of the representation of endosomatic entities is not, as with visual objects, by the replication of their appearances. In general, we signify an endosomatic entity by its antecedent or consequent, by stimulation or expression rather than by depiction. If I say, "Taste this . . . !" I represent an experience to you by indicating its cause. Representation of the inner world is first of all a matter of contact with its continuous transformations.

Though sound might seem to belong to exosomatic phenomena, it is ambiguous. Sound lacks precision of location in three-dimensional space. (It is not clear that the location of a sound is the location of its source.) The endosomatic world is not a world of auditory appearances, but vast parts of it seem able to establish contact with sound and able to shape or be shaped by sound. This holds, with attenuation, even for the sounds of words. Words are stripped of auditory value by their incorporation in a fully articulated system. But language includes a good deal of expressive sound which is not the sound of words in its inflectional contours and interjectory vocalizations. In these and in moaning, sighing, yelling, clapping, and elsewhere, we see expressions isogenous with certain musical gestures. The auditory sign is, in the first instance, a transformation of an impulse ("expression" in its root sense of pressing out) or, for the recipient, a stimulus. Sound, which the body produces by more or less strenuous effort, shares a general field of reference with expressive muscular gesture both in expression and in reception. These communications must be regarded as immediate influences which invoke somatic changes—microscopic perhaps for a sedentary auditor—informing rather than transforming. The feeling of these changes is perceived as the quality of the gesture which provokes them.

8.3. Musical and Muscular Gesture

Gesture has a privileged status in the expression of somatic states, for gesture appears to have no function outside of its communicative one. One fundamental fact supporting auditory and gestural expression may be easier to grasp in the integral calculus than in English, since language segregates representations of time and space more dogmatically than mathematics does. Gesture is a temporal shape set by an instantaneous condition. Linguistic habit has us think of conditions and behaviors as quite distinct, but in some cases they are like two sides of a coin. A hungry animal is one that seeks food, a sad man one who sighs, and so on. Sound appears to us as a kind of behavior, but its behavior is integrated as a state or condition.

The equivalence of musical figures with gestures is widely observed. Coker (1972) takes gesture as a general category encompassing all of music. His exposition allows for inclusional hierarchies of gesture—gestures made of smaller gestures—and gives the concept enough scope to include syntactical structures. Tarasti (1979, following Adorno) takes the "gestural" in a narrow sense related to the heroic manner. My meaning is restricted and conventional. Gesture encompasses all brief, expressive molar units of motor activity, be they of the limbs, the digits, the larynx, the torso, units which are whole but not readily subdivisible.

The essence of a motor gesture is readily represented in music by a brief group of notes. The small gestalt of a few notes, a motive or ornament or single figuration, is the atomic level of signification in music. Smaller units, notes, or even cells of two or three notes have syntactic and sensory values, but they do not usually constitute units of expression in the way slightly larger shapes easily do, as representations of gesture with a certain solidarity and wholeness and, at the same time, the capacity to possess individual character. This view is conventional, though not universal, and is supported by the terminology and practice of musical pedagogies. D'Indy (1909), for example, devotes a chapter to analysis of the musical "idea" as the first level of significant invention. The role of diminution in Baroque ornamentation is comparable, as is the use of the term "subject" (fugue subject), which can, but does not always, refer to larger groupings. The rhetorical theorists of Baroque music attend to short figures as a privileged level of expression. The riff in jazz, the *gamulka* in Carnatic music, appears comparable to the European examples as minimal but important units of expression. As Nattiez (1975) has shown in detail, there is no neutral basis for defining this level of structure. He failed to note that, like the morpheme, it must be defined by its significance. It is simply the first level of structure in which the somatic behavior we call gesture finds a correlate.

To say just how musical figures translate muscular gestures is obviously problematic. I suppose that musical and muscular gestures are isogenous, linked by an inner behavior correlated with a state or feeling. Clynes's train or investigation, reviewed in the preceding Introduction, gives some substance to this hypothesis. Though his thought is largely restricted to one type of psychosomatic state, the emotion state, it is sufficiently pertinent to a great deal of music that it merits careful attention. I quote Clynes's example from the Ballade Op. 47 of Chopin (Figure 8.1). I give his description without comment here, but I will return to it later on and consider the same musical excerpt in its musical context:

> The first half of this theme can be felt to embody longing, yearning, and ecstasy. It begins with a sense of being attracted, a pull expanding, and at the second bar, there is a continuing sense of floating upward after the C is struck. This apparently limitless feeling of being carried upward is accompanied by a sense of ecstasy, lasting for a moment, till we are gently carried back to the ground by the following F–E flat phrase.
> The inner form of this feeling and virtual body image . . . is produced only if there is a slight acceleration in the second half of the bar, and a corresponding lengthening of the first part of the second bar. (Clynes 1976, p. 230)

For any of us who read this description with a sense of recognition, Clynes's research supplies interesting evidence that a very private and apparently ineffable experience realizes shared, determinate, and measurable biological reactions. The notion of expressive gesture interpreted as the surface form of an underlying neurological function gives us a logical connection between somatic and musical experience, one which shows a basis for cause and resemblance in the relation of music to feeling. Of course, music is not simple expression, and the musical sign is of another order altogether than that of such physiological mechanisms as may inform it.

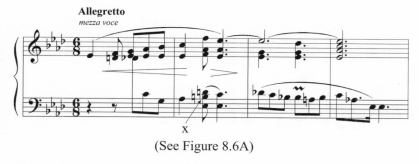

Allegretto
mezza voce

X

(See Figure 8.6A)

Figure 8.1. Chopin, Op. 47, mm. 1–4.

8.4. Music's Representation of the Body

The moment it takes musical form, the somatic sign is veiled by complications and its source obscured. It evolves through networks of qualification, ambiguation, and manipulation from a mode of reaction to become a mode of ideation. The word "evolve" denotes a progressive series, and this idea is appropriate, but all stages of the progression persist as aspects of the whole. The terms *index*, *icon*, and *symbol* in this context are applicable here to simultaneous and coexisting aspects of music, not to distinct segments.

The Musical Index

The index is the most transparent sign in music; it is all too transparent. The interpretation of speed, dissonance, vibrato, loudness (or their opposites) in terms of bodily excitement or repose arouses academic distrust; the brush stroke is too wide. Therefore, neither the quick incisions of Barthes's brief forays in musical hermeneutics nor the laboriously documented survey of Lomax's *Cantometrics* wins academic confidence easily. The learned musician has a great stake in sublimating the obvious meanings of the musical body.

But it is as much a mistake to reject the raw facts of somatic investiture in sound as it is to value them too naively. An acquired taste in sound (nasal singing, operatic vibrato, the rough attack of the harpsichord) is incomplete if it is merely an acquired tolerance which hears through the noise to pertinent relations but fails to participate in its material values. On the other hand, there is a methodological pitfall in appreciating material values too naively (for example, ascending pitch expresses increasing tension). Not only are these simple relations negated or supplanted in some measure by composition, but they also acquire internal imbrications of structure which make their meaning complex.

Consider, for example, how opposites compensate: *staccato* may cause us to hear connections; *piano subito* makes us intent. Meter displays subtle variations in so-

Figure 8.2A. Chopin, Op. 47, mm. 210–211.

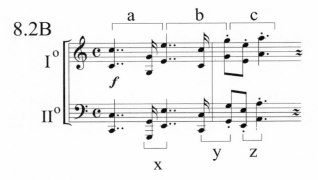

Figure 8.2B. Mozart, K. 521, mm. 1–2.

matic value through compound pulse (not compound meter: simple meter with recurring downbeats at one rate and beats at a multiple of that rate).

The variables of pulse are speed and intensity. Naively, speed is exciting. Intensity is involving. Strong, foreground pulse as in folk dances and marches controls movement directly. Attenuated pulse is a factor in the sublimation of somatic force. The import of a compound pulse that integrates two or more sets of values according to the relative intensity of the levels of beat within the same flow is less obvious. My observation is that the more subordinate rate of pulse characterizes a more contained or introverted factor of the somatic state, while the foreground or dominating rate refers to the more overt factor. Subordinated rapid beating within a predominant slow pulse (an extreme example, the extended trills in Beethoven's slow movements) indexes an inner, contained excitement. Subordinated slower beats, hypermetrical accents over predominant fast measures, also index an internal state, a relatively calmer framework in which the faster action is perceived. As the orchestral scherzo evolves in stature, regular four-bar metrical groups add monumentality at some cost to its motor compulsion. To attribute indexical status to an element of music means that its effect is direct but not that it is necessarily simple.

When the theme from Chopin which Clynes describes returns at the end of the

Ballade, one of the reversals it expresses is an inversion of the relative prominence of the beat and its subdivisions (Figure 8.2A). The faster pulse, originally weak, moves to the foreground or at least competes for the foreground. What we took as a sign of sentiment, inward feeling, in the theme's first presentation—the relative rhythmic weakness of its eighths in comparison with the larger beat—becomes by its reversal a sign of a physical embodiment, a realization or enactment of previous desire or fantasy.

The Musical Icon

If Clynes's report suggests that he has located a trace of neurological codes of emotional expression in musical composition, this is not the case. He does not deal with musical composition but with muscular responses to real or fantasized performance. His work argues only that performances, not composition, can include indices of somatic behaviors. It seems patent that pure composition does not have the indexical force of performance, which uses its access to the unarticulated functions of nuance to cause responses which are at most merely hinted by composition. On the other hand, thoughtful performers of thoughtfully composed music really do rely on composition as a guide to interpretation. They do not add expressive effects arbitrarily. The icons of gesture in composition are abstract but sufficiently telling to permit and suggest interpretation.

Nevertheless, it is one thing to assert that the icon of sentic expression occurs in the score and another to demonstrate it or pinpoint it. Take Clynes's example from Chopin. Is the shape he describes in the melody? Is it in the harmony? Could the quality of longing possibly be a function of the abrupt expansion of the texture from one voice to the full chord spanning a tenth (like the opening of the *Tristan* Prelude)? We might suppose that we could deduce the force of a motive from its components, but when we analyze the separate compositional features, we sometimes find them opposite to the shape of which the whole seems to be iconic.

The motive shown as Figure 8.2B, from the Sonata for Piano, Four Hands, K. 521, should be easy to analyze being an incipit (no prior context) and a unison. It is a unified shape which rises and accelerates with an unbroken thrust. Now, it is obvious that the figure rises in pitch and that the speed of the slower notes of each pair increases, but these changes are not regular or accelerating. They decrease! Each of the groups of analogous intervals marked by sequentially lettered brackets is a *decreasing* series. It is true that the half-note pulse is doubled in the second measure, but the sixteenths yield to eighths, a reverse and equally abrupt change. The last note is the first departure from the tonic triad, clearly a factor in the tension, but what sort? The integration of all these changes into a unified, vigorous gesture is so palpable that the analysis of its components is annoying. The fact is that we have no idea what makes the components sum the way they do. We can say what we hear but not why.

Hornbostel, in an article about the choreographic style of Isadora Duncan (1975), suggested that the dynamic gesture of melody, which he has illustrated

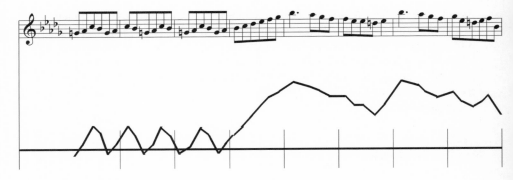

Figure 8.3. Hornbostel's graph of "melodic dance."

with his own sketch, is equivalent to the line drawn by connecting the note heads (Figure 8.3). The sketch I have added below the staff is the line which results when the note heads are mechanically connected. That is literally what I did: I imposed the line on a widened staff. Obviously it is not the same. Hornbostel's line does observe, quite faithfully, the proportions of staff notation. But his spontaneous, freehand line is entirely different in feeling from my result. Hornbostel's drawing, with its particular sweeping *curves,* really does mirror this Chopin waltz. Those unaccountable curves would do so even if the proportions to the staff were less accurate.

The interpersonal codes which interpret the musical icon may be secure intuitively but are largely opaque. We do not even know if they observe a fixed system of dimensions, such as those broached in the musical psychology of Kurth (weight, contour, mass, etc.—divisions which are themselves somewhat arbitrary and opaque). If we consider the musical motive in its musical context rather than abstractly, its somatic value is not just a function of its own structure but also of its relations with other patterns. In situ, musical combinations take their values in so rich a matrix of relations that a code established in four to sixteen notes is capable of surpassing complexity and individuality.

Should we try to decode the musical icon systemically, we enter a methodological labyrinth which may have no exit. Seeger's project of a syntax for musical contour is as impossible as a deductive procedure for determining the subject of a picture from a geometrical inventory of its color patches (Seeger 1975). We recognize the gestural import of a melody much as we recognize a visual image, holistically. The particular cannot be predicated of the articulate on the basis of its formal structure alone. The relevant rules, if we could find them, would have to do with representation, not just structure.

In music, expressive gestures are represented within a mobile flow of movement which can maintain an attitude without always projecting it aggressively. The expressive icon in melody is a special moment. Nothing in the several measures which follow the first two in Clynes's Chopin example above equals them in expressive force. On the contrary, a form is established, the eight-measure phrase, which alienates the icon from its indexical substrate by framing it. The density of iconic contents within the flow of music is variable. Though we cannot elucidate the code of the icon itself, we can appraise expressive densities and analyze the tensions between expressive iconic shape and neutralizing symbolic formality.

The Musical Symbol

As the icon and index in music are manipulated by composition, they lose their expressive transparency; they become symbols. The issue conventionally proposed as musical meaning lends itself to equally productive analysis as loss of meaning. An affinity of sound with significant neural-motor impulses is given a priori; it is natural. We cannot comprehend the power of music if we do not grasp its capacity to neutralize this affinity and thus its power to free thought from the slavish compulsion of the body toward self-expression. Composition wrests intellectual freedom from that determinate function by the free play of articulations imposed on the continuities of expression. In terms of a semiotic hierarchy of freedom, the systems of music are a double achievement. First, they disconnect expression from its source; second, they provide unlimited scope for its transformation through the devices of variation. A musical figure engendered as the icon of a gesture can be arbitrarily inverted, reversed, lengthened, shortened, and otherwise deformed. This is exactly what is impossible for immediate expression. It is impossible to sigh backward or repeat just the second half of a yawn.

The abstract character of the musical figure as an articulate structure allows for the construction of meaningless figures as well as meaningful ones, but the general association of musical figures as a whole with the field of gesture as a whole also allows for the possibility that any musical construction, no matter how arbitrary, may support an expressive interpretation. The deliberate use of standardized and neutralized thematic materials is a pervasive technique in composition, from traditional counterpoint to twelve-tone method.

Music has the option of exploiting its intellectual capacity for variation in the fullest, and thus moving toward autonomy and logical closure, or of restraining these possibilities to attach itself to external determinants. It is not laziness or a lack of invention that restricts contrapuntal elaboration in Baroque opera or restrains developmental variety in nineteenth-century program music; monotonous elements in music are deictic in force. When clues to interpretation are withheld, monotony, if not rejected, appears transcendental and spiritual.

Music's polar capacities for expression and abstraction bear witness to fundamental dilemmas of civilization, the negotiation of instinct and control, of impulse and reflection, the achievement of intellectual freedom and its price in spontaneity. We cherish expression in music in relation to our own commitments, great or small, to civility. For some this constraint may exclude subjective imagery from music; for others without such inhibitions, a radical expressive anarchy is inviting. Most interesting in this perspective is perhaps that music is not entrapped in a strict social dogma, but is, as the product and the sign of a real consciousness of the values at stake, participating in a dialectic where it represents the unsettled questions of its own society. The Ballade, of which we have regarded so far only one phrase, is such a work.

8.5. Chopin Ballade in A-flat Major, Op. 47

> This Ballade, the "Undine" of Mickiewicz . . . is too well-known to analyze. It is the schoolgirls' delight, who familiarly toy with its demon, seeing only favor and prettiness in its elegant measures. . . . Forsooth, it is aristocratic, gay, graceful, piquant, and also something more. Even in its playful moments there is delicate irony, a spiritual sporting with graver and more passionate emotions. Those broken octaves which usher in each time the second theme, with its fascinating infectious, rhythmical lilt, what an ironically joyous fillip they give the imagination. "A coquettish grace—if we accept by this expression that half unconscious toying with the power that chants and fires, that follows up confession with reluctance . . ." [Ehlert] The episodes of this Ballade are so attenuated of any grosser elements that none but psychical meanings should be read into them.
>
> —Huneker (1966), p. 108

There is a recurrent waltz movement in the Ballades. The meter has only a nominal relation to the six-eight of the English ballads which Mickiewicz claimed as a source, but the reliance on waltz movement would be, perhaps, the nearest thing in Chopin's palette to a colloquial idiom—not in the specifically nationalistic sense of the mazurka and polonaise but as a familiar language suggesting some allegiance with low style rather than high. The waltz in Chopin's hands has little naiveté to be sure and nothing coarse in it, but this does not mean it has lost its history or lost touch with its origins.

In its first ascendance the waltz was an intervention of the body in the formal ballroom. No less scandalous in the period of its emergence than rock in the 1950s, the waltz was the dance of aggressive speed, hypnotic entrancement, and close embrace. Its rise coincides with the French Revolution. The waltz, in the form in which it seized Europe by force, was coarse, erotic, and democratic. Ladies danced with servants. Though Chopin refines, formalizes, elaborates, and sculptures the waltz, its native force is sensed as what has been resisted and sublimated, its sexuality transferred from the torso to the head through a virtuosity of harmony and figurations whose whirling movement is faster, smoother, or more deeply entranced than merely corporeal dancing could be.

The young Mickiewicz was more directly attuned to the vulgar. Though not yet consistent in his hold on popular language in these early ballads, his stylistic direction, away from literary refinement, is already clear. (I rely primarily on Weintraub 1954.) Perhaps this is a reason why Huneker (1966) and many others have had little interest in Chopin's involvement with Mickiewicz's ballads, but our authority for the source is Schumann. It would be fantastic to suppose that Schumann falsified his conversations with the composer in this respect.

Tracing Mickiewicz's tale in Chopin's Ballade would be of interest on historical

Figure 8.4. Chopin, Op. 47, thematic materials.

grounds, but my point here is to take advantage of it as a key to the discourse in somatic imagery intrinsic to the music. Even acknowledging "Chopin's known dislike for the translation of poetry into music" (Gavoty 1974, p. 388), there are too many specific correspondences between the verbal text and the score to ignore or dismiss. What I mean to show is that nearly all of these hinge on somatic imagery of all sorts—sentic shapes, indices of excitement, imitations of the respiratory and articulatory exertions of speech—as well as the neutralization of these by abstract form. To be sure, the Ballade has something like a narrative tone but not because it translates. Narrative quality is achieved, first, by a speechlike pace of melody (again a somatic reference) and, second, by the melody's reliance on the scant handful of figures collected in a few lines of score in Figure 8.4. Though handled so deftly as scarcely to attract notice, this minimalism of thematic content goes well beyond any requirement of unity or economy and thereby acquires the speechlike implication of extrinsic significance which excessive repetition evokes.

"Switezianka" (as Mickiewicz renames *Ondine*) is the story of a catastrophe of sexual enthusiasm which bifurcates the feminine, interpreting it first as virginal and charming and then as sensual and disastrous. A youth is deceived by Switezianka, who appears first as a wood nymph, fleet, alluring, but not quite natural. She extracts an oath of eternal fidelity but rejects him with prophetic warnings. She flees, he pursues. Reaching the lake, he sees a veiled maiden dancing over the water who mocks his distress and promises much more than the wood nymph. Overwhelmed, he yields to her. The underworld opens. Only as he hears her rebuke does he realize that the two maidens are one and his doom fulfilled. Even in translation one catches the banter, the sense of an irrelevant here and now, the invention of pseudo-balladic formulae which ensure Mickiewicz as much distance from his material as Chopin achieves very differently through the neoclassic aspects of his art.[1]

The form and tone of the first four stanzas have a reasonable counterpart in the form and tone of the first four eight-measure phrases. Both texts announce a romantic theme (Clynes has given us a somatic analysis of Chopin's) but absorb it in formalities, stylized stanzaic groupings in Mickiewicz, period structure with elaborated cadences in Chopin. There is a heightening of rhetoric both in the poem's third stanza, a shift from present to indefinite time, and in the music's third phrase (Figure 8.5A), where the musical change is embodied in melodic and registral elaboration mimetic of the motor patterns of passionate speech. In both the poem and the music, more bravura and ritualistic closing figures follow ("Whence came she? Who knows keeps still. / Where will she go? None go with her.").

The poem's next two groups of four stanzas are the first dialogic episode; the first four, the young man's suit, the second, Ondine's rejection of it. Both center on her, first as addressee, then as addresser. Do the closing sequences of mm. 41–43 amount to a gesture of imploration such as he makes? I shall not stickle for that, but the presentation of Switezianka in her first guise as wood nymph in the passage which follows is unmistakable (Figure 8.5B).

The broken octaves which introduce the theme are a gesture so minimal as to belong necessarily to the eyes, a wink or a glance, or to a fairy creature. The theme's somatic image is formed by a gently dancing meter which has its slight weight removed from downbeat to upbeat. The sustained conflict of grouping between iambic melody and trochaic accompaniment, a prolonged gestalt ambiguity, is indexical of entrancement. This is the dance of a nearly weightless body—a body without real flesh. A key sentic pattern (not one in Clynes's set, but Darwin [1873] describes it and we recognize it) is the shyness gesture, normally realized by a brief blush with the glance deflected downwards, the head slightly to one side. In a context of sexual arousal it seems coquettish or flirtatious. The inner shape of this gesture is given to the melody of the semi-cadence in mm. 55–56 (marked X in the figure).

Of course, any surmise of parallelism in the music and the poem is conjectural. Chopin would not use the poem rigidly. Yet, there are grounds to wonder if Chopin did perhaps approach some passages of the composition almost as if he were setting the poem. The correspondence between the four eight-bar phrases beginning at m. 65 and the four stanzas in which Switezianka rejects the youth is remarkably detailed. In the appearance of the minor mode at this point we have, perhaps, a cultural symbol rather than a somatic sign (Figure 8.5C). Denial is light and mocking in the first of her stanzas, more vehement in the second. The thematic exposition with its darker intensification parallels this change. In the third stanza the youth interrupts her with his fateful oath. Chopin interrupts the melody

---

1. I do not read Polish and relied, first, on the 1821 translation into German by Pietraz (Mickiewicz 1976) and, second, on the critical assistance of Marcia Ostashewski. The Pietraz translation is appended to the original publication of this article.

Figure 8.5A. Chopin, Op. 47, mm. 22–23.

Figure 8.5B. Mm. 54–55.

Figure 8.5C. Mm. 66–69.

Figure 8.5D. Mm. 88–90.

of the third phrase (at m. 87) with a fragment recalling mm. 17–24, material which seemed there as it does here mimetic of heightened rhetoric (Figure 8.5A). Her fourth stanza is a warning counsel and a veiled pronouncement of doom. Correspondingly, the next musical phrase (Figure 8.5D) is a somatic image of posture rather than gesture; the prophet is immobile, ponderous, and statuesque.

A reprise of Ondine's entrance theme follows. Mickiewicz uses Ondine's flight—and the youth's bootless pursuit to the shore of the lake—to characterize her further, and the reprise of her entrance music is perfectly in keeping with that scheme. The correspondence of poem and music inferred here suggests that motion onto or toward the tonic is a correlate of the poem's principal narrative moments. The instance I read most tentatively is the first one. The first theme recurs and restores the tonic in m. 37. One might fancy it as *colla voce* here and pianoforte solo at m. 1—though the measures are identical—the voice being that of the youth who here speaks his first lines. More obvious are the turn from F major to minor for Ondine's refusal, the pivot through A-flat at m. 58 for his oath and her pronouncement, and the new episode at m. 116 (Figure 8.6A), which must be understood, even if all other programmatic interpretations are rejected, as the appearance of Ondine in metamorphosis as the goddess of the lake, veiled and hovering over the water.

If the performance provides the requisite tension, there is a special kind of waltz movement in this passage which is inverted in its somatic reference. The icon of the body is truncated: The bass notes are registrally disjunct and occur on only about half the strong beats (of triplets), conveying the slow movements of deep water rather than the steady beat of feet. The dance rhythm of the episode depends on the florid, elegant, aristocratic roulade in the treble. This latter is formal, courteous rather than emotive in its gesture. It covers a compelling, seductive movement in the middle voice, amplifying it by what stage magicians call misdirection. This tenor motive (marked X in the figure) seems to fit Clynes's description of the sentic form for sexual emotion, a fairly abrupt forward pressure peaking in about half a second and relaxing more slowly. Our intuitive sentographs might link this figure with another ascending iambic eighth-note semitone marked in Figure 8.1.

Now word and music become more disparate. In the poem Mickiewicz allows his water nymph five stanzas to taunt and cajole; the young man's fall follows abruptly. Chopin's proportions are reversed. A hint of speech rhythms (m. 132) climactically interrupts Ondine's water dance, but as the body is already represented by the dance in its full seductive power, an extended icon of her speech would be musically superfluous. On the other hand, the youth's stages of abandonment, just sketched in the poem, are drawn out. Abandonment is a mind-body theme. Music can unfold it in much more literal detail than words.

As the youth hastens to the shore of the lake, a solid bass line is regained (m. 134, Figure 8.6B) with middle register arpeggios gesturally iconic of heaving breath. As he loses direction, the passages which follow abandon articulation in a rising flood of physical power, movement from psychic to corporeal energy. There is an obvious, slightly ironic correspondence of texts here. The sprite's theme is transposed and transformed as she, transformed, effects her magic. The bass becomes a confusion. Before the final catastrophe there is an instant of paralysis or blindness, the

Figure 8.6A. Chopin, Op. 47, mm. 116–117.

Figure 8.6B. Mm. 134–135.

Figure 8.6C. Mm. 162–163.

crushing but static figurations of m. 162ff. (Figure 8.6C; compare "He starts and stares, stares and starts"). Two complete diatonic cycles of fifths (mm. 176–180), a perpetual and automatic motion, act as a compositional sign of the abdication of composition, or of losing one's head. The rhythm of the rough bass ostinato which follows is the least articulate and most extreme image of physicality in the Ballade. Then, like the recognition which comes too late, the final reprise is, as we observed above, drained of its prior affect and somatically and semantically inverted to become the *embodiment* of a previously sentimental excitement (see Figure 8.2A).

Paradoxically, what constrains the iconic force of the theme on its return is the melody, the same melody which had seemed so pregnant with gestural content at the opening. The melody undergoes an inversion of values. The pulsation felt there in absentia is here supplied. The register changes from middle to outer (from vocal to nonvocal range). Thin texture becomes rich, soft becomes loud. The melody, for all its sensuous concreteness, is abstracted from its former character and is much more neutral in somatic content. The executor who attempts to retain its former accents in this passage will only paralyze and bowdlerize the performance. The melody now is a mental property with the particular function of evoking memory and the strange deformation which memory works on our reception of the present.

The last narrative image is of the drowning, where the youth swirling in the water is drawn into an underworld, but neither artist ends his work with this tumultuous image. With one shift of tense, Mickiewicz's last couplet repeats the formulaic second couplet of the third stanza:

> Two passing shadows here,
> A maiden and her youth.
> She dances over the silver sea.
> He drifts among the pines.
> Who is the youth? A hunter in the woods.
> And the maiden? I know not.

Chopin, equally formal, quotes first the water sprite's dance (m. 116) and then the cadential formula of his introduction (m. 28). Is this not an extraordinary degree of parallelism? Can it be other than evidence of allegiance to Mickiewicz on Chopin's part?

Quotation and abbreviation render these previously expressive figures as more abstract in both works, and we see here at what level they are most significantly allied. In both discourses the centripetal subjectivity of instinctive action, desire, and impulse is balanced by the centrifugal embellishment of an objective and digressive cultural reflection which views myth as ornament and physique as symptom. The poem acts within an order to which Chopin was always loyal; he keeps us in mind of the body without abandoning thought.

9 *Opera Operta:* Realism and Rehabilitation in *La Traviata*

Finally, Violetta dies of tuberculosis, but luckily for us, her voice is not overly injured. We are spared the suffocation of listening as we must in *Tristan* to a rasping *voce suffocato* (for nearly an hour it seems) or even the more tastefully brief indulgence of this verismo technique in *Otello.* So where is the realism? Certainly not at the ending, for there is a long coda here. Violetta dies twice, first with "Addio, del passato." Here her tempo and collapsing melody relay her expiration: "The musical image central to 'Addio, del passato' is that of a collapsed or distorted death-dance. ... The 'lame' accents on the second beats ... with their stresses on unaccented syllables ... car[ry] a signal of disorder, strain, and weariness" (Hepokoski 1989, p. 262). We don't require the extra track of quiet coughing that adorns the third act in Toscanini's recording. Violetta needs no other special vocal techniques than the weak final notes Verdi specifies (*un filo de voce*), and when, after her "tutto finì," the jubilation of Carnival is heard passing her window, we can understand that she is no longer in our world. The rest of her music is posthumous, light years from Paris. Her second death will be enacted *parlando.*

We have no lack of precedent for a confusion of space-times of the last act. (To go back to the root, this is a story of a prostitute with a heart of gold, and the original myth from which the type is drawn ends posthumously with the resurrection.) In the great final duet, we feel that Alfredo is living inside a fantasy and Violetta is singing from Heaven. Violetta calls for, but cannot achieve, a return to life. She fails as the father enters. Her final donation of the medallion begins with a strangely troped topic of a funeral march in triple meter, a version of the *topos* Noske (1977) identifies with death in Verdi, but here, in three, an otherworldly effect further enhanced by the *tuba mirum* of a brass choir. Apart from one flash of melody that follows her *parlando* exit, her last *sung* words, "from among the angels," simply confirm the unreality of time and place.

In language, we take the independence of signified and signifying times for granted:

> Papa Germont persuaded Violetta to abandon Alfredo.
> Before that she went to live with him in the country.
> That was after they finally met at a party,

This chapter is based on a paper read in June 1995 at the annual meeting of the International Semiotic Association in Berkeley, California. I am grateful to Dorothy de Val for comments on a version of this chapter.

Following Alfredo's long, silent infatuation,
That had begun with his first glimpse of her.

Since mentioning things in an order reversed from what happened is easy, let us not be chary of according to music its own contribution to a rearrangement of time or to effect a dream sequence. Though the break is patched over with narrative detail (Annina returns through the warp-lock to announce that the starship will dock presently with Alfredo and his father) the final scene is outside the principal time of the action; we must bracket the entire ending when we assess the narrative attitude of *La Traviata*.

So the coda, in a fundamental sense, is not part of the realism, though the separation of hero and heroine, one alive, one dead, even as they sing, is the extreme consequence of a psychological verity we will find well prepared. It was realism that put a courtesan on stage, that put tuberculosis on stage (however suspiciously convenient to the story), and above all, realism that selected a libretto where money triumphs over love.

Realism in *La Traviata* is a now well ventilated problem in musicology, like voice-leading analysis in music theory is for that poor little A-major variation theme, which, for no fault of Mozart's, has finally become tiresome. Sad, but, realistically, why would Verdi get off any easier than Mozart? I do not imagine for a moment that I can add fresh observations to this rich discourse, but it seems to me worthwhile to show where and how the musicology of *La Traviata,* a discourse in which references to gesture and symptom are frequent, contacts the method we undertook in the previous chapter. We are almost where we left off—still in the middle of the nineteenth century, still listening to the waltzes of Paris. I continue to exploit the counterpoint of text and music to emphasize the pertinence of somatic imagery to musical semantics, but with one difference. In Chapter 8, where the music of the Ballade was removed from the poem, I argued for a coherent meaning. Here, where the words are embedded in the music, we might expect to anchor musical semantics with even less ambiguity. The opposite obtains. The opera, a compelling but porous chain of fragments, is open to divergent constructions by its audiences. "Like almost every musical dramatist of any standing who is aware of the inherent contradictions of opera . . . [Verdi] was not consistent": Dahlhaus (1985, p. 68) responds to this inconsistency with a persuasive stylistic analysis, but to deal with operatic realism only as style, even allowing this approach the wide scope that he does, has the consequence of putting questions of meaning aside. If we want to appreciate ambiguity in characterization and motivation in the opera without yielding to vagueness, I think we need a fully *functional* grasp of gestural expression in music. What I mean by functional here is a semantic analysis that is scrupulous in distinguishing the expression of the part from the expression of the whole. Dietrich Schnebel summarizes his stunning rapprochement of Verdi to Wagner by a comparison of Verdi's reliance on gesture to Wagner's reliance on symbols (2001, p. 66). Such an invocation of the notion of gesture works well for his broad mural, but for my sketches of details I need a finer brush. Like language, with its words, phrases, sentences, paragraphs, and arguments, music has various strata of significations and hierarchies of signifiers. What and how words mean is not what or how sentences mean. Within the present genre, still *opera seria* if we accept Dahlhaus's reassurance in his analysis cited above, we might keep various levels in mind: the level of figures, the level of phrase or period, the level of the verse or stanza, the level of the complete number, and the level of the whole opera.

Sometimes a short figure will serve as a conventional term. Noske discusses a number of these in his work on opera mentioned above (Noske 1977). In addition, a short figure, effectively performed, can embody a spontaneous expressive gesture. Gesture, in my sense, belongs only to this minimal level. At the level of the phrase which encompasses the figure, we find an essentially cultural form. A phrase readily supplies reference to a socially constructed feeling rather than to a raw emotion. At the level of the aria or, let us say, of the whole number, we get a much more elaborate reference, typically a *pris de position.* Personality dynamics come alive; territory is marked out; interpersonal psychology is diagrammed. The cliché that recitatives provide data and arias emotion is very inadequate. Arias show entire egos; duets, entire relationships. At the level of the whole work nothing is definite and everything is possible. Of course we have a whole narrative, but was it the music that gave it to us? We may sense that the music has established a viewpoint, what we call informally a philosophy of life, surely something that the component parts are not adequate to convey on their own.

What a playground for semiotics we have in *La Traviata!* First, there is the famous chain of interpretants. Alexander Dumas, *fils,* appropriated Abbé Prevost's novel *Manon Lescaut* as a sign of the life of the real Marie Duplessis and fashioned his novel *La dame aux camélias* as an interpretant of that sign. (The first novel is cited in the second.) Then we have a play as an interpretant of the novel; the opera as an interpretant of the play; Garbo's movie as an interpretant of all of it, plus two operas on *Manon,* biographies of Dumas and Duplessis and naughty Verdi himself, all interpreting and reinterpreting the same story. And that is not all: the topic of codes is highlighted from the inside. Dumas's roman à clef is absolutely frank on this point right from its opening scene at the auction, where there is much to decipher. Indeed, frankness and coding are motivic, beginning with the flowers of the title that persist, without all the petals, in the opera:

> For twenty-five days of the month the camellias were white, and for five they were red. No one ever knew the reason for the colors changing, which I mention though I can't explain it; it was noticed by the habitués of the theatres she frequented and by her friends like me. (Dumas 1963, p. 37)[1]

When our heroine says to her young lover (whom, by the way, she has just compared to a puppy dog), "Our sort, when we have a bit of spirit, we accord words

---

1. Pendant vingt-cinq jours du mois les camélias étaient blancs et pendant cinq ils étaient rouges, on n'a jamais su la raison de cette variété de couleurs, que je signale sans pouvoir l'expliquer, et que les habitués des théâtres où elle allait le plus fréquemment et ses amis avaient remarquée comme moi.

and objects a range and elaboration other women don't know," what semiotician will stand aloof?[2]

We won't trace the opera scene by scene here. For a first close-up, let us begin with "Ah, fors'è lui che l'anima," Violetta's response to "Un dì, felice." If the number is not shortened, Violetta alternates two moods and two tempi. Take the strongest gestures, brief motives from each, perhaps those of Figure 9.1. In isolation, the somatic images are not what they will become when integrated in the whole, and in isolation they quite exceed the requirements of the text. In her Andante, the halting breath of the opening staccato and the desultory, feebly reiterated, hapless leaps up to F, almost like sobs, are the stuff of real depression or grief. In the Allegro, the trills and chromatic passing tones touch the opposite pole of delirious, manic enthusiasm. (In Figures 9.1A and B, where I thought some comparison was possible with the sentic forms of Figure III.1 in the Introduction to Part III, I have indicated a two-second duration with a horizontal bracket, according to the Parenti tempos, as noted in Figure 9.1.)

Of course, the aggregate expression of the song is not so extremely polarized as the expressions of its extreme gestures. The phrases are symmetrical, balanced, and resolved. As absorbed in the larger whole of the phrase, the emotional indicators of the leading gestures are reconstructed to accord with nineteenth-century literary psychology. A depressive, but sweet and touching, sadness alternates with a girlish giddiness.

Even with these more gentle, reconstructed sentiments, the aria *as a whole* reveals a psychological pattern whose truth has not escaped those who appreciate Verdi. The aria represents Violetta's instability and vulnerability. Violetta does not appear to contemplate alternatives and then thoughtfully elect frivolity. The separation of the tempi by recitative denies musically logical motivation to the cabaletta. In consequence, she seems compelled, trapped by her modus vivendi rather than exercising decision. The aria as a whole reveals her condition as more than a sum of its parts.

There are more parts. This is the aria in which Violetta recalls Alfredo, first singing his hook from "Un dì, felice" in its original key of F and then hearing him in her imagination, represented by the off-stage serenade in A-flat. We cannot deal with this recollection in terms of part-to-whole relations alone. First, there is the part-to-part relation with the original. Note that when Alfredo sings "di quell'amor ch'è palpito" he sounds truly infatuated, if not necessarily lovable. When Violetta sings the very same tune and words, she may sound lovable, but she does not really sound infatuated, at least not with him. The phrase she repeats began on F, the upper tonic. It is the crest of his opening phrase, his highest downbeat. In her case, the high F was already established, but in minor. The phrase enters not as a crest of her line but as a diversion, an extended *tierce de Picardy,* and the D♭, which is a new color for Alfredo, is simply a retreat toward the prevailing minor for Violetta. Where he gave vent to rising feeling, she embarks, tentatively, via recollection, on

---

2. Nous autres, quand nous avons un peu de coeur, nous donnons aux mots et aux choses une extension et un développement inconnues aux autres femmes.

an escape fantasy. The phrase itself is malleable—too weak to resist the reinterpretation of its context.

To see why the phrase itself is for all its attractiveness fundamentally spineless, we can compare it to Violetta's personal version of this hook in act 2, "Amami, Alfredo," which I have written out with Alfredo's in Figure 9.1 (examples C and D, with parallels marked). Her variation is much more powerful for obvious reasons. It is not chopped up by full cadences. The dominant is held back. The first E (x in the figure) is treated as a passing tone rather than harmonized as a leading tone; indeed, the following dominant is merely indicated over the bass's incomplete neighbor note as a six-four-three, the four-measure groups ending without harmonic resolution. The high A (z), which is merely a cadential flourish in "Un dì, felice," serves to build a climax in "Amami, Alfredo," and the flat sixth, the D♭ (y), which is a memorable but essentially arbitrary digression in Alfredo's tune, is taken by Violetta to announce the one dominant harmony that really counts, making the whole one irregular phrase. This anguished passage is the one place in the opera, excluding recitatives, where a personal expressive figure takes full priority over social conventions of phrasing. The melody is a breakthrough for Violetta, a moment of real strength even as she retreats to her doom.

In stark contrast, Alfredo's version, in "Un dì, felice," is a perfect miniature portrait of the tender vacuity of youth. He may look or sound like a gorgeous left tackle, but Alfredo cannot hold back the leading tone with its dominant root. The most solidly heartfelt phrase of "Un dì, felice" is the first one, the opening fifteen measures and especially the first four measures (Figure 9.1E). At the level of the figure, we hear an expression of pure reverence. It is only the cadential turn on A which confesses the least hint of eroticism, a hint of desire. The shortened repetition with its rapid modulation builds a compelling tension which seems ready to thrust us into an entirely different emotional realm, but here and throughout the opera Alfredo is *incapable* of sustaining tension. He has no self-control. Hence this symptom of premature E. The dominant chord arrives, at a minimum, one measure too early, a unique event in this opera. (In the act 3 repetition of this tune the leading tone is supported by a tonic pedal, more like the harmony in "Amami, Alfredo.") This unclassical, folksy harmonic rhythm, I-V-V-I (instead of I-I-V-I or I-ii-V-I, etc.), occurs in only one other number, the bridge phrase of "Addio, del passato," where Violetta recalls Alfredo with the same melodic cluster of pitches.

Alfredo's quickly erupting and collapsing tune displays in miniature, as a synecdoche, the same sort of behavior that the Finale of act 2 will enlarge, when Alfredo, enraged, explodes in anger, spilling his coins and immediately collapsing in remorse. (After the brutal ostinato which underlies the preceding duet in act 2, his briefly militant posture in the quick and tidy revenge aria that Alfredo musters for his fit sounds patently childish.)

Here and there I am exploiting exaggeration as an analytical method. This may be irritating, but brief figures, motives, little parts, considered in isolation, do permit us to read into them a reference to highly profiled emotional charge which the musical stanza, containing the figure in a greater whole, does not authorize. Alfredo's verse in "Un dì, felice," taken in its entirety, is considerably domesticated.

Horizontal brackets indicate durations of approximately two seconds (based on the tempi in Mario Parenti's edition of the piano score Ricordi--also the source from which the lyrics are quoted) to allow comparison with the images of Figure III.1

Figure 9.1. Motives and phrases from *La Traviata*.

Its gestures are confined and mutually neutralizing. They sum up as the socially constructed, idealized emotion of innocent adoration, a fib that cannot last.

"Ah, fors'è lui che l'anima" ends as a duet. Translating Marguerite's wit in Dumas's novel as Violetta's *fioriture* in the opera, Verdi ensures that Violetta will show no response to what Alfredo sings except in his absence, when he is a fantasy. Here, at the end of act 1, the reference of their duet, regarded as a whole, is not just to her wit or to his adoration, but rather, it is our first full diagram of territorial relations between two persons. What is notable at that level is that there is nothing going on. They do alternate and do harmonize, but neither of them responds to the feelings of the other. This is the way it always is with them. There had been no truthful interaction in the gay duo of the opening party scene. Their drinking song does not by any means establish the rapport between Alfredo and Violetta, which it does, however, tempt us and them to imagine. Groos (1995, p. 242) observes an argument (but perhaps "disconnection" would be better than "argument"): He sings of fleeting pleasure as a prelude to love: she of love as fleeting and pleasure as all. They part on a misunderstanding, for she has given him a flower which he receives as a token of love and which she still intends, more or less—yes, we can qualify it just that much—as a business card. The brief moment in act 2 when they sing to each other in the country is a moment of deception. In the dramatically ironic and genuinely terrifying duet of the second scene, they no more communicate than they would with a glass wall between them.

We must note here the options of musical dialogue. When someone writes a complete theory of the musical images of dialogue, he or she will need to note at least two fundamental schemas. With Alfredo and Violetta, we have type B, perhaps the more common but more surprising type, where identical or nearly identical melodies mean different things. In instrumental music the same melody may land first on the dominant, and then on the tonic, and we speak of question and answer. Compositional identity sets the stage for expressive difference.

I find the most pointed display of this principle in the third-act duet's cabaletta. Where Violetta protests that she is too young to die, Verdi has provided for a moment of pure bitterness. Bitterness evokes the gesture of anger but cuts it short. Her upbeat dissonances left by descending leaps, twice from B, first over an F-major chord and then C major, precisely capture a flash of resentment ("io che penato ho tanto" in Figure 9.1J). Alfredo sings the tune next but cannot echo the sentiment; it does not fit his words or his situation. Such discrepancies are easy to attribute to Verdi's routines, as if he failed to characterize Alfredo. Perhaps we should imagine that Verdi knew when to let the system do its work. Alfredo, not Verdi, is inadequate to the occasion. The performers, rather than attempting to unify their expression (which will bowdlerize both) may allow the difference to show. The reprise, which gives the last word to Violetta, should not be cut.

What the couple share and what their melodic agreements do display is their common level of excitability or distress, which must not be confused with rapport. Her fear in the second part of act 2 has nothing to do with his anger; they are equally worked up, and therein lies the irony of the scene. Their identity of melodies merely signifies and dramatizes their deafness to each other. How different it will be when Violetta sings with Alfredo's father! Alfredo and Violetta sing the same tunes and mean different things. Germont Senior and Violetta sing different tunes and each responds with unerring accuracy to the feeling of the preceding.

The opera, *La Traviata,* is not a closed world, autonomous and self-sufficient. It lives as an adaptation and demands to be understood as an adaptation. The story was already on everyone's lips. Our reading must take the other versions into account as we do when we watch a movie based on a novel we know. The dances of the Gypsies and the matadors have been criticized as extraneous concessions to the demands of French fashion. But the criticism may itself be an extraneous concession to a Germanic fashion for autonomous coherence. The dances function as adaptations. At the same point in the story in the novels of both Prévost and Dumas, the life of the young man becomes sordid by contamination with the underworld of gambling. That *narrative* element is omitted in the stage versions, but replaced here by what is in effect a musical *description.* Urban high life is darkened by the shadows of southern and oriental low life conveyed with these conventional motifs of the matador and Gypsy.

Insisting then on the propriety, even the necessity, of translation as a process that belongs to the modus vivendi of *La Traviata,* let us now imagine the characters in modern dress. We give Wagner extra marks for anticipating Freud. Nothing in Verdi's characterizations suggests a psychological blind spot. Violetta (Marie Duplessis in translation) would appear to carry the weight of childhood abuse and probably incest. She is brilliant, sophisticated, daring, and yet addicted to the admiration of others, and she is looking for what she is utterly lacking, a sense of self-worth. (Casini [1985] remarks that Violetta is characterized by her dependence on men.) Alfredo (Dumas *fils* in translation) is suffocated by a selfish father, and he is looking for what he will never obtain, which is to take his father's place with his mother. Verdi has good reason never to show us any mutual relation between Violetta and Alfredo except misunderstanding. In reality, they have no common ground. She wants self-worth. He wants unconditional love.

Germont, who owns the most powerful and self-sufficient ego of the three principals, needs no psychoanalysis, but we do need to notice what he is. For Kimbell (1991) he embodies the *raisonneur,* the standard type of the moralist in the fiction of the period who represents bourgeois values. Well and good, but we need to note also that, for him, these values are entirely self-serving. Groos's fascinating analysis of references to tuberculosis in *La Traviata* (1995) shows that they saturate the opera and would have been obvious to its contemporary audience. A consequence that Groos does not mention would seem to be that no contemporary audience could have possibly imagined a Germont who did not already know, when he approached Violetta with his embrace and about-face in act 3, that she was about to die. After all, he enters with her doctor! (The quick moment of shock Verdi accords him when he is face to face with her final agony—just one quick measure on a forte deceptive resolution—does not suggest a total surprise! Personally, I'm quite sure he had caught on by the end of act 2.) Germont is a realist. Barzun, who says that the exploration of reality was the fundamental intention of Romantic art, wrote that "Realism meant force without principle" (1943, p. 64). Once Germont gets the medical facts straight, he is at liberty to be sympathetic—his problem is resolved. Before he gets the picture, he has a job cut out for him, and he shows no scruples.

He does the job in his great duet with Violetta in act 2. In the novel, this scene is one of two dramatic moments of argument. The first is Marguerite's long and elegant self-justification to the young man who has become impatient with her professional obligations; that's where she compares him to her lost puppy. The second, this dialogue with the father, has, in its words, exactly the same logical content in the novel, in the play, and in the opera. However, in the play it is a quick four pages, a thunderbolt. Verdi, impelled by his obligations to the voice, stretches it out with striking consequences. It is as if Germont knows that his son cannot really touch this woman the way he can, selfish Germont, tireless in his nagging, pompous in his consolations. Whatever the status of his own satisfaction or dissatisfactions, he is able to control and sustain his expressions of feeling, and on his own terms, he has his way with the young woman. They really do interact; she cannot resist him. Change the words of this scene and the music could convey nearly any intense encounter between a dislocated woman and a manipulative man. The music would do for a seduction, a plan of elopement. Drawing on a tradition which is both his engine and his obstacle, Verdi does not need the logic of social consequences which Piave has transposed from Dumas. He captures all the dynamics on the plane of misplaced desire, and there, it seems to me, you have Verdi's most original contribution to the received story. What I find interesting here are the divergences of word and musical gesture.

Kimbell says Germont begins equitably, without emotion (p. 663), a possible reading, but I will suggest another. His steady, limpid, pure arpeggios as he sings of his daughter convey the stance of one boasting. Notice how every two-measure or four-measure phrase of "Pure siccome un angelo" ends with an extra little lift, a puff of pride (marked in Figure 9.1F). Germont is restrained, but perhaps not so much in the manner of a philosopher as of the middle-aged man who does not need to mention money as his finger lightly brushes a bulging pocket. There is an emotion here, and its unfolding, in authoritatively symmetrical periods, constitutes a male display. Violetta responds ("Non sapete quale affetto") in distraught, interrupted fragments—contractions of *fear* that finally rise to a wail (Figure 9.1G). Her emotion is not directly indicated in her words. The words are about Alfredo and a future suffering, but her melody addresses and responds to the man standing before her who has displayed power. He, absolutely unyielding, acknowledges her sacrifice without any nuance, in a descending line totally devoid of motivic gesture, and then follows up her fear with an actual threat: "Un dì, quando le veneri": The separated sixteenths are like a jabbing finger, and the trill, a menacing shake. All that Germont expresses in his motives he controls and restrains in his phrasing. The *raissoneur* masks brutality with reason. The gestures wear the courtly dress of cadenced periods—a gangster in a three-piece suit.

When Violetta is entirely reduced to submission ("È vero!" with no tune, for she, too, is a realist, but had tried to take a vacation) then his melodic figure becomes caressing (Figure 9.1H). Now he invites her to become "the consoling angel (of my family)." I place "of my family" in parentheses because it is of no consequence to the music. The musical relationship is a relationship between Violetta and Germont, who now proceed to sing a love song. The duet is asymmetrical in that her relatively uninflected line is a melody of devotion, and his chromatic ornaments take sole possession of the only blatantly erotic element, but still, if you disregard the words, it is a love song. It is *his* letter she will read in act 3 with the love motto in the orchestra. The letter speaks of Alfredo, but Alfredo is a fantasist. He was good for daydreams, illusions, false hopes; for her, Germont is absolutely riveting.

Germont has less success regaining control of his son on his first try, but the power relations are clear. Alfredo, cornered by the old man, is denied any substantial opportunity to spell out his anguish when he receives her letter. Dahlhaus reminds us that the conventions of *opera seria* deny Alfredo an aria here, but Verdi retains the conventions that work to his purpose and modifies what he needs to. The self-assertion of a full aria in the presence of his father would have been psychologically unrealistic. All that is possible is the arioso of self-abasement that will follow in the next scene, when Germont pushes the right button to get the young fellow in tow. (We might notice that Germont appears at this unlikely venue, the equivalent of a fraternity house party, for only one reason, to take control of his son. We have no need to regard his mutterings of sympathy for Violetta in the ensemble finale as a change of heart; they are inconsequential except in helping him feel that he has rehabilitated his own sensibilities.)

Does it make sense to look for an object of reference for the opera as a whole? Would we dare reduce this opera to one "message" or to the exposition of a unified *Weltanschauung*? I do not want to overly appreciate *La Traviata*. Its realism is easier to see because its fantasies no longer merit much of our investment. (Better the soaps for that!) It has been called a tragedy of free love. That hardly does the job. And why would Verdi, of all people, take a tragic view of individual liberty? The most genuinely, most realistically tragic moment may be the second-act finale where we are immersed, not in the failure of a love affair, but in the genuine misery of the false and failed sociality of a circle of friends, but this point, more strongly emphasized in the novel and play, is not the main point either there or in the opera. True tragedy, be it of noble persons or the lumpenproletariat, requires heroism, and there is no heroism in *La Traviata*. The form is perhaps parable rather than tragedy, the parable of a realist who tried to escape reality. If a parable must have a moral, we can find one. When Germont finally arrives in act 3, Violetta sings "Ahimé! tardi giungeste!"—You have come too late! She sings this simple phrase over a suddenly pulsing accompaniment that expresses the harmonies which Hatten, in his Beethoven studies (1994), identifies with self-abnegation; they are not exactly that here, but a heart-breaking acknowledgement of defeat, for me, the most poignant moment of the show. The moral, a good moral for a realist, is that sometimes we really are too late.

The opera is an imperfect marriage of two sign systems, French romance and Italian opera. There are visible fault lines, as with the swollen cabalettas and the whole loss of Violetta's or rather Marguerite's acid wit. But the faults do not impair the virtual world and virtual personae constructed. Verdi's agility preserves the passion and pathos of the story and, at the same time, allows the intersecting genres to engender a mutual critique. Verdi does not hide Violetta's ultimate, involuntary prostitution, which is to the father, not the count. Verdi permits us to see what a pompous infant Alfredo really is, and Verdi never demands we believe that Germont, making a tardy about-face in act 4 that may help his image but hardly save his soul, is more than a scoundrel. But, of course, these are not readings on which the opera insists. Image is certainly an explicit issue in *La Traviata*. Dumas himself had already been criticized for writing a book that aimed to rehabilitate a courtesan. All the characters in *La Traviata* have their spin. Verdi, who was a realist when he had to consider his multiple audiences and censors, had no intention to demythologize, but he is not Germont's or Alfredo's or Violetta's spin doctor either. Verdi, who asked his librettist for a contemporary subject, calculated what he could get away with. He gave us an ambiguous opera that, as a whole, allows us to understand his characters as representing people as they really are, if we really want to.

10 A Monument in Song (1996):
Beverly (Buffy) Sainte-Marie's
"Bury My Heart at Wounded Knee"

Beverly ("Buffy") Sainte-Marie's song "Bury My Heart at Wounded Knee"[1] commemorates the American Indian Movement, brutally repressed by the FBI. The song is a defiant and moving reminder of the incarceration of Leonard Pelletier and the assassination of Anna Mae Aquash. She first released the song in 1991 on her album *Coincidences and Likely Stories* and reissued it in 1994 on *Up Where We Belong*. The lyric, musical, production, and arrangement credits are all Sainte-Marie's.

My desire to write about the song arose from my admiration and from the power it holds over me, but I confess to feel some doubt whether this song needs an academic essay appended to it. The song is forceful and clear, easily commands attention, and appears to offer no barriers to interpretation. My rationale for going ahead notes that when a work of art is attached to an emotionally loaded historical event, we might wonder skeptically whether our involvement is aroused by the artwork itself or by our own ideas of the history recalled. Perhaps my analysis will help show how the song measures up to the task it sets for itself.

The task is daunting, for the history the song recalls is devastating to recollect: it concerns the unequal contest in which uranium mining companies, protected by the U.S. federal government, squashed reservation communities who were trying to protect their health, properties, and identities. The specific events alluded to poetically in the song are documented in detail in *Agents of Repression* by Ward Churchill and Jim Vander Wall (1988). The Micmac political activist Anna Mae Aquash was found shot in the head at close range from the back and abandoned in the desert in February 1976 after repeated threats from FBI agent David Price. He claimed not to recognize the body; her hand was severed and sent to Washington for identification. The incarceration of Leonard Pelletier was achieved by tricking Canada to cooperate in a deportation (later officially regretted) and then excluding from his trial all evidence and testimony which could cast doubt on the witnesses against him. A hundred years earlier, the original massacre of Wounded Knee, where the American Army deceived and killed a band of three hundred, had marked the effective end of armed resistance by Native Americans to the continual

---

This chapter combines papers read to the International Conference on Musical Signification, Bologna, 1966, and the Semiotic Society of America, Philadelphia, 1966.
1. Buffy Sainte-Marie, *Up Where We Belong*, EMI Music, Canada.

forced transfers, dispossession, and cultural destruction that was their lot as the victims of colonization.

Sainte-Marie's musical response establishes linked but contrasting attitudes of grievous rage and indomitable spirit. Despite the elaborate commercial co-option and exploitation of rock and folk styles in recent decades, it is still easy to impute a socially critical orientation to folk-rock style, a latency readily evoked here. The music also draws on its immediate context in an album which includes powwow singing and derived material to allude to Native American drumming and chanting.

By the currently conventional academic divisions of musical territory, an essay on this song would seem to belong to what we call "popular music studies"—a rather awkward category which includes rock groups you'll never hear of, while excluding some Mozart played all around the globe. Be that as it may, popular music studies is not my field. I have very thin knowledge of the repertories that would provide the most natural comparative context for this song. My contribution here, fragmentary of necessity, leaves out of the account comparisons of this song with others that are stylistically similar, and I will bypass some very important questions of aesthetics.

To discuss this song, I draw on the theory of musical gesture and a conception of *modality* which allows us to address the song's rhetorical or pragmatic function as a memorial.

The song has an introduction followed by five verse-chorus alternations. This is a common enough prototype, but it is not a neutral container. As we move from a *parlando* introduction or a recitative into an aria or a proper verse, we have a sense, within the music, of "breaking into song," and as we move from verse to chorus, and also sometimes as we move from aria to cavatina, we have a further sense still, at another level, of "breaking into song" again. "Breaking into song" means, quite generally, I think, a move from speech to expressive action. Typically, in the verse, words are more dominant, and typically, in the chorus, melody is more dominant. My sense is that in most songs these shifts of balance between words and music are highly determinant of the overall representation. Most often the two subgenres, verse and chorus, are mutually confirming. For example, the verses may present separate incidents, and the chorus a moral or common thread. The present song is of a less common type in which the verse and chorus establish a powerful opposition. That opposition is the very crux of this musical memorial. The choruses, following an established convention in rock,[2] build in length and intensity. The first chorus is eight measures, but the fourth chorus is doubled and the fifth doubled twice.

As we turn to details of structure, we cannot analyze the song without holding the words and music apart momentarily, but to do so only emphasizes their interweaving. Syllabic groupings are so richly varied that without the music, the poetic sound patterning of the verses would be irrecoverable at certain places. For example, the emphatic rhymes of "these" with "companies" or of "uranium" with

---

2. Here and elsewhere I am indebted to my colleague Rob Bowman for preventing *some* ignorant errors. Those which I continue to insist on are not his fault.

"dumped" depend on their musical parallelism in abrasive resistance to unequal syllable weight. Similarly, it is essential to the delineation of attitudes in the music itself that the more complex syntax of verbal declaratives and interrogatives appears exclusively in the verses, while the chorus is limited to simple imperatives. Emotional irony in the words suffuses the music, partly because of Sainte-Marie's virtuosic ability to maintain very specific speech tones of voice while singing. The allusions to Indian song and drumming in the later choruses permit verbal economies that would otherwise lack point. (Imperatives appear within the verses only as indirect speech: "I learned a safety rule, I don't know who to thank ... Don't stand between the reservation and the corporate bank. ..." in verse 1, or as an auditory graffiti: "Get rich! Get rich quick!" in verse 2.)

Verses and choruses contrast by the opposition of dialect to idiolect discussed in Chapter 3. It will be critical in the present instance that dialect (or grammar) which exploits socially established, abstract categories is aligned with the society that determines those categories. Idiolect (or design) derives from perceptions of resemblance and contrast inherent to the music where we encounter them, and its valence attracts the expression of independence from social constraint. Here grammar is dominant in the verses, design in the choruses.

The introduction establishes a backdrop essential both to the narrative and the harmony, but both are left incomplete. There is no formal closure there in the tonality or in the story. The verses are each seven measures long, with an eighth measure pickup to the chorus. The first four measures present a rhymed couplet based on an underlying pattern of trimeters: {3, 3, 4+3}. The final three measures of the verse vary widely in structure but always offer additional internal and or external rhyme. The verses are harmonically oriented by the introduction in E-flat major but they move to C minor. (A deceptive resolution of the dominant is transformed to a tonicization of the submediant.) The possibility describing such a conventional harmonic syntax demonstrates the grammaticality of the verses. The lyrics are similarly aligned: The verses display fully formed sentences in an integrated narrative and argumentative discourse.

The choruses, by contrast, build idiolectic structures. There is no internal grammatical movement within them, but rather a gradual aggregation. Harmonically, the choruses sit on one pounding A-flat chord, a "SUS chord," in lead sheet terminology, a $\frac{7}{4}$ by the old figured bass system. The G♭ and D♭ in this chord contrast maximally with the preceding harmonies while suggesting interpretable relationships with them (including the Neapolitan relation and blue notes) which are not resolved. For words we have only short phrases, the title phrase repeated and, less often, the second imperative, "Cover me with pretty lies." The sense of aggregation mounts with the length changes mentioned above, the doubling and double doubling of the fourth and the fifth choruses. The entrance of a backbeat in the chorus increases the feeling of speed, energy, and length. There is a very complex evolution of sound in the choruses, which build a dramatic and meticulous textural crescendo through techniques of mixing and production, but one cannot refer this development to any a priori grammar. These are structures of design—repetition, resemblance, difference, and process.

Gestural expression is more immediate and more forceful in the choruses than in the verses. The verses still show a negotiation with a social system that, in this instance, we will understand as brutally repressive. For all of their bitterness and irony, the verses follow grammatical rules and are essentially civil. The choruses are raw and unconstrained. But the two are not merely different. The chorus is felt as unleashing what the verse is felt as holding back. That holding back enacted by grammar is metonymic of social constraint in general. The association established in the music of the verses between restraint of gesture and the governance of grammar complements the perspective of the lyrics on the corporate state as tyrannical and oppressive, for grammar, even when we are at peace with it, is an anonymous, global system. While the verse is subject to an abstract authority, the chorus behaves as if there are no rules but its own rules. The choruses are rebellious.

Because gesture is more constrained in the verses, it is difficult to fully identify its character. The gestures are, for the most part, incomplete, and what comes through is their dammed-up force, straining almost to the point of breaking, a force that will show its identity in the choruses. You can easily move your jaw, neck, knees, or heels in response to the musical emotion of the verses, but I think any genuinely responsive full movement of the torso or limbs will be spasmodic if not altogether inhibited, unless you listen to the bass only and ignore the voice. The strain between intense feeling and constricted expression is revealed partly in the tense relation of words to musical meter, partly by the vocal vibrato where it becomes uvular. The strain is revealed most calamitously through the symptoms of the graffiti or riffs which occur ornamentally, like the interspersed squeal "Get rich quick" at the end of verse 2, the synthesizer comment in verse 4, and most explicitly, the final stuttering of verse 5.

The gestural content of the chorus is fully spelled out, however difficult it may be to denote adequately with words. Here you can easily move your limbs or your whole body to the music. The pervasive gestures of the chorus are pounding and wrenching motions, reiterated despairingly, angrily, defiantly, triumphantly.

The principal text figure of the chorus, the title line, which is also the title of Dennis Lee's historical study of an earlier century of Indian massacres culminating at Pine Ridge, derives from the last stanza of Stephen Vincent Benét's poem "American Names." In this strangely complex, introverted poem, the phrase has more lassitude than energy:

> I shall not rest quiet in Montparnasse.
> I shall not lie easy at Winchelsea.
> You may bury my body in Sussex grass,
> You may bury my tongue at Champmédy.
> I shall not be there. I shall rise and pass.
> Bury my heart at Wounded Knee.

The rhythmic and stress implications of the poetic verses here are difficult to pin down completely. There is a complex hesitation in the balance of the first and second stressed syllables and between the third and fourth. The result is a sound hesitant, thoughtful, tinged with regret. In the song the accentuation is unambiguous and decisive. The result is emotional and gestural; linguistic subtlety is no issue. Sainte-Marie treats the phrase with an aggressive indifference to the tempo, stress, and inflection it most readily calls up in normal speech, furthering the tension between social authority and personal gesture in the climactic refrain.

We have to consider what happens to a gesture, or the representation of a gesture, when we repeat it. Repetition is the first ordering principle of music, but continuous repetition in music and in dance can be the catalyst by which, or represent the catatonia in which, "a perfect order [becomes] a perfect disorder." Demarcated symmetries can mute representations of gesture, making them more abstract, but within a certain range repetition can intensify gesture. This happens here not only in the chorus but with the abrupt motion we experience four times from the chorus back to the verse, which has for me the effect, stronger each time, of a boxer who won't go down for the count, picking himself up to come out swinging again. Repetition beyond a point of maximum intensity leads to saturation and a further muting. This is a factor in the final chorus.

The repetitions of the choruses keep increasing, but they play against an ongoing development of the mix. They are achieved partly by sequenced loops and then doubled as the whole chorus repeats. There is no vocal repetition in chorus 1. In chorus 2 an ostinato refrain is added. In chorus 3 there are further texted background tracks with historical commentary ("an eighth of the reservation . . ."). The double chorus, chorus 4, introduces first a new vocal obbligato and then a synthesizer chordal ostinato, and in chorus 5 all this returns except the spoken text. The repetitions have a double import. They threaten chaos, but by the entrancement of saturation, they also represent a spiritual transformation. Or to put it more melodramatically—but I do think the language is justified—the representation of unleashed, unrelenting gesture confronts disintegration but achieves transcendence. To show why this is not loose talk, I invoke a notion of *modality*, and to this end I take up the question how a memorial signifies.

A memorial is a sign of a past event or person or persons, and it is a sign which refers to its object in two related ways, both of which have a totalizing or summative effect. First, it refers to its object in a particular and striking attitude or perspective; and second, it refers to its object in such a way that this object can itself be taken in turn to signify a more general situation or condition. For example, a gravestone refers to a person, normally in an attitude of respect, and in providing dates also allows the life remembered to stand for a period in time. It is the attribution of an "attitude" such as an "attitude of respect" that implicates us in a conception of modality.

I am using the word "modality" with reference to its rather complicated philosophical heritage and without any thought of the distantly connected technical usage in music. In a very cursory summary, I think we can distinguish three strands of meaning for mode, outside of music theory. In analytical philosophy, mode is associated with multivalued logic and possible worlds. In grammar, the modals are a class of verbs or verbal modifiers. And in psychological semantics, mode is approached as a relation between the enunciation and the enunciator. Greimas fixes a system of modes, intended as universal but closely tied, I believe, to French language models. Tarasti, in his *Theory of Musical Semiotics,* retains the Greimasian system but provides a strictly psychological interpretation. All in all, modality is a jungle.

When we walk into a jungle, it is useful to carry a machete. I will adopt a simple notion that seems to me to serve music well but is also suggestive in many other contexts. *A mode is a world into which a sign projects its object.* A sign extracts its object from a given context and may project it into another world, a world of fact, of hope, of fear, of possibility, of doubt. With this definition, we do not need to tie ourselves to any preconception of psychology or to any particular linguistic scheme.[3] "Bury My Heart" evokes two modes, two worlds. I would caption them as a world of events and a world of power. The verses project the American Indian Movement into a bleak world of finite events. The chorus lifts us up because, in all its darkness, it projects the American Indian Movement into a world of eternal forces: a world in which its defeat, however bitter, feels far from final. This is what many great memorials do. They give us a sense that what they represent is both part of the events of past and the living force of the present. Here then we come to the crux of one accomplishment of this song. In the chorus, repetition finally approaches a point of saturation, a point of exhaustion, but a transformation has been evoked by the subtle and gradual identification of the repeating rhythm with the drumming and singing of the powwow music which precedes it earlier in the album. The modalities of the verses and the choruses evoke a dialectic of fatality and destiny. The universe represented by this monument is not simply the cruel and terrifying world in which the American Indian Movement was torn apart, but also another where eternal force and righteousness of its cause survive.

---

3. For a somewhat fuller discussion of mode in my personal sense, see my *Elements of Semiotics* (1999).

Part Four: *The Messages of Methods*

The naturalism of the signifier in European concert music from the Renaissance through the nineteenth century determines that we should attend to techniques only by exception. On the side of composition, fugue is an exception. On the side of performance, bravura. The one represents invention and learning, the other, magic. For the rest, *poeisis* must give rise to a "natural" result so that *poeisis* will be invisible to *aesthesis*. This ideal does not hold for the twentieth century, a time when *how* things were made took on more significance in composition. How things were made was always significant to the artists making them, we can be sure, important both on a strictly private level and in their professional relations. But even where pride in craft and novelty are evident, the good cobblers may not want you to notice their stitches unless you are a fellow cobbler. With the Neoclassicism of the 1920s the *how* of composition, no longer mythologized as inspiration or humbled as unconscious craft, became part of the public aesthetic object, as a sign of artistic intention. The method-sign remains entrenched where composers want a sign to indicate that their work is not aimed at popularity.

I do not think the change in sensibilities was always clear to those composers who were themselves most involved in according a higher degree of philosophical significance to their own technical orientations, orientations constructed with more individuality and a wider sense of options than ever before.

So far as I have been able to notice, the four papers which follow, though bearing on this theme, have no distinctive common method, and *their* methods, as methods, have no message.

11 Bartók the Progressive

The argument I happen to illustrate in this chapter via a commentary on the first movement of Bartók's Second String Quartet could probably take as its starting point any of his major works that follow this one of 1919. I was drawn to this particular quartet by the accident of discovering a recording by the Budapest Quartet, who recorded none of the others. The Budapest's Beethoven was a major influence in my early musical life. I find their recording of this Bartók quartet insightful, and it has, I am sure, influenced my reading of the work. However, it is the accidental aspect of my choice that I would emphasize, and I make no case for one performance as against another.

The first movement is a thematic sonata form. The snippets cited in Figure 11.1 may serve to recall the music to readers who have studied it, but, except for the first phrase, only a few initial motives of themes are shown, and provide only an orientation for memory. The tonal relations between exposition and recapitulation are singular, they do not govern. It is the type of sonata form that responds to the nineteenth-century quest for some kind of continuous evolution—be it variation, development, or, as we are readily tempted to say, narrative—that takes precedence over formulaic symmetries. Every element when recapitulated is fundamentally changed. You could easily put a story to the music, most probably one with an intimate setting, with more conversations than speeches, and with passionate moments but no fighting. We needn't propose any story, but let us take a quick tour of the movement. (My letters for sections refer to the figure. The references tabulated in the figure indicate rehearsal numbers in the Boosey and Hawkes pocket score with measures counted from each rehearsal number.)

I don't think I know any E♭ in the whole literature of music that sounds as apprehensive, so in a hurry to leave the room, as the one in the measure of accompaniment that precedes the first theme, A. The very graphic first gesture of the melody (m. 2) is, for me, a perfect image of a shrug. This is what so struck me when I first heard the Budapest recording, but I have heard the shrug with others. (I don't mean that I thought of a shrug when I heard the music, but that on reflection the musical gesture seemed equivalent to one.) A shrug is not the vehicle of one particular emotion. My pocket dictionary defines a shrug as a hoisting of the shoulders, but I think the shoulders incidental. What you say with your shoulders you can also say with your eyebrows. A shrug is abortive. It casts doubt. There are all flavors of shrugs, but there is always an element of disconnection, of not knowing or not owning something. We begin here with diffidence, a shrug followed by a quiver and cadencing (falling) in futility. That opening motive proves to be the most prevalent and characteristic figure of the movement. A splendid demonstration follows, however, that a motive, however gesturally specific, is not tied to its initial feeling. In

	Exposition			Recapitulation	
	m. 1	Theme A	R16	m. 8	Theme A
R1		Development of A	R18		New development
R2		(Peroration)			
R3		Development of A			
	m. 6	Theme B		m. 5	Theme B
R5		Theme C	R19	m. 3	Hint of theme D
	m. 5	B enlarged		m. 4	Theme C
	m. 8	Theme D		m. 8	Theme B
R7	m. 3	B, C, D in counterpoint	R20		Theme E
R9		Theme E	R21	To end	Coda

	Development
R10	Like R3
R12	New motives from A and B
R14	Climactic episode
R15	Loud, static dissonant chords
R16	Bridge to recapitulation

Figure 11.1. Bartók, Second Quartet, themes.

the ensuing phrase, of which Figure 11.1 provides a representative sample (R1, m. 3), it rapidly "morphs," stretching toward another character. The brief ostinato of octave G's at R2 blazes above a rising scale of parallel six-four chords to a peroration in one of the brightest textures of the movement. Then, the same motive, in another developmental phrase, "morphs" again to the descending scale theme, B, related to sobbing but much more gentle and inward. Motive C responds; its expression is broader, perhaps entreating. (The augmented triad introduced here— C♯, E♯, A—will return with just a spelling change as the final sonority of the coda, sustained over an indefinite modal bass line.) An expansion of theme B culminates with the presentation of a new idea, in a strikingly open texture, a diatonic melody neither *parlando* nor *cantabile,* but chantlike, with prominent octave doubling and prominently continuous eighth-note motion in additive rhythms. The closing theme, E (R9), the nearest we've come to an actual tune—abab'cc'—is almost catchy.

The development section juxtaposes the movement's driest, most academic contrapuntal workout (of a new rhythm derived from the first motive by a metric shift) and its most dramatic, lyrical and dark-textured passage. This latter has the structure of a slow duet between high violin and low cello surrounding the rapidly circling accompaniment figures of the second violin and viola playing at first in parallel thirds and then in parallel tritones. The duet brakes suddenly; loud, repeated, static dissonances dissolve into a bridge to the recapitulation.

The first theme A is now, in its return, much more at peace with the world, for its accompaniment has relaxed into harmonious augmented sixths. The little development that leads away from it is completely fresh. Theme B exchanges its old ornaments for a new set. There is just a hint of theme D before theme C reappears, restaged as a cross-register dialogue. The developmental phrase from R3 is recalled next, but now over wide-spaced triadic arpeggios in the cello. Finally the nearly tunelike closing theme, E, comes out of the closet; there had been, after all, a full-fledged folk-song topic waiting for this moment of unveiling. The cello supports it with *pizzicato,* guitarlike major chords. For the coda, more counterpoint, a *ritardando,* a cadence that does not quite deny our hunch that A was, overall, the tonal center, especially when we recall Bartók's penchant to clarify tonality more in the middle of a movement than at the very ending.

What did we learn from this tour? Perhaps I had enough verbal ingenuity to keep it entertaining, but I have not conveyed much of an idea of what the movement is like, and I have explained less. Running through it this way, I had in mind the striking closing remarks which Raymond Monelle offered to the Fifth International Congress on Musical Signification, where there had been much talk of gestures associated with emotional expression and topics as vehicles of cultural reference. He said that if we wanted to consider the basis of musical signification, we ought not to forget texture, equally fundamental. Surely it is. As the term itself suggests, "texture" is a rich domain of synesthesia and often significant because changes of texture may convey a variable affinity with or distance from the human voice. Take those three categories—gesture, topic, texture—and add a fourth for rhetorical functions (like peroration), and you have the elements with which I organized my survey: topics of folk song, chant, or academic development; contrasts of dark and light, smooth and abrasive textures; and gestures (but really often muted) of shrugs or stretches or sobs. I risked exaggeration to ferret out these possibilities; yet even with that advantage, my account doesn't amount to more than, at best, pulling some raisins out of the raisin bread and neglecting the dough. Surely we must all agree that it can be a bit trivializing to reduce music this way. My shy shrug is five notes. The first movement of Bartók's quartet is around thirty-five hundred notes. And it is not like a wallpaper where, once you have grasped the principal figure, you know the rest. Don't blame Monelle. That wasn't his idea at all. What he always emphasizes is that musical significations in any work of substance comprise a complex and unbounded network, and that "every musical gesture and syntagma, of whatever length or complexity, carries a signification which can be incorporated in the pattern of cultural units which make up the world" (1999). That network of significations, for a composition, for a composer, for a person, or for an epoch might be what we mean by a style. But how are we to get at the semantic networking if it is to be more than just a collection?

It is much easier to write of musical signification today than it was three decades ago. At that time, even if our history books were happy to recognize various resonances between the development of musical style and the general history of culture, theoretical constructions of musical meaning were not on the agenda. Musical studies tended, with extraordinary homogeneity, toward uninterpreted structuralism—which, by the way, we are extraordinarily good at. Since then, the growing prominence of ethnomusicology and popular music studies (fields where the notion of autonomous music sometimes appears outlandish) and various interpretive efforts in historical musicology have somewhat renewed our focus on mimetic elements which contribute to musical significance.

An open mind about mimesis does not substitute for a clear head about form. Would we make a better case for the Second String Quartet by sticking to issues of structure than we do by appreciating the "raisins" of signification? It is certainly not clear that this is the case. Bartók's style was probably better known in the middle decades of the century than that of any other avant-garde European composer of his generation except Stravinsky. It was an influential style and remains highly respected. But it seems a little less in favor academically at present (I'm not completely sure about this), and if its prestige has declined, I think this is because of its intractability to pure structural analysis during a period in which structural analysis dominated academic assessments of music. It is a style which offers neither a system, as Schoenberg's twelve-tone compositions do, nor a dogmatic insistence on intuition, as Stravinsky's blocklike forms generally do, nor any pervasive gimmick of constructive method.

Bartók did realize daring innovations in structure, such as the symmetrical architecture of the Fourth Quartet, and seems to have probed highly formulaic procedures, as in those works which conform in their proportions to the Fibonacci series. But these structures do not offer a general key to his style. On the contrary, they appear as singular and sometimes as isolated from the minutia of deciding one note after another. There are many passages in his music (and a few in this quartet) that exhibit an extreme discipline of motivic unity; yet such motivic discipline is not a ubiquitous characteristic of his music but a resource for characterizing a particular texture over a particular duration.

Our example, not a radical work at first view, encapsulates the conundrum. It seems to be more or less tonal, but perhaps also more or less atonal. It follows a sonata form, but a loose one. It is contrapuntal, but not in any thoroughgoing way. It shows intense motivic working out, but the composer is ready to jettison that technique at any moment. It has some elements of folk material, as we have already seen, but what are these doing side by side with post-Wagnerian chromatic sequences? A purely structural appraisal might find it wishy-washy.

Just such an appraisal—which, I will argue, is wrong—seems to lie behind the prevalent conception of Bartók as the most conservative of the stylistic pioneers of his generation. The judgment might seem suspect if you consider the composer. I don't propose to substitute biography for technical analysis, but there is no harm in turning to biography for clues. Bartók in his early twenties had already formed a deep commitment to secular humanism. He wrote to his friend Stephanie Graf, in a letter where we can feel the passion of his desire to bring her into the conspiracy, that for him the only trinity was art, science, and nature. He explains his conviction that the soul is mortal and the body immortal in terms that seem straightforward to the present-day ecologist. How different from Schoenberg's long tug-of-war with Judaism and Catholicism or Stravinsky's dogmatic insistence on dogma or even Ives's nostalgia for American transcendentalism. He was also a practicing scientist both in ethnomusicology and lepidopterology. In politics, he identified with the anticolonial vanguard in Hungary. In the long run, his initial interest in Hungarian nationalism, motivated more as a resistance to German imperialism than to any atavistic passion for pure roots, was subsumed in a broader vision of internationalism. His interest in folk music, as Cowell emphasizes (2001, p. 155), was not an interest particularly centered on Hungary. It began there and became a vehicle of his internationalism. The ideal of secularism or worldliness that resounds in the writings of Edward Said was fully embodied in Bartók's response to the German subjugation of Hungary.

Bartók was a progressive with his own idea of progress. It corresponded neither to Stravinsky's talent for reaction nor to Schoenberg's teleology of economy. His ideal was synthesis. His essay welcoming Schoenberg's atonal harmonies cautions that we must not on that account abandon consecutive consonances where those are appropriate. He was slightly scandalized by Stravinsky's confession that he reached middle age without having a thorough knowledge of Beethoven's piano sonatas, for he did not accept the idea that his appreciation of German music contradicted or compromised his political position. Progress for Bartók meant access to what was new and everything of value in tradition, all at the same time.

If we take this position as a guide to style, then at first encounter it is nonsense. You can speak many languages, but you cannot freely mix their grammars, which Bartók seems almost to intend. His solution must be understood in relation to the assemblage of phenomena that constitute for me the locus of the deepest and most fundamental investigations in comparative semiotics, the properties of articulation. I think it is impossible to give a good account of Bartók's style in strictly structural terms; yet attention to articulatory premises, a quintessentially structural concern, provides us a conceptual handle on his stylistic position while demonstrating how his solution was progressive.

Carl Dahlhaus's *The Idea of Absolute Music* (1989) instructs us that this phrase from Wagner, which we usually treat as a slogan, evolved through several debates that accorded it different meanings. In the early-nineteenth-century conception of what we later came to know as absolute music, the dialectic of plastic and musical art was central. Music, having inherently structured materials, does not rely on imitation for form, whereas painting, which has no such intrinsic structure in its material, takes its form from what it represents. The opposition posited here has wide validity. Those "inherent structures" are what we have often referred to as categories in this book—the notes themselves, the intervals, chords, regulated durations, as well as composite structures freshly assembled, motives, themes, and figurations, that we hear as compounds of more elementary "inherent structures." Painting lacks such definite articulatory elements as a general rule, and our initial perception of sense in pictures is recognition of what they represent. But the ratio of music and painting proposed by this debate is exaggerated, and it can be reversed. The most rigidly articulated music reveals fluidity of shape at certain levels, and some paintings depict nothing. In some highly stylized genres of painting, forms and colors are as solid and recurrent as our scales. (The red of my favorite Flemish painter, Hans Memling, seems to me as definite and articulate an element as a D-major triad.) In music, from the early Classical style to the post-Romantic, the general drift of European style is away from inherently structured materials and toward more and more blending and fluidity. Expressionism reaps the harvest of an evolution that affords music the possibility of a free wash of color and perfect flexibility of contours.

In the dry, technical perspective of articulation theory, the change is from categories to quantities: not dissonant or consonant but more or less dissonant, more or less consonant. There are passages in Berg and in Ives where the very intervals themselves seem to shrink or stretch.

Yet, while recognizing the variability and interchangeability of "plastic" and "musical" traits, we should also acknowledge some common sense in assigning plastic representation to painting and musical articulatory schemata to music. The musical freedoms of expressionism and other styles of that time which accepted comparable "license" appeared chaotic even to the composers who breathed those tendencies. The new chaos seemed ungoverned and ungovernable. The trade-off for painting, where formal articulation is not autonomous, is to "take its form from what it represents." Schoenberg rejected that option explicitly when he insisted on confronting the problem of form in non-texted music, and he responded by returning (dare I say "retreating"?) to inherently structured material, his row. Stravinsky had approached chaos from another side, but he, too, needed a reversal and found inherently structured materials in the restraints and borrowings of Neoclassicism. Bartók is not the only composer who remained unswervingly committed to the resources of plastic sound, but his interpretation of the medium is unique.

Let us look first at the craft of sustaining plasticity and then return to its sense and its purpose. Consider the unfolding of the first theme as a whole, starting with the diffident shrug and ending with its transformation into the decisive, patterned peroration. I borrowed "morph" from digital *visual* design with prejudice; the melody evolves by gradual stages into a figure of opposite character. The bass begins as a pedal point and unobtrusively becomes melodic. The inner voices begin with a murmur and evolve to a firm choir. The harmony is fogged at first, but clear shapes emerge. Abrupt contrasts occur, but it seems possible in this style to modulate smoothly from any sound or rhythm to any other. An extraordinary sensitivity of ear is requisite to the motility of the sound, for this is a condition quite unnatural to music. This music is still composed of materials regulated by discrete equivalences, twelve pitch classes, six interval classes, and eighth and quarter notes. Normally one class would not slide into the next, but in Bartók's adroit handling, we hardly notice when the parallel thirds of the development's climactic episode become tritones. There is no simple translation between visual and aural shapes. Nothing like a straight line except, perhaps, a series of octaves. Pitch space is curved and multidimensional. Middle C is right next to the D♭ above it and the B below it, but, in another dimension it is right next to the G above and F below. These intervals and others both cycle and interact in highly differentiated relations of tension and attraction. In detail, the technique depends on maintaining harmonies sufficiently complex that we hear them quantitatively instead of categorically, or as we sometimes say, hear them coloristically rather than functionally, but also in maintaining niceties of voice leading that compensate for the fundamental inhomogeneity of pitch space while avoiding its mechanization. (Elsewhere Bartók uses mechanical patterns as well, but these "primary colors" are not featured in the movement selected.) The triads and sevenths with added tones that we could name chord by chord in the phrase shown are constructed to ambiguate or mask the tonal functions suggested in simultaneous, but incompatible, harmonies. Yet these harmonic implications, though muffled, are always allowed some room for negotiation. The first harmonic second, D against E♭, depends for its effect on the incompatibility of the fourth and third degrees in a system not sustained here and would be too muddy an octave lower, too mild an octave higher. What is extraordinary is how Bartók keeps it up, continuously adjusting the weights for a flexibility of sound that does not disregard the harmonic values it contradicts.

This craft is not Bartók's alone, though I might argue that his fluidity and acumen are rare. We find comparable technique in Ives, in Shostakovich, in Britten, and in many other composers. Perhaps there was a period, say, from 1908 to 1925, where everybody had a turn with this technique, but not everybody had the same understanding of it.

According to the ancient debate, plastic art makes sense by representing. Exploiting plasticity as a principle of unity, Bartók makes a syntax out of representations. He makes allusions. He alludes to tonality without subscribing to its rules. He alludes to song without rounding out his melodies. He alludes to imitative procedures and developmental procedures which he is quick to abandon for fresh gestures. He alludes to folk music without accepting its constraints. To put it another way, he has turned all these other styles into topics. Collectively, these topics constitute networks of oppositions which are mediated by the possibility, in a plastic sound, of a modulatory progress from any one pole to any other. Stockhausen (1961) recalled that he glimpsed the principles that would become characteristic of his own composing when he prepared an analysis for Messiaen's class of the *Music for Strings, Percussion and Celesta*. Stockhausen wrote an academic thesis on Bartók's Sonata for Two Pianos and Percussion before going to France to study with Messiaen. I recall reading (but cannot retrace my source) a memoir by him or interview in which he found that Bartók composed by devising mediations between opposite values in all parameters. Such an appraisal justifies a more radical summary of the technique: Bartók remains in a world of shape and color to which he can afford structure by adducing principles of geometry—lines (scales) that connect opposite points and, on occasion, by arbitrary symmetries. Danuta Mirka's analysis of Penderecki's "sonoristic structuralism" (1997) echoes Bartók's method of according what we loosely call "color" a structural role that is not subordinated to any harmonic system. His syntax leads historically to the tape studio and the digital studio. Schaeffer (1966), who does not acknowledge Bartók but acknowledges Messiaen, is very precise about the role of plasticity of sound in his vision of a new music. Not that we should demote Bartók to the class of "forerunners"! He is still composing with notes. His plastic surface must be won chord by chord from heterogeneous materials, and his purposes are philosophical, requiring an interplay of topics with more abstract formal arrangements.

Bartók's "night music" informs us of a further dimension of his ideals which is not contradicted in this quartet though it is perhaps harder to demonstrate here. The evocative image of the night is obviously not a literal copy of night sounds. As a stylized representation it presents both an image of the sound and feeling of night outside the city, and an image of listening. Listening has as much attitude as speaking. Listening in Bartók's night music is alert, intelligent, and poised. It is neither submissive nor domineering. Bartók's synthesis via allusions to topics and his organization of these via his geometrical tendencies is neither a passive acceptance of whatever sounds come along nor a tyrannical *Gesamtkunstwerk* bending all materials to one unified and encompassing idea. His synthesis is receptive. Consider as a case in point his relation to folk music. This string quartet movement has little to do with folk music in its global style and architecture, but folk music appears as a topic in the first and second movements. It is clear from his essays that Bartók regarded folk music as a more pure source of musical thought than more elaborated styles as well as a source of renewal, but folk music does not function here as the emblem of a reform; its topic is received into a community of musicalities.

The form of the first movement of the Second Quartet is less radical than its style, though it, too, represents a synthesis between the rationality of sonata form and the nineteenth-century aesthetic ideal of musical form as a psychological drama or an intimate confession. We begin with the isolation and introversion of its shrug, move through varieties of expressivity that evoke the psychology of relationships between individuals, and arrive at a kind of resolution to the more public sociality of accompanied folk song. The possibility of narrative translation cannot really tempt me very long. In suggesting that a purely structural analysis could go nowhere, I did not mean to imply that a purely semantic analysis would fare any better. We must be oriented by the dialogue of structure and representation which is fundamental to the music itself. Bartók's style establishes a humane music that is at once both autonomous and implicated in experience, a music that moves rapidly between extreme representational moments of gesture, texture, topic, and rhetorical manner within a unity that exploits the purely structural craft of plasticity, a music that sidesteps the debates between Classical and Romantic to assert (as is often remarked) its acquisition of the problems bequeathed in Beethoven's late style. We must reclaim a word for his progressive synthesis that has, perhaps, become discredited: "serious." It is a word that may grate upon post-modern sensibilities, but no other word will do.

12 The Art of Music Theory and the Aesthetic Category of *the Possible*

The recounting of structural relations which we can sometimes produce for twentieth-century music, with more or less security, rarely sparks the flash of illumination that characterizes a good technical analysis of eighteenth- or nineteenth-century compositions. Paradoxically (or it may be more a corollary than a contradiction) the twentieth century was one in which composers invested a good deal of work in technical formulations. Suppose we do not confine our appreciation of these theories to the context that they would seem to affiliate with on first view. Music theory before the twentieth century is usually intended for instruction in a shared craft; it is often also intended as a polemic promoting certain aesthetic values that, though in part controversial, are also presumed to be shared by an extended professional community. The tradition of such writings created a form of discourse which continues into the twentieth century, but perhaps not always with the same purposes. I cannot see Messiaen's *Technique de mon langage musicale* as either a polemic or as a recipe book for further generations of Messiaens. The alternative we explore here will suggest that Messiaen's theory might have another relation with his music than those.

My focus here is on the music within the Western European and North American concert tradition that was more or less avant-garde in its time of composition though not necessarily radical. The movement of thought I propose to delineate might be dated from Busoni's *New Aesthetic* and continues to have repercussions today. Much twentieth-century theory has a very marked aesthetic temperament. It is audacious and frequently virtuosic in its own domain, displaying a conceptual or mathematical bravura, as we see in Xenakis, rather than corporal athletics. Along with some tomes worked out in a thoroughly pedagogical or even pedantic style like Schillinger's, Hindemith's, and Schoenberg's, we have other fragmentary and oracular statements, sometimes seeming to revel in darkness and abstruseness, like Wolpe's. Some new theory is more than a bit brazen. It is often self-consciously iconoclastic. Above all, and of this more later, it points toward new kinds of transcendence. This transcendence is sometimes understood morally as when Busoni or Ives link technical difficulty with integrity. Sometimes this transcendence is projected onto the very act of hearing, as in the discipline of listening experiments developed by Schaeffer or, in a very different way, by the postulate required by the time-point theory of Babbitt and attractive to many others that the ear will learn

An earlier, rather different version of this essay, originally a paper read to the ICMS in Helsinki, 1988, is listed in the References (Lidov 1995).

to follow where the intelligence shows the way. In musicology, a temperament which blends audacity, virtuosity, hints of obscurity, and transcendentalism is called romantic.

My experiment here is to acknowledge technical theories as aesthetic objects. Whatever label we might ultimately want to stamp on their temper, if any, the evident fact is that many technical pronouncements seem to be conceived for and injected into the domain of aesthetic perception. In fact, theory in the first half of the twentieth century takes on a role parallel to that of literary texts in the century previous, the texts of songs and musical programs. To be sure, some of those texts may have been quite inessential, as theory is to some contemporary music. One may not need a program for the Pastoral Symphony. But one does need to know the texts of Schubert's *Lieder* and to understand the titles of Liszt's tone poems, or else something of their point is lost. Where Stockhausen (1961) says of "Refrain," "Those who wish to understand what I have written . . . must read the score. . . . Those who simply wish to hear (not understand) . . . need only listen," his position replicates, in another mode, that of the nineteenth-century composer of programmatic music.

To point out that a theory has its own aesthetic character is not to impugn its technical content as irrelevant or incorrect. To hear a work of Schoenberg's when you have studied its row is a much richer experience than hearing it with technical naiveté. Schoenberg was quite ambiguous in his statements about the role that knowledge of his technique should play in musical understanding but not at all ambivalent about the value he placed on studiousness in listening. To hear Stockhausen's *Stimmung* is pleasantly intoxicating. To perform it, which means to master its theory—the notation entails novel theory—has quite a different fascination. These experiences, for which we could find parallels in dozens of compositions, establish the pertinence of composers' musical theories to structure and structural perception. In this regard, recent times may be no different from many other epochs—music theory remains pertinent to musical activity as a correct description.

But my particular interest here lies in functions of theory that exceed description. I would like to distinguish two functions that cannot be entirely separated. As a first approximation, I will designate them as syntactic and semantic. On the syntactic side, articulated theory has the function of promoting the attitude of *theoretical consciousness*. We can bring theoretical consciousness to the music of any place or time, but the artistic prominence and aesthetic function of theoretical consciousness change from epoch to epoch. Theoretical consciousness includes attention to inventive notations, attention to procedures of a patently experimental character, or alertness to structures whose novelty is an attraction in itself. It also includes an involvement, felt in active listening though not usually explicit in consciousness, with the prospective possibilities of an evolving structure. I will return to this last point toward the end of this chapter. For music to depend on theoretical mediation is frequently seen as a fault. *Augenmusik* remains a pejorative epithet; Dahlhaus has demonstrated how overhasty the condemnation may be (1970, pp. 53–56). We can't separate out pure listening from a listening informed by and

The Art of Music Theory and the Possible 195

imbued with concepts and notations. However, the value of theory in hearing is variable. Technical theoretical consciousness could be a destructive intrusion in listening to nineteenth-century grand opera, but we find an enthusiasm for theory in works like *The Art of Fugue* or Stravinsky's late serial writing.

The other function, tentatively "semantic," is more especially characteristic of the stylistic period we have in view. Theory imposes a context which makes any specific music merely an example of a general principle. Whereas music is an actual instance, the theory of that same music delineates the universe of possible instances. The odd development a hundred years ago was that it became aesthetically important to associate actual music with imagined possibilities.

The parallel, suggested above, of music and text correlations in nineteenth- and twentieth-century music is a parallel of semiotic structures: sound plus poetry as a single sign in the first case and sound plus technical theory as a single sign in the second. On the side of the signifier, a difference is that the correlation is more specific with program music. We know which program and which particular piece are paired, whereas a theory might attach to a style rather more firmly than to one particular work. On the side of the signified we can compare two entirely different ideals. With the risks that attend brevity, I suggest that poetry and programs when correlated with sound in the nineteenth century generally have the function of directing musical reference toward intuition and feeling, or toward an abstract notion of the *poetic*. The corresponding, general bearing of technical theory when correlated with the music of, roughly, 1910–1960 was to direct reference toward what I will call the ideal of the *possible*. "Possible" is a specialized term here, though, like "poetic," not an absolutely precise one. The *possible*, as an aesthetic ideal linked often to an optimistic conception of scientific technology, encompasses a broad family of related musical conceptions, some of which are quite vague, others more specific. Along with the flowering of interest in what was, so far as I know, a historically new aesthetic category, we should also be alert to contrary reactions, dilutions, and reversions from the aesthetic back to practical technique.[1]

The defining opposition is not between the possible and the impossible, a topic previously foregrounded in nineteenth-century virtuosity (which magically accomplished the impossible, technically and expressively), though this precedent is not without relevance. We deal with the possible in opposition to the actual or the known. And where everyday possibility, standing for genuine options, is always given within limits, we must recognize an ideal of absolute character, like the "sublime" or, even earlier, the "artificial." The American composer Kenneth Gabura is said to have remarked that any definition of music is a pretext for a composition that doesn't fit the definition. That is a good emblem for the possible. The many shaded meanings that possibility took on in musical thought collectively represent a very distinct and unprecedented emphasis. If it is one which, in the last forty years, has lost some of its allure, it should at least merit historical appreciation.

---

1. The pedagogical and public relations thematization of "creativity" perpetuates a secondary and epigonal residual of this aesthetic, though there are other factors as well. My completely unoriginal criticism of creativity will be found in the chapter of *Elements of Semiotics* on education.

The idea of possibility became prominent in the most varied musical discourses. The idea of discovering new possibilities of harmony, color, rhythm, or form was widely understood (and, for some, still is) as self-justifying. Novelty has always, or at least often, been appreciated in music when it was a question of new details or new nuances or even new characterizations within an existing grammar. The change was that innovations of detail became almost disdained in comparison with inventions which opened up fields of possible future action. "The purpose is to show the coordination of all *possible* musical materials within a certain overtone radius, *regardless of whether or not the materials are yet in actual use*," wrote Henry Cowell in 1930, introducing his widely influential *New Musical Resources* (1996, p. xi, my emphasis). Consider such unlike documents as Stiller's *Handbook on Instrumentation* (1985) in which thorough attention to the most arcane methods of sound production replaces the corresponding attention to characterization found in Berlioz or Rimsky-Korsakov, the massive compilation of possible permutations in Schillinger's system, or the harmony textbook of Persichetti (1961), who states flatly at the beginning that any combination of notes can be a chord and any chord can follow any other.

We are not to mistake unlimited possibility as a value which needs no justification for *libertinage*. The theory of unlimited harmonic possibilities emerges explicitly in the aesthetics of Busoni as a mark of courage or adventure in the pursuit of truth. By 1911, the year he published *Sketch of a New Esthetic of Music*, his technical speculations (and experiments) had already extended to new modes and sixth-tone scales. Yet he was not composing with these materials. This early statement signals two characteristic themes, first, that, like Cowell above, he is writing very abstractly about music of the future (not as with Wagner, *my* future, not programmatically but speculatively), and, second, that his thought is influenced by the physical science of sound, specifically the "Dynamophone" of Thaddeus Cahill (Busoni 1962, p. 95).

"Theory" and "possibility" are related. A theory is a specific representation of abstract possibility. The theoretical concept of a C major chord represents the unlimited possibility of its realizations. Similarly, in linguistics a grammar defines a universe of possible utterances. Theory as an aesthetic sign represents possibility as an aesthetic topic. There is also a slightly more difficult inverse relationship. Where we can downgrade the actual to the status of a mere example of the possible, the actual *as one possibility* represents theory. Both these relations operate in twentieth-century musical aesthetics. Open notations invite the two-sided understanding that what is written represents unlimited possibility and that what is played is merely an instance. We must consider a composer's turn toward theory as representing, sometimes, a pedagogical intention—probably the case for Hindemith— sometimes a normative intention—probably the case for Babbitt—but also as an artistic expression which develops the affiliation of that composer's music with the aesthetic ideal of the *possible*. In these latter cases, by no means exclusive of the others, we can regard theoretical texts as part of the artistic oeuvre conditioning perceived sound much as literary texts had done in the previous century.

This seems to me to be the case for Pierre Schaeffer, whose writings spell out an "aesthetic of possibilities," for he has been insistent from the beginning that his methods of experimenting with sound permit an approach to composition which does not proceed from a priori intentions. The question here is whether his music makes its point, as he implies, simply as a sound object which we confront openly and naively, or whether instead we can understand his compositions more fully if we link them to his theories. His own desire to have the sound do its work unassisted cannot be doubted. He described his discipline of "acousmatics" as having the purpose of "not allowing either musical instruments or social conditioning to prevent our *confrontation with the sounds or 'possible' sounds of music*" (1966, p. 98; italics in the original).[2] Yet the sound surface which is typical of Schaeffer's work does not seem to me to be one likely to involve the listener in a romance of new possibilities. It is a very polished sound, like an exhibit of pretty acoustic toys. The sound is more significant when one understands it as the result of its theory, that is, when one hears it as the product of the systematic experimentation and manipulation of sounds discovered in the world. In that context it signifies a project; its sheen entrains our imagination in the prospect of a new infinity. To hear the music richly, we need to know the theoretical project. Schaeffer's insistence on the priority of hearing over any theoretical knowledge is a fundamental motif of his work, but this contrary motif is no more than what another century would have called his poetic conceit. A truer account of the real situation of his art is that the sound and the theory together represent a sensibility which neither could convey without reference to the other.

Messiaen presents us with two aesthetic positions, for he speaks of works one way and of style another. "The questions of aesthetic language and of the sentiment expressed belong to two different domains" (cited in Samuel 1967, p. 12).[3] His works offer us a contemplation of personal emotion or religious subjects, but his own discussions of stylistic development, whether it be his appreciation of his predecessors and colleagues or his condemnation of jazz, hinge on questions of novelty (see, for example, Samuel 1967 throughout, but especially Chapter VII).

The theory in Messiaen's *Technique* (1966), leaving aside for now the poetic features of its style of presentation, which are considerable and which identify it as an aesthetic object, is essentially a generative theory. Unlike, for example, Schoenberg's analytic essays and textbooks, which aim at a comprehension of syntactic functions, or Hindemith's, where assessments of roots and densities provide a system of classification, Messiaen's theory aims to show how resources can be indefinitely enlarged. Like Schaeffer's practical theory of experimentation and transformation, Messiaen's theory is a pathway toward unlimited and unpredictable possibilities. His own insistence on the "charm of impossibilities" simply holds the motif of his research in a mirror.

Obviously one cannot argue that his music is pointless without its theory, for his style continues to achieve success with audiences who are not familiar with his book. Nevertheless, in the context which excludes the theory, his work can readily

2. nier l'instrument et le conditionnement culturel, *mettre face á nous le sonore et son "possible" musical.*
3. La question du langage esthétique et celle du sentiment exprimé son deux domaines différents.

be criticized for an excessive length and dependence on arbitrary colors that un-critically extend Debussy's palette. These are, of course, the very features which Messiaen seems to intend as signs of the transcendental. Here a serious regard for the theory really contributes to the music. By uniting the sonorous surface with an infinitely generative system, the theory gives more substance to the music's tran-scendental vision. Is this not a good reason for the author to have wished to place the theory itself before the public, as he did, in such an attractive format? Even the insistent images of birdsong, otherwise tainted with a suspect sentimentality, take on a meaningful role in their theoretical context where they serve to mediate between subjective intention and objective discovery. All in all, Messiaen's work is more compelling and significant if we regard its theory and sonorous configuration as a unified project developing an aesthetic of possibilities.

I think it is American composition, especially but not exclusively that of the ex-perimental schools, that shows us both the quickest flowering and most construc-tive criticism of the aesthetics of possibility and its liaison with theory. The idea of composing to find out what a piece (or technique) will sound like, often a very particular and finite venture, cannot be entirely identified with an idealization of unknown possibilities (an ideal that is sometimes much more vague), but the mu-tual sympathy of these attitudes is evident. Cowell's book cited earlier in this chap-ter flowed from his work with Charles Seeger, who claimed a co-authorship of some of its ideas (see David Nicholls's introduction to Cowell 1966). Seeger's theo-retical construction of dissonant counterpoint is a more modest but very thorough speculation which produced in Ruth Crawford's music a subsequent style. This de-monstratively productive speculation seems to have proceeded from no motivation other than to explore and concretize a reversal of actual practice and thought—that is to say, from an idea of a possibility and the idea that a new possibility is a justi-fication in itself. Cowell's book was written speculatively, but its speculations be-came experiments in his work or in the work of others. Yet, from the beginning, there is an opposite thrust. Cowell asks with unprecedented boldness what might be possible, but he also asks of all that is possible, What is correct? One has the impression that for his colleague Carl Ruggles, who was equally open to experi-ment, it was only the latter question that really mattered. The bare idea that yet unknown musical worlds were possible (and might be contacted by speculative theory) was in itself a source of motivation, but it was also open to critique. Stra-vinsky recounts his terror on beginning a composition, where he finds himself be-fore "the infinitude of possibilities" (1947, p. 65)—not the sentiment of a composer who must produce one more minuet, but also not a sentiment that any composer could have thought to voice in the age of the minuet.

The most pointed critique of the aesthetic of possibility is embodied in the mu-sic of Edgar Varèse, who provides a striking counterexample with regard to the tendencies traced here. It is true that he said he devoted his life to the liberation of sound, but he certainly did not mean that phrase as Shaeffer might have. To liberate sound meant to put it as his disposal, to control it. He insisted that his compositions were not experiments; a composition is a particular statement which has nothing to do with what might have been or could be. It should be noted in this connection that for all its novelty Varèse's style does not promote a theoretical consciousness. He does not generally entrain the listener's attention in the development and transformation of motives. We are not asked, as listeners, to experience a tension between the actual shapes of his materials and their potentials. In the music of Varèse, such transformations can be discovered, but they are increasingly tenuous. The relation of this pioneer to the aesthetic of possibility is that he rejects it through a style which continually affirms the value of the particular over the general. On a practical level, no one worked harder than Varèse to obtain support for new technology and new institutions for music. But his novel music does not invite us to participate in a dialogue of the actual and possible: it says, "I am precisely and unalterably what you hear." It followed that Varèse had no need to share a theory of his methods with the public and seemed to want to cut his compositions off from any explanatory context. Nevertheless, music does not operate in a desert, and the context of *Déserts* is that tendency toward generalizing which is nearly ubiquitous in modern thought and which his music forcefully opposes.

After a new aesthetic conception blooms and fades we notice its hybrids, which are always perennials and even tend to acquire earlier histories. Perhaps it would be as rare today as two hundred years ago for a composer of first-rate intelligence to be enthusiastic about a musical construction merely because it is possible, but in combination with other ideals, the *possible* may be as permanent and renewable as the *poetic*, the *artificial*, the *natural*, the *austere*, the *exotic*, and so on. I will conclude by noting two manifestations which blend this idea with others. As we do so, the reason why earlier I bracketed "syntactic" and "semantic" will become clear—a musical syntax represents an attitude, which is to say that any musical syntax has a semantic aspect, and, conversely, any semantic act in music, any representation, inflects its syntax. We need surgical tools to separate musical syntax from semantics if it can be done at all.

First, I think that a sensibility for experiment gave rise as early as the Baroque to a particular syntax which took a more independent form early in the twentieth century. The early form occurs in developmental passages. I describe this syntax as a cycle of three phases, "projection," "amplification," and "saturation." The syntax depends on theoretical *consciousness* (though not on theoretical texts). In "projection" a generative cell is associated with a mode of extension which suggests its virtual future; a variation process comes into play which is both sufficiently salient and sufficiently open to invite participation. Projection suggests continuations but does not imply the "necessity" of a particular continuation or any specific outcome. (As I would understand "implication" to do: True implication seems to be limited to specific and familiar contexts, tonal and/or formal. Implication weakens projection to the extent that it shifts attention from immediate to final prospects.) In the second phase of the cycle, "amplification," the unfolding suggests a much wider range of possibilities, so that the generative material seems to acquire an infinite potential. In the third phase, "saturation," variants proceeding from the generative element fail to capture the larger universe they seemed to promise and accumulate in harmonic or rhythmic redundancy. Saturation may motivate either a new generator or an enlargement of the mode of variation. I published a brief illustration of this common syntax in the paper from which this chapter is derived. It studies the "Elegia" from Bartók's *Concerto for Orchestra*. It is an unlikely example in the sense that the movement as a whole is not limited to the aesthetic of the possible and does not share the optimism typical of that aesthetic. The "Elegia" is humanistic and pessimistic, but my point is that there are links nonetheless because of the shared culture of experimentation and rapidly changing horizons which ties modernism to this aesthetic. Bartók's interval games develop theoretical consciousness as a characteristic way of hearing his music

To cite just the very beginning of that analysis, the first generator is the opening pair of descending fourths, F♯-C♯ and D♯-A♯, a minor third apart. The continuation which they suggest is a third descending fourth, C to G (see Figure 12.1a). The next pair of notes Bartók writes amplifies the projection because it neither continues nor abandons the pattern which was initiated (Figure 12.1b). The pitch, G, and the interval, an ascending fifth, connect these notes with the initial projection but introduce several new possibilities of variation. At this point we hear a line which seems to have a definite principle of unity and yet infinite possibilities of extension. It is inviting to imagine more—not that we necessarily have a melody of our own come to mind, but we get a sense of identification: "I could be expressing/inventing this." (This sense of a participatory syntax linked to theoretical consciousness and an awareness, at least dimly, of possibilities, is precisely what Varèse chooses to suppress by severe limitations on isochronous pulse and discontinuous procedures of variation.)

With the entrances of other parts, the range of transformations and the suggestions of possibilities grow larger (m. 4ff., Figure 12.1c). But where the initial growth of the generating melody seemed to promise boundless possibility, we sense very rapidly that its space is filling up, that chromatic symmetries are suffocating the harmony. The space of the first generator has become saturated. Therefore, there is immediate relief with the appearance of a new generative cell at the entrance of the clarinet at m. 10.

A very different manifestation of the idea of the possible arises with the incorporation of chance and aleatoric elements in music. It has become a commonplace of musical criticism today to identify the perceptual results of total serialism with the perceptual results of chance operations. Although there is a moment of intersection, the two technical attitudes are very different. If there are some particular works which seem to arrive at the same sound world, and many others which programmatically mix techniques, it is still the case that the impetus of their traditions remains distinct in a larger perspective on style. Serialism defines and controls its total universe. Chance operations represent a sampling of the unknown. I do not think John Cage was very excited by the romance of infinite possibilities, at least not for very long. The idea that for music everything had become possible was a condition of music that seemed to be, for him, a fact absorbed and mastered early in his thinking, well before he began to exploit chance operations in composing. The question he moved on to was how to respond musically to a universe in which all possible sounds and silences could be music. In his work, unlimited possibility is not an ideal but rather a material to be shaped by forms of attention. We have

Figure 12.1. Bartók, "Elegia" from the *Concerto for Orchestra*.

had various occasion to observe that notation is theory (as in Chapter 5). Cage's meticulous, highly inventive, highly personal autographs are the theories which express in generalities the possibilities of which the works as performed are instances. Any doubt that the score functions both as theory and as aesthetic object is settled by his own publication of the anthology *Notations*. His musical score is addressed in the first instance to the performer, but images of scores have also found their way into the iconography that helps to frame and interpret his music to its wider audiences.

Composers whom Cage has influenced, such as Walter Zimmerman, whose work is briefly discussed in the introduction to the final chapter, are the most inventive of all composers in directing attention to very limited ranges of possibilities, but ranges of possibilities that remain open. We might speak here of infinitesimal rather than infinite possibilities. The technical acquisition of structures that evoke possibility will be as permanent as counterpoint or harmony, and when you pass a wind chime, you know that this "new" acquisition is the more ancient.

13 Technique and Signification in the Twelve-Tone Method

In the 1920s, late in the fourth decade of his life, Schoenberg developed a new for-mulation of compositional technique which he called the "method of composing with twelve tones related only to each other." History has made the forcefulness of Schoenberg's invention obvious. Was his new formulation purely a technical matter—a matter of means but not ends—or did it express a change of aesthetic, a change in philosophy? And, if so, what change? For semiotics, the question is whether the twelve-tone method as deployed in his music is a *sign*. Note that we do not ask whether the method is governing or organizing a sign *system*—a ques-tion of a very different order. We ask whether the method invented by Schoenberg may be conceived as the audible vehicle of a meaning specific to it in its *totality*.

Schoenberg did address himself to this question. His answers—not entirely consistent—seem to favor the negative: "Form in the arts, especially in music, aims primarily at comprehensibility. . . . Composition with twelve tones has no other aim than comprehensibility" (Schoenberg 1951, p. 103). And in a letter to Kolisch he writes despairingly of twelve-tone analysis, saying that people must see what his music is, not how it is made (Schoenberg 1965, p. 164; cf. p. 267).

I would not have chosen to raise this issue if I agreed with Schoenberg that his method is semantically neutral, and I am comforted to find at least some ambiguity in Schoenberg's own theoretical writings that supports my belief that a master-ful technique is necessarily a communicative sign. He once wrote, "Every man has fingerprints of his own and every craftsman's hand has its personality; out of such subjectivity grow the traits which comprise the style of the finished product" (Schoenberg 1951, p. 47). However, the personal and expressive traits of Schoen-berg's technique are not entirely subjective. Here I will be concerned with their objective formulation and the meanings that attach to them.

For me, the objective presence of values (aesthetic, moral, and intellectual) in Schoenberg's techniques is illuminated when we regard them in the light of a dichotomy which runs as a *leitmotif* through the poetics of Roman Jakobson, his opposition of selectional relations—leading to *metaphor*—and combinational relations—producing *metonymy*. Building on the Saussurian view that sentences combine words that are selected because of their differential values in different paradigms, Jakobson held that artistic communication characteristically exagger-ated the proportions of the two principles, with poetry inclining to stress associa-

This essay was published in *Degrés* VII, no. 18 (1979), and in Wendy Steiner, ed., *The Sign in Music and Literature* (Austin: University of Texas Press, 1980).

tion (that is, paradigmatic, selectional relations) and narrative tending to stress the syntagmic or combinatorial relation. I will invoke the dichotomy of combination and selection in proposing a homology between musical form and philosophical principles (a form of musical explication discussed by Ruwet [1972, p. 14]).

In comparison with melodic gesture and harmonic color, so immediately expressive in their sensuous aspect, the more abstract musical facets of form and structure may often seem to have a purely technical or merely cabalistic content. In the case of a minor composer, formal questions do slip to the background; form becomes the first aspect of musical expression to be automated. With philosophically original composers formal considerations or consideration of technical procedure enter the foreground. This is the inevitable fact in Bach's music, Mozart's, Beethoven's, Wagner's, and certainly Schoenberg's. With composers of the first rank, form and technique become homologous with forms of discourse or structures of belief. They involve music in issues of philosophic stature.

One of the domains of reference particularly accessible to music is that of qualities of consciousness. Images of consciousness are readily evoked by music because, like consciousness itself, music is temporal, continuous in its extent, and without spatial boundaries. We will find a key to the philosophic dimensions of Schoenberg's musical thought in the qualities of consciousness imagined within the aesthetic frameworks of his styles, beginning with expressionism and proceeding to the twelve-tone method.

Expressionism brought to a climax the development of an idea which was germinal for the Romantic movement, the idea of exotic associations.[1] The early Romantic theory that a state of enthusiasm enables a poet to transcend the logical surface of thought is pushed to new consequences in expressionism. Enthusiasm becomes a frenzied agitation approaching derangement, and freedom of association leads not only to exoticism but to an imagery seemingly shorn of all civilizing inhibitions and to what we might term a consciousness of the unconscious. Various writers including Schoenberg himself have suggested a link between psychoanalytic concepts and the aesthetics of expressionism (Schoenberg 1951, pp. 86, 182). This link is not casual hyperbole. A close analysis of the musical technique shows this psychological content to be as deeply rooted in its stylistic procedure as it is in the literary texts and subjects with which it is allied.

Musical and literary semiotic structures in expressionist style are homologous with each other in that both proceed by a gross exaggeration of associative or selectional relations and the near eclipse of combinatorial grammar, by a domination of metaphor over metonymy. For music the principle of grammatical combinations resided in the principles of consonance and tonality. In terms of Schoenberg's theory of monotonality (a theory which does not seem appropriate for the music of earlier composers but which gives us essential insights into his), all chords belong to every key as representatives of its immediate or distant regions. The distant relations of the tonic are normally comprehended through the mediation of closer

---

1. I am indebted to discussions with Tillock Banerjee, York University, regarding Romantic aesthetic theories.

chords via an established logic of harmonic progression (the combinatorial grammar). The technique of expressionism is to skip past the mediations—the preparations and resolutions—on the basis of the enthusiasm or agitation captured in the *Einfall,* the first inspiration of an expressive motive, a figure that may then be freely varied to bring distant harmonies and dissonances into immediate apposition.

An early and relatively straightforward example appears in the opening of Schoenberg's Second Quartet, a passage which can even yield its pitches, if not its secrets, to a prolongation analysis. Elements of F-sharp minor are established in hierarchically crucial positions throughout the first forty measures, but the rapid excursions from the tonic key express neither linear nor harmonic requirements. Harmonies switch on and off like stage lights: the tonic minor for four measures, the unison E♮ of mm. 6 and 7, the A minor, C-sharp minor, and F major which follow. One can speak of a plan, but it is as tenuous and complex as the plots of dream imagery and equally compressed.

The phenomenon of compression is crucial. The oppositions of harmonically distant regions or dissonant pitches take their specific semiotic character from their sensuous temporality. Presented in time so that their rapid sequence and short duration are imposed on our perception, these contrasts provoke a division of attention and defy memory. Ultimately, it is this music's choreography of our own mental movements between concentration and recollection which becomes its most intimate sign of a knowledge beyond ordinary knowledge. Of course, our understanding of the composer's historical situation, his literary allegiances, and his philosophical commitments play their natural role in our understanding of his musical language, but both the structure and phenomenological character of the technique support our interpretation. The fleeting and irrational harmonies have the form and tempo of free associations in the psychoanalytic sense, those subliminal glimpses of an unknown part of our mind which are available to us when we are in a condition to abandon the inhibitions of rational control. And what are the conditions under which we do abandon rationality? For the early Romantics, the condition was enthusiasm, but they had only scratched the surface of free associations. Here we have the madness of *Pierrot,* the insanity of *Erwartung.* Knowledge is gained at a price. The advantage of Schoenberg's harmonic theory is that, unlike Schenker's, it does not portray all possible departures from the key as ultimately strengthening the dominion of the single tonality. His theory of monotonality is compatible with a concept of a weak and fading center. Expressionism accepted weakness as a condition of knowledge. We hear the equation in the "Litany" of the Second Quartet as the poet sings, "Schwach ist mein atem rufend dem traume."

What happens to these signs in twelve-tone compositions? The new method first appears in a series of works that have the external trappings of Neoclassicism. Is this an apostasy? A retreat from brave adventures to the easy comforts of scholastic routine?

Liebowitz has demonstrated the continuity of Schoenberg's melodic and harmonic manners as his style moved through phases of tonal, freely atonal, and twelve-tone technique, but obviously Schoenberg's style experienced significant changes (Liebowitz 1975, pp. 74–77). Schoenberg's expressionism was part of a widely shared and forcefully articulated aesthetic movement, but the philosophical commitment embodied in the new technique was entirely his individual achievement. We have the difficult task of deducing it from the sound and logic of the method itself. I think we must begin with some attributes of the technique which were more evident to its critics than its proponents.

The sound of the twelve-tone method is willful and contrived, and we can hear, if the music sounds artful and spontaneous, that this is so despite the bias of the system, not because of it. Schoenberg threw us off the track with his insistence, rather defensive it seems to me, on the inevitability and naturalness of his invention, as when he offered the unpersuasive simile that compared the manipulation of the tone row to the rotation of a table knife in the visual field (Schoenberg 1951, p. 113).

Not only is the argument patently false (the inversion of a theme always changes its character), but other marks of contrivance must not be denied. The rhythm wrestles against the constraints of number magic. Groupings of pitches into 5 and 7, 6 and 6, four times three and three times four—felt as present or as nearly avoided—establish a subliminal obsession which but for his consummate artistry would become a prominent nuisance.

Another false defense of the method was to speak of it as an alternative to tonality. The quality of naturalness in the developed tonal system is an effect or, if you prefer, an illusion which results from values that are largely foreign to Schoenberg's method. His own spontaneity and warmth impose a natural quality on his musical expression, but these are entirely subjective and personal qualities. His naturalness does not result from the twelve-tone method, and furthermore, his analytical essays show no favor to the techniques, such as simplified accompaniment—techniques won gradually through decades of experiment—by which Classical compositions had objectified the concept of musical nature.

Although Schoenberg speaks of the twelve-tone method as a substitute for tonality, it is fundamentally unlike tonality in its level of abstract representation. Both are abstract, but whereas a tonality can be represented in the mind in terms of the qualities of a single tone or chord, the tone row is irreducible. In the abstract form of a sequence of twelve pitch classes, mental representation of the row as a precise, single, molar unit is always just beyond reach. I don't mean that you can't memorize a tone row. I have memorized lots of them! I mean that, even when memorized, the row does not shrink to one simple and complete gestalt, like a tonic chord. Perhaps this has something to do with the capacities which psychologists ascribe to short-term memory. All we can grasp securely are the concrete realizations of the row which impose temporary hierarchical groupings on its elements. Even in its concrete form the consequent tends to obliterate the aural memory of the antecedent. The principle of continuation in twelve-tone music, which Adorno claimed to be missing, is the need to hear the row another time so we can get it straight, the need to regard a complex object from another angle and for another moment (Adorno 1973, pp. 73–75). Schoenberg enunciated the principle: "An alert mind will demand to be told the more remote consequences of the simple matters he has already comprehended" (1951, pp. 55–56).

Whereas tonality is abstract in the manner of an environment, an orientation, an objective place where things happen, the tone row is abstract in the manner of a *personality,* a subjective force unifying the character of its manifestations but itself never wholly visible or wholly conscious. Considering the twelve-tone technique as a sign vehicle, we find then that two of its most obvious characteristics are its quality of artificiality or unnaturalness and the intangibility or ephemerality of its kernel structure.

However, the very intangibility of the row makes it a suitable vehicle for Schoenberg's discourse on unconscious or transcendental knowledge, which continues with heightened profundity in his music. The discourse is further elaborated through the row's thematic content. Schoenberg never abandoned the concept of *Einfall,* which sees the theme or perhaps the row as a vehicle of unconscious inspiration and hence a talisman of associative power. Through the pervasive presence of the row the conscious content of one theme becomes the unconscious content of all others. We find subliminal motivic associations in all sorts of music, but in this music such associations are so dense that all categories of themes, accompaniments, developments, and ornaments blend in a constant meld. Every figure has more associations than we can bring to mind.

The difference is that we now find the process of bringing a richer range of associations to mind is not conditional on weakening of rationality. The genius of the method is to draw its rationality from within the associative process itself. Expressionism opposed motivic association to tonal combinatorial logic, but the new technique takes its logic from the selectional discipline of continuous transformations. To fully grasp this point we must step outside the scholastic conventions of those "twelve-tone analyses" which show merely how the twelve-tone composition can be reduced to transforms of its row. Actually, Schoenberg's compositions in the technique use at least three dimensions of transformations. One is transformation of the concrete form of the row. Another, derived from the first but not identical to it, is the transformation of compositional functions: themes gradually change into accompaniments and vice versa (a prominent process in composition since at least Robert Schumann). And finally there is the transformation of roles in the row as different portions of the row become identified with each other through the resemblances of their concrete forms.

Here are specific and typical examples of these three types of transformation from the Third Quartet, Op. 30: transformations of the concrete form of the row—ubiquitous, but mm. 1–8 (original) versus mm. 9–12 (inverted retrograde) will do; transformation of functions—the cello's *melody,* mm. 13–18, is immediately identified with the opening ostinato *accompaniment* by virtue of row identity *plus* contour identity and registral proximity (one octave lower than the viola, m. 2); association of distinct row elements—the same cello melody associates original pitches 1, 2, 4, and 5 with inversion pitches 5, 3, 2, and 1, respectively.

In the density of these associations which cut freely across the boundaries of materials and in the potentially irrational contiguity of the variants, the method establishes a further homology with the quality of unconscious thought. But there is a censor. Despite the density and extremity of variation, all those natural, spontaneous variants of the theme—even very close ones—which do not conform to the row must be excluded. We have a new discipline, purely selective but very tough and very severe. Such a method can have no pretence of imitating nature. What it imitates is the moral will:

> [Moses:] Dienen, dem Gottesgedanken zu deinen ist die Freiheit. (*Moses and Aaron,* act 3, scene 1)

Perhaps we have been so gleeful about the evidence of megalomania—the quarrel with Mann, the too-autobiographical portrayal of Moses—that we have failed to confront the moral content of Schoenberg's technique. The hyper-romanticism of his early compositions yields to a moral imperative in his later work. The willful and contrived sound of the method which we observed before must be understood not as a forgivable fault but as a sign—the index and the icon—of moral will. An idea of will, the given law, the commandment, has taken on the role which Classicism had ascribed to nature and the Romantics to enthusiasm. The most intense participation is demanded of the listener, who, following an ideal which is evident in all of Schoenberg's writing on music, must become a student in order to hear anything more than aural wallpaper. What the student hears, provided he or she is in touch with the associative relations of the row, is, as in certain earlier music, appropriately construed as an image of consciousness striving for transcendence, a transcendence which Schoenberg himself identifies most often in religious terms. Those who knew him report that he was obsessed with an urge to know.[2] The consistent principle in all of his styles is that the idealization of transcendental knowledge is encoded in the overriding dominance of the selectional principle over the combinatorial grammar. With the twelve-tone method, the urge to know, which had earlier broken the boundaries of consciousness through the medium of madness, becomes elevated to a moral principle.

Adorno has criticized this style for its element of mechanical procedure and its reliance on neoclassical reflexes. His criticism singled out the Fourth Quartet. We cannot deny the nostalgia for a simpler style conveyed by the phrase rhythm of the opening melody (Adorno 1973, pp. 73–75, 103). How easy it makes the row seem! But our job as listeners is also to hear the accompanying chords, which are made of the same stuff, though not so clearly sounded. The music demands constant effort. If, as Adorno suggests, the music sometimes seems academic, it may be because we have retreated from it. The complexity, the intensity of vision and of pain in this music, are sometimes more than we can take.

---

2. This theme recurs throughout Reich (1971), especially in the second half of the biography.

14 The Project of Abstraction and the Persistence of the Figure in Twentieth-Century Music and Painting: On the Music of Elliott Carter, with a Postscript on the Ninth Symphony of Beethoven

"Abstract" is the opposite of "concrete." But the *musique concrète* of Pierre Schaeffer, which was intended to strip away all reference from sound, was, in a familiar sense, an idea that belongs to abstractionism. The English poet Dame Edith Sitwell described her work *Façade* as "abstract" poetry, but it is largely the same as what others call "concrete poetry." There is not necessarily any paradox here, for you might say one term refers to the signifier and the other to the signified, but we can take note that abstraction, which is with us everywhere, is an idea that resists definition.

The *New Princeton Encyclopedia of Poetry and Poetics* includes a brief entry on "Abstract Poem." It says, with reference to Sitwell's concept, "She may have meant 'abstract' as . . . in painting (i.e. non-representational) or as in music, in the sense which music is said to be abstract" (Brogan 1993). Apparently, then, abstract painting and abstract music are not abstract in the same sense, or at least not at Princeton.

Langer (1957) defined "symbol" as anything we use for abstraction. Abstraction is always with us, and it is fundamental in some way to all intellectual and artistic work. It is perhaps all the more striking then that, at around the turn of the last century, a movement toward radical abstraction was felt as a desideratum or even as a necessity in so many sectors of culture. Abstractionism in the arts, an aspect of modernism, is roughly coincident with the most abstract treatment of mathematics and logic as well as physics. The invention of quantum mechanics posed such a devastating challenge to intuition that the Copenhagen school, Bohr and many colleagues, insisted on abandoning any attempt to construct a mental picture of physical relations. I don't think these historical coincidences should be attributed to an inexplicable Zeitgeist. All of these movements were reacting to an-

A version of this chapter was read as a paper to the International Congress on Musical Signification in 2001 in Imatra, Finland.

tecedent exaggerations of materialism, realism, and naturalism, and various cross-influences have been suggested, not just from science to art, but also in the other direction.[1]

If all music is abstract, it is not all equally abstract.

I believe that music's firmly rooted domain of representation is kinesthetic. Just as the color and shape in painting may represent bodies in the lifeworld, the perceived motion of sound may represent human bodies, not their visual appearance, of course, but their kinesthetic experience, the appearance of movement from within. It may also represent other kinds of motion which, typically, we anthropomorphize—Schubert's spinning wheel, which is holding back tears; Debussy's perfumes in the evening air, which are evoked in a rhythm linked both to the slowest of palpable breezes and to nasal inhalation; or Elliot Carter's sandpiper in *A Mirror on Which to Dwell,* with its humanly urbane and neurotic strut. But I don't mean to interpret a psycho-physical propensity as an artistic universal! In some music, despite hearing sound in motion, we do not hear its motion representationally, certainly not anthropomorphically. I find this to be the case, for example, in much of Xenakis. Schaeffer's program for *musique concrète* aimed to arrive at this state. There is also music where we have a very wide choice of listening attitudes in this regard. The difference between abstract and figurative hearing is not erased, however, if the listener makes the choice instead of the composer.

I think of the second variation in Stravinsky's *Variations* as abstract. I believe this is the variation Stravinsky compared with pride to the sound of glass breaking, but that does not make it less abstract. In contrast, I hear the Prelude of the *Requiem Canticles* as kinesthetically specific. I don't know whether the violin is wringing its hands, beating its breast, or pulling its hair, but the general form of these high, trembling contractions is common to all three of these self-lacerating gestures, and it is captured precisely, along with, of course, the emotion in which such a behavior or representation is implicated.

There are parallels and differences between musical and visual abstraction.

Victor Grauer, a multimedia artist and ethnomusicologist, has published a series of articles (now available both in print and online)[2] that deal with modernism in painting, film, and music comparatively. His perspective centers on a highly generalized notion of syntax and on what he calls "antax," an opposite of syntax that he holds to be cognitively more fundamental. I am particularly indebted to his understanding of stylistic developments in the work of Cézanne and Mondrian.

Cézanne's style was formed in his attempt to record visual experiences anterior to the integration and adjustment which the brain imposes on perceptual data, a stage of visual perception that is normally bypassed by consciousness, yet not entirely unavailable. You can sample the experience in question by arranging to look at a complex scene with just one eye, using a fixed peephole that immobilizes your

---

1. Regarding possible influences on Bohr's physics from the humanities, see Selleri (1989).
2. Grauer's papers are listed in the References as originally published. To view these and others online, access his homepage from his site list: http://worldzone.net/arts/doktorgee/home.htm. His most extensive writing on Cézanne can be found in chapter 4 of his book *Montage Realism and the Act of Vision* at http://worldzone.net/arts/doktorgee/MontageBook/MontageBook-intro.htm.

head. When Cézanne drew exactly what he saw, he found it didn't balance pictorially. Thus, a further root of his style was his commitment to restore balance to the painted image of this visual experience by manipulating the signifier in ways that compensate for intelligibility lost in the represented object. These manipulations are abstract in that they serve only an aesthetic, not a representational, purpose. Cézanne's art demonstrates that what we call abstraction can arise from a pursuit of verisimilitude. Grauer provides other, parallel cases.

In deleting some of the process of integration and interpretation that the mind supplies to vision, Cézanne begins to undermine the representation of a fully formed and integrated perceiving subject. Something quite different but not unrelated occurs in musical expressionism, which presents raw expressive gesture as literally as possible and without syntactic contextualization. Here, too, representation engenders abstraction.

We cannot deal with the disintegration of the represented object and avoid considering the disintegration of an implied expressive or receptive subject. Expressionism, fascinated by madness, is linked thematically to the breakdown of the socially integrated personality.

If I may glance back one last time to *Façade,* the poet's brother, Osbert Sitwell, reported in the liner notes for her recording that the speaker in the first performance was hidden by a curtain. He wrote, "The project was to present the poems in as abstract a manner as possible. . . . When the speaker is seen, . . . personality obtrudes and engages the audience" (1949). Thus, the project of abstraction impinges on the construction and representation of the "self," of what we often call "personality" or what recent French discourse designates as the *sujet.* The disintegration of the represented subject is a theme dramatically theorized by Julia Kristeva in her *Revolution of Poetic Language.*

Adopting a perspective informed by Freudian and Lacanian theory, Kristeva understands both the symbolic domain and the distinct, ever-evolving subject who will express it or be expressed by it as arising from rupture. The infant, rudely separated from its mother, must assert its desires despite its own apartness. As repercussions of this rift, signifier divides from signified and both become alienated from the *chora,* the body's native rhythmic manifestation of primary drives. The alienation is not final or absolute. The revolution in poetic language is a recurring intrusion of biological drives into the social, symbolic domain, yielding what she calls, in her peculiar usage, *le sémiotique.*

My own theoretical image of the soma is not built around Freudian primary drives. Even if I have often emphasized certain neurological hypotheses, I start with the large bones and the large muscles—the ones that walk, breath, cringe, or lash out. Kristeva's soma reduces quickly to genitalia and orifices, with mouth and tongue showing a special flair to represent the others. I reject this reduction for music, and I suspect it is also a disservice to Mallarmé. Her brilliant distributional analysis of the phonetic constituents of Mallarmé's *Prose*—tracing what she, following Mallarmé himself, calls its "rhythm"—does not in the end address the very basic question of its metrical form: Why fourteen quatrains of perfect octosyllabic verses? Even if the poet himself speaks dismissively of the discipline he adopts, are these stanzaic forms merely, as he did suggest, dead fossils of Greek feet? In fact, the rhythm would have no force without the meter, the ground of the rhythmic elasticity that permits it to possess our body.

My caveat is neither very small nor very great. Kristeva's theoretical framework for regarding the dialectic of identification and dis-identification of the subject is entirely compatible with a richer appreciation of meter than she provides. I dwell on meter here because it is a critical factor in the musical control of identity. In essays which have been very influential, Schoenberg analyzed the obstacle to the reception of new musical styles as a problem of intelligibility, but I think the problem of identification can be more decisive. At least in music, but I do believe this of poetry as well, meter establishes a *participatory* schema of cyclic movement— bodily movement, large muscle movement—which is expressive, entrancing, sensitizing, and orienting for rhythmic structure and nuance. Of the two Stravinsky examples I cited, the more abstract has a meter only in notation; the more representational is patently metrical. Since the representation in question is a representation of bodily movement, we can adopt a term from visual artists—figural art. A central question of this chapter is what it means that Elliott Carter, who has clearly achieved an ambitious program of figural representation in music, has done this without metrical support.

From the Renaissance through much of the nineteenth century, an ideal of personal identity develops which envisions a specific individual, possessed of a potentially continuous and coherent memory of his or her own experience, confronting a universe which also has a continuous and integrated history. As we approach the twentieth century, this ideal is upset—in science, in art, in philosophy, and in social and political relations. Kristeva schematizes this social and psychic change and its image in art by recourse to the most perennial and productive device of structural semiotics, the concept of articulation, the division or separation that makes one into two but also joins two as one. My corollary will suggest that abstractionism, in revising articulatory structures in music and painting, tends to exchange their typical valence with respect to the engaged subject.

In what we call realist painting, the space in the picture and the space of the viewer are entirely distinct. I do not stand in Vermeer's room or in Constable's meadows when I regard their paintings. I may want to. The painting evokes a desire to share its point of view and encourages us to imagine being there, enjoying the sight. But we don't confuse our space with the picture's space. The space which Rothko or De Kooning creates is, by contrast, part of my own space as a viewer; the painter is now, in effect, using vision to enter my kinesphere, possible in their styles because the system of visual articulatory boundaries has been withdrawn.

In music, the reverse holds. In the music which is historically contemporary with realist painting, the space of musical motion can be fully identified with the listener's personal space of kinesthetic perception and imagery. One part of the difference is a difference between the visible lifeworld and the experienced kinesphere. Vision asserts a background and a foreground, and foreground objects have bounding surfaces. In the visual world my boundary is my skin. There are no such pat boundaries in interior perception: not for kinesthetic images, not for emotions, not for the sense of personal territory.

But another part of the difference is the articulatory structure of the corresponding representations. Realist visual art reproduced the boundary effects of the visual lifeworld. "Realist" music, on the contrary, encourages identification by allowing us to participate: We feel the beat, orient ourselves by the tonic, keep tabs on motives. Lending ourselves thus to music we may hear it sing on our behalf. This effect is highlighted when the orchestra at the opera, echoing or enlarging the phrases of a grieving aria, expresses sympathy for the character on our behalf. But this same phenomenon is pervasive. We are asked to lose our personal boundaries, at least much of the time, when we listen to Schubert's music or to Morton Feldman's. We are usually asked to maintain them when we listen to Stravinsky's or Carter's. I don't think these four cases are very ambivalent, though I could mention others which are. Music which abandons participatory mechanisms (or, in Stravinsky's case, fragments them) may invite us to adopt a greater aesthetic distance, to step back, as it were, to become observers rather than participants.

This thought struck me when I first heard Elliott Carter's *Symphony of Three Orchestras*. The chords at the end were the most terrifying moment of orchestral music of any I could bring to mind since Beethoven, but with a strange difference. In the most turbulent moments of the Ninth Symphony, my sense is that I am swept up in the storm, that something is happening of which I am, myself, a part. (The symphony is discussed in the Postscript to this chapter.) But those mighty crashes in Carter's *Symphony* seem to impinge on me from a safer distance. My pity is aroused, as if for the instruments themselves. Although the four great chords are scored exactly nine seconds apart and surely gain stature and authority by their equidistance, I do not catch a beat. If I did, the violins weeping in the interstices would throw me off it. I do not participate in the meter, though I may notice it. I am moved by the music, but I do not identify with the music.

The century's adventure with abstraction played against a continuing desire to represent the figure. In the 1930s, Picasso returned to the human figure, stylized, schematized, but in no sense obscured. That decade also finds Schoenberg turning down the thermostat after the brief climax of his radically brittle sonorities in Op. 25, and returning to a more humanist style of gesture. Bartók, in a radio interview in that same decade, called for "an inspired simplicity." One can adduce social and political motivations, but there is no reason not to respect a need within artistic thought to recur to spontaneous imaging of the human body as a necessary fount of imagination. The movement is not all on the side of production; reception also changes, and imagination gains new powers. We learn to see and hear organic form where less complete evidence is offered, to interpret fainter suggestions more richly.

A pervasive motive of Carter's performance instructions and of his explications of his work is that instruments or groups of instruments are characters. Carter's music evokes figural effects in a new way. The musical representation of kinesthesia is usually a joint responsibility of composition and performance. We know from computer synthesis that discrepancies of a very few thousandths of a second make a palpable change in the feeling of a metrical beat or the import of a melodic motive. Composition does not normally deal with thousandths of seconds. Beats which are a tenth of a second different in actual performed duration can routinely be treated as nominally equivalent for the relations of composition. Like many of his contemporaries, Carter composes into the temporal space of performance nuance. He writes fairly intricate patterns with notes that are as short as a twentieth of a second, and the time between attacks of notes in different pulse streams can be less than 0.02 seconds (though usually not). Unlike occurrences of similar or even greater levels of notational finesse in Stockhausen, Boulez, Ferneyhough, et al., we cannot possible dismiss these as wishful thinking or polite fictions, for, in Carter's music, the difference is critical to formal schemes of multiple tempos. We might ask, first, whether composition itself is supplying the level of nuance that other styles relegate to performance, and, second, whether the performer still retains responsibility for kinesthetic representation. I can't answer either of these questions, but I would suggest that, in part, the scene of the action has shifted. I believe it is not the play of nuance against meter that evokes expressivity in Carter's music but rather his exploitation of what I would call peripheral hearing.

Both because his melody is often fragmentary and because attention is divided by counterpoint, Carter exploits some effects of peripheral hearing which are like peripheral vision. The images that flit by in the corner of our eye are often subject to extravagant interpretation: a vague blip turns into a mouse running through the grass or maybe a golf ball. Auditory streaming is like that too. Intent on a conversation with one person and oblivious to the background noise, I suddenly whirl around when I hear somebody mention my favorite semiotic theory—it turns out to be a cake recipe, instead.

My impression is that, in Carter's music, interference and competition for attention between simultaneous strands of music amplify our interpretive propensities. When I isolate one line, playing from the score, I find frequently that much of the magical suggestiveness it works in context evaporates. The expressive features are very skeletal; with the floodlights on, the line is abstract, it doesn't maintain its representational force. It is not the same as taking away harmonic support, and I don't know any consistent parallel in music, though there are hints of it in Schoenberg, who is another very fast thinker. Restore the line to the full texture, where it must be heard "in the corner of our ear," and its representational force is restored.

The image of the human figure persists in Carter's abstract sound world represented in a new way but also represented in a new social context. At the time she wrote *Revolution of Poetic Language*, Kristeva believed that the more symptomatic of social and psychic crisis a work of art was, the more important its historic role. This is a challenging perspective, though I reserve full endorsement. It seems to me to tip the market, pushing the Mendelssohn stock down (too heavily invested in civilized voice leading) and pumping the John Field stock up (highly exposed to volatile, high-tech sensuality). But perhaps Kristeva's perspective is one we must maintain as a heuristic.

If the central intellectual crisis of the twentieth century was one of fragmentation, de-centering, and the relativization of its orientations and values, we can ask in her perspective how music has both represented and responded to this crisis. There is music which cannot be said to take it into account at all. There is music which embraces and celebrates chaos. There is music which creates a space of communal order by abandoning memory in favor of a continuous present. (Philip Glass has described his own music in exactly those terms, and please remember that without memory there can be no distinctness of persons.) There is music which reconstructs focus and order on a purely sensuous and/or technical basis, excluding any constructed role for interpretive imagining. I do not disparage any of these lines of work; they have all given us some beauty. The attitude of Carter's music is to encompass fragmentation and chaos within orderly and very abstractly defined processive forms.

There should be no mistaking his encounter with psychic fragmentation. The simplest cross-rhythm, let alone multiple tempos, initiates a split in personality. I say to my own hands, "You play in five. You play in seven. We'll meet at the bar around the corner."

Carter acknowledges this, for according to his own explications of his technique, which are accurate and pertinent, he presents a scene of movement that corresponds to a group, sometimes a multitude of individual actions or actors, or, as he has said on at least one occasion, regarding *Night Fantasies,* to the actual disarray of our own thoughts. From the standpoint of dream analysis the two cases are the same. The crowd of individuals is a projection of our divided consciousness. I find it very telling that Carter has characterized his music as cinematic because the difference I have just described between two listening experiences appears to obtain between theater and cinema as well. The space of the stage continues into the space of the audience. The space of the screen does not.[3] But the cinema is certainly a domain of figures. Carter has never abandoned figural representation:

> The combinations of rhythm . . . arise from the fact that I do not want to give the impression of a simultaneous motion in which everybody's part is coordinated like a goose step. . . . I want it to seem like a crowd of people or like waves on the sea. (Stone and Stone 1977, p. 36)

> I think my music is very much like the kind of thing you see in the moving pictures, in which the camera will show you a big scene, and then focus on one part of it, and then move over and show you something else. (Ibid., p. 43)

The notion of a crowd of individuals and the problem of the artist's identification with such a crowd may be a particular theme of American art, one we recognize, for example, from the poetry of Walt Whitman. The social crisis and *le sujet en procès* are manifest in Carter's music, but perhaps with less of the sense of turbulence and despair Kristeva associates with that theme. When Carter set the poetry of his friend Robert Lowell, a poet of continuous crisis, he provided appropriate images of disturbance, and we can see his capacity to do so elsewhere, but this

---

3. My comparison of cinematic and theatrical space draws on conversations with my colleague Evan Cameron.

vein of imagery doesn't dominate. Perhaps, as in the poetry of Robert Frost, some of the turbulence is covert. Some of my reaction to Carter's music and my involvement with it reflects the fact that I was born in the United States but have spent thirty-five years becoming a foreigner. His stylistic solution seems to me very much a Yankee solution. Adducing a Kristevan perspective on this very confident and sometimes ebullient style of music sounds a discord which I would not choose at present either to prolong further or to resolve. When the time comes that Carter's music is studied as much to understand its personality as it is now analyzed in pursuit of its technical methods, then I think such outside angles will have something to tell us about its construction of national character: about the problems it recognizes, the problems it solves, and the problems it tends to hide.

Postscript

The "disaster" in Beethoven's Ninth Symphony to which I compared Carter's work is, as I think you probably know, the beginning of the recapitulation of the first movement, referred to in another context in Chapter 8. In the present chapter, which recalls this musical moment and also evokes Kristeva's development of the problematics of subject identity, it is a pleasure to recognize my indebtedness to the well-known commentary on Beethoven's Ninth Symphony in Susan McClary's *Feminine Endings*, the book that may have done more to reinvigorate discourse on musical interpretation than any other original work of English-language musicology to appear during my career. Although her commentary is brief, it is dense and careful, drawing together threads developed throughout the essays collected in her book. It is difficult, therefore, to summarize it fairly. She argues that European professional music after the Renaissance tends to be predominantly involved in modeling and exploiting libidinal appetites, and that it develops archetypal forms and images of libidinal narrative structure which enact men's problem of maintaining masculinity (McClary 1991, pp. 124–25). She considers the alignment of tonal tensions with the arousal and satisfaction of desire, perhaps not separating sufficiently the roles of tonality and representations of gesture. The case she builds serves as an exegesis of Adrienne Rich's poem "The Ninth Symphony of Beethoven Understood at Last as a Sexual Message," which attributes to the symphony the rage of sexual impotence. McClary writes, "The problem Beethoven has constructed for this movement is that it seems to begin before the subject of the symphony has managed to achieve its identity: we witness the emergence of the initial theme and its key out of a womblike void," and later, of the recapitulation:

> The desire for cadential arrival that has built up over the course of the development finally erupts, as the subject necessarily (because of narrative tradition) finds itself in the throes of the initial void while refusing to relent: the entire first key area in the recapitulation is pockmarked with explosions. It is the consequent juxtaposition of desire and unspeakable violence in this moment that creates its unparalleled fusion of murderous rage and yet a kind of pleasure in its fulfillment of formal demands. (p. 128)

And she finds in the anger of this passage the motor of the remainder of the work.

This reading develops in a book about gender and sexuality in music, and it would be beside the point to criticize the reading on the basis that the author has not undertaken comparisons among alternate possible interpretations. Within the orientation assumed it is astute. If we are to undertake such comparisons in response to it, we must consider how her mode of analysis interacts with them, and not simply bypass her perspective. I suggest that her account may be arbitrary to the extent that it relies on two schema that are excessively rigid. One is a notion of narrative movement in sonata form that, despite various qualifications, remains too pat, and the other, a baldly technical conception of "desire"—hardly a mistake original with her—that serves the arts badly.

Approaching this latter from the side of the signifier, I would hold that the natural way to describe the desire evoked by tonality would not take the final tonic as the object but rather the specific melodic movement, the voice leading which achieves the tonic. The final chord itself is an index of what we already achieved. It is where we live happily ever after. If we recognize this distinction, we can understand that half a dozen subdominants pointing toward the same tonic construct half a dozen different objects of desire when we add their own colors to the voice leading they induce us to project.

The nineteenth century inherited and developed constructions of many different desires, and I insist on the plural—desires, not desire: the desire of the hungry to be fed, the desire of the tyrannized to be liberated, the desire of the sick for health or for death, the desire for justice, the desire for knowledge. With the exception of death, all these objects of desire, when taken in the abstract, tend to be personified as feminine, and all these desires attract libidinal energy, especially on the part of those who are not actually too hungry, too tyrannized, or too sick to participate in that energy. Yet libido may enter as a surplus and not take the role of prime mover. For all that sex in car advertising may influence brand selection or frequency of replacement, I would not be ready to concede the place of needing a way to get to work as a major reason for buying cars. It is a non sequitur to jump from a recognition of libidinal forms as pervasive to the conclusion that, wherever we see them, libidinal desire is the dominating source of meaning and energy. It is often observed that a man who fails to provide his family with food, authority, or justice (for example, when required, revenge) feels his failure as an insult to his masculinity. The insult makes a good story, but this insult is the insult added to the man's injury, not his primary problem. (Even Freud, who invented a reductive conception of desire, came to acknowledge a death wish as the consequence of egoistic drives that were not subsumed in the libido, and contemporary physiology, more modular than the one he drew on, leaves us without his scientific excuse for amalgamating all our drives.)

While McClary speaks of Beethoven as exercising a critique (p. 129), a question that remains to be developed is whether and how and how much composers who work with forms that appear to be derived from constructions of libidinal desire may have directed them to other purposes. If we are to hear Beethoven's first movement as referencing desire, we must not prejudge, without attention to its specific weights and rhythms, what specific sorts of desires might be at play. Of course, any particular performance will tell us more of this than the score does, but perhaps there is a hint in the diatonicism of the development's episodes in major that the solace envisioned is not primarily sexual.

Regarding sonata form, we must always bear in mind that in its fundamentals, the repeatable exposition and recapitulation, it is no friend of narrative. When a composer adduces narrative motivation to such a form, various options are available, though if he or she is loyal to the form, these will be at some level merely ornamental. The impossibility of a full accommodation between narrative and sonata is a guarantee of flexibility because there is no one solution that yields a full fit. Beethoven is a master of the narrativization of sonata, but he takes an exceptional course here in his Ninth Symphony. Most typically, the classical first subject is a tonality-creating theme. Here the process of tonal grounding begins first, before the theme takes shape. The theme does not emerge from a void—a true void is entirely empty—but from the interstellar matter of a stable fifth. (McClary's phrase "the throes of the void" doesn't make sense.) I suggest that we can hear a second agency here, the vaguer agency of the subject's environment along with the agency of the subject. The melodic material of this movement remains for the most part highly fragmented, often expressed in motives that seem to fall below the horizon of definite gesture. The flow of harmony sometimes takes on a life of its own, as in a prelude or etude, a giant continuo to which the melody must accommodate. The narrative consequence is that Beethoven is able to develop a tension between tonality and subject. The subject does not seem to fully control its tonal environment, hence our feeling that the subject is subject to a fate. When McClary speaks of "narrative obligation" as determining the onset of the recapitulation, she seems to mean a need external to the story, motivated by social and historical convention. But I think Beethoven has newly reimagined this need as a force *within* the story. (While Beethoven had been working with the technique of foregrounding the harmonic flow at least since the D-minor piano sonata, Opus 31, no. 3, I can't think of any exact precedent, but McClary's analysis of Monteverdi's *Orfeo* suggests a comparison: when he orates, he directs the tonal flow, and when he is insane, it overcomes him [p. 46].)

The independence of this second agent is declared where its rhythm and direction do not take their cue from thematic unfolding. I think Beethoven cuts the development a bit short of any natural, organic peak. We are just beginning to enjoy F major (m. 283) when an emergency telegraph from the dominant summons us home (a scant six measures, 295–300). It was harmonically foreshadowed, but not thematically or gesturally motivated. What we really desired was an authentic cadence in F, even the briefest. The debt is owing from the exposition, which afforded us only the submediant, not the relative major. Sonata form would have allowed the pause. Thematic identity would not have felt threatened by the request. Schubert would have let us do it. In fact, the notion of a final goal in tonality has been overplayed. Tonality is like a voyage: where you go may be more important than coming home, which is sometimes merely an unproblematic necessity. But this particular D-minor tonality of Beethoven's is implacable and will not let us touch down.

We have no resolution here. The tonality sweeping us home is an intervening doom, not a culmination of desire. The subject is dragged back to its key, furious and, yes, impotent above the wrong bass note, F♯, the yawning chasm of the subdominant narrowly avoided. But is this the fury of the aggressor or the victim? The sexual narrative proposed does not seem to have a slot for what the subject is up against, for this second agent—the tonal environment with a will of its own. The archetype of quests with enemies (dragons, sorcerers, and so on) will come to mind. Usually there is also a maiden to be won, but sometimes she seems like an afterthought. (In Schiller's little ballad *Der Handschuh,* she is rejected in the end for causing too much trouble.)

The best word I know for the kind of anger I hear in this movement is "dismay." Historically, that word carries a connotation of impotence, but not the sexual impotence that Rich's poem ascribes to the symphony. The decade of this symphony was one in which the secret police of Vienna were unleashed in a crackdown on revolutionaries, exceeding, so far, even our new homeland security. I hear a dismay most conventionally identified with the recognition of fate, but for me, personally, it is very akin to my own dismay and impotence before those persons who would make an imperium of the democracy that I had thought my birthright. I am not sure what McClary means in contending that this anger is the motor of the whole work. In this energetic symphony I also hear sheer gusto, stoic humor, mirth, and even energetic joy. But apart from these possibilities (and apart from the fact that we impose a higher pitch on our poor sopranos than was intended), why would Beethoven's hymn not exhibit an excessive vehemence if "joy" had become a code word for liberties repressed by his state?

If I was correct in Chapter 1 to claim that instrumental music is inherently biased by a solipsism, first-person singular or plural, that blocks the specification of the *other,* then we cannot say that the contest in this movement is not sexual or not political or not against the ravages of time and illness. The story of its sexual message needed to be told, needed courage to tell, and must not be dismissed.

Of course, Rich wrote of "finally understanding" that message in the symphony, not of a final understanding, or *the* final understanding, which will inevitably elude prose or poetry. Do we overburden the music in elaborating such complex interpretations? I am fully convinced Beethoven was responsive to his physical and social world and knew all these ideas but less in words than as relations of tone color, movement, mass, and gesture. I must note, as it approaches my own topic, that when Beethoven reduces the figural specificity of thematic shapes to involve us more fully with images of force, color, and mass, another process of *abstraction* is entailed, leading here to the language of musical idealism. The orchestra is its most natural medium, but we find it elsewhere in his late work and in the work of those he influenced. This sense of abstraction (an enormously complicated idea) exceeds the focus of this chapter and would need a book I don't know how to write for its explication, but the development of abstractions which discard detail to articulate general ideas is not confined to language.

For a highly illuminating historical critique of the myth of Beethoven's "chauvinism," national and masculine, presented as a very old story that was never well grounded, see Riethmüller (2001).

Part Five: *Resisting Representation*

Walter Zimmermann, a composer presently working in Berlin, transforms philosophical conceptions into music via an inexplicable alchemy. The transformations are unpredictable and sometimes as astounding as the magic by which Schubert draws melodies from poems. In his music we hear sounding forms as idea and ideas as sounding form, and yet, you must never "accuse" Zimmermann of composing program music. I have seen that it makes him anxious. He is not alone. No composer who acknowledges the heritage of Western European art music can be immune from the prestige of absolute music or deaf to its real achievements. Our art is infinitely capable of representation, but to its glory, it resists.

Figure V.1 is a schematic score of the opening of Zimmermann's *Randonnée No. 1, Northwest Passage,* corresponding to the first forty seconds of a ten-minute piece. The group who commissioned the work, Toronto's Arraymusic Ensemble, have recently completed a stunning recording of it, still awaiting distribution but available at their web site.[1] Zimmermann's score, for practical reasons, is notated in six-eight measures and with transposing instrument parts in their own keys. To display one aspect of its structure in the simplest manner, I have redrawn it ametrically with *Mensurstrichen,* without showing the rests, and I have omitted the cymbals. The visual alignment of the parts in my version is slightly compromised. The texture illustrated, except for the heightened activity of the double bass at the start, is a fair sample of a sonic format that continues throughout the work. Most of the time we hear only groups of repeating notes at one pitch. The groups overlap and differ in the speeds and numbers of repetitions. The texture is audacious in the simplicity of its premises, challenging in the complexity of its resultants.

The two-part title would seem to allude to incompatible directions of this composition. *Randonnée* (hike or excursion) fits the arbitrary, autonomous technique, where Zimmermann overlays the map of Canada with a derivative of his "magic square" of pitches, a cycle of fifths taking one edge of the square as fundamental tones and their twelve lowest partials filling the perpen-

---

1. The recording is planned to be released with the title *Array Live* on the Artifact label.

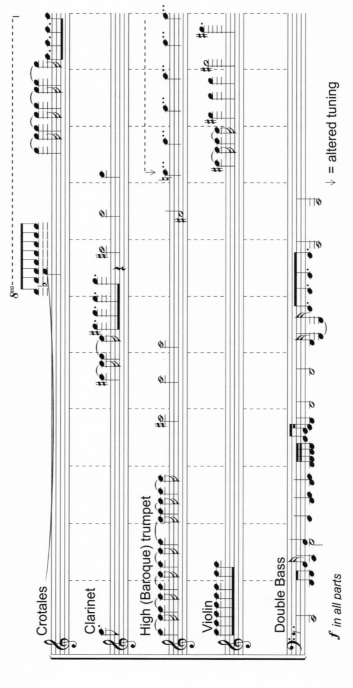

Figure V.1. Zimmermann, *Randonnée No. 1, Northwest Passage*, mm. 1–11, schematic score (cymbals omitted).

diculars. The slow march of tones across the square follows the route on the map of the ill-fated seamen who attempted for three years to navigate a northwest passage only to perish, trapped in ice floes, ending a voyage which Zimmermann asks us to contemplate as a tragic quest for knowledge. An arbitrary square and an arbitrary procedure thus interpret a factual map and historical narrative. How can they have any mutual relation that matters to the ear?

In truth, it is not difficult to account for representational elements of *Northwest Passage,* in part depending on somatic images and in part on *dangerously* literal figures. Recurrent washes of cymbal rolls immerse the boat in an icy storm. The timbre of high trumpet, with the violin and clarinet also in extreme registers, the double bass and metallic percussion is freezing cold. The boat, nearly blocked, slowly lurching, slowly turning, is immediately present as a mode of movement felt in the slow and abstruse cross-rhythms of the bleating, repeated tones. There is a charmed and elevated innocence in the conception of an extended music where, as if children dreaming a fairy tale, we feel throughout that we are moving in the manner that a huge ship moves (not its wobbling passengers but the ship itself, as when while parallel parking my body becomes a car). But the demise of the boat in a gradual, very prolonged diminuendo is tragic and entirely adult.

What are we to make of the literal citations—the wood rods that the percussionists snap as the ship breaks apart or the ship's bell that sounds in the second half? These intrusions from another world are at once so poignant and sound so perfectly fitted to the music that one would expect to find a strictly musical logic in them. I cannot! A paradox is evoked that we are more familiar with in the visual arts, as when a painter glues a bit of newspaper to the canvas. The scrap may or may not represent newspapers in general, but either way it is not a *likeness* of newspaper. The sample of newspaper would be capable of referring to newspaper in general, or news in general, or scraps in general—samples are the most ambiguous of all signs—but the new context of the sample, the surrounding colors and textures with which it joins in new relations, may overwhelm its referential potential. Quite likely the painter so intends. Whatever the discourse, the painter's pride will be the kaleidoscope of sensuous distractions. Representation is resisted. Although the sounds cited are literal, they, too, resist representation.

The force of the narrative image constructed in *Northwest Passage* is inseparable from the representationally irrelevant fascination of its nearly meaningless sensory and logical relations, the subtleties of speed and grouping changes in the slow progress of the twisting chords that change one voice at a time, and the strange aberrations of displaced Pythagorean relations in the intervals of its trichords. Perhaps I should feel no special affinity for Zimmermann's style. It conveys an appreciation of purity and mysticism I would not normally share. He takes risks with monotony that irritate me, even when the reward is as enthralling and surprising as in his *Patience and Opportunity* (*Geduld & Gelegenheit*) for piano and cello with curved bow, where we wait a year, it seems, for one B♭ with miniscule variations of timbre to turn into a garden of harmonies. Yet the discomforts disappear in the radiance of his endlessly inventive sound world that nourishes and is nourished by a novel and energetic contest between structure and reference.

Neither the style nor the tone of the composition analyzed in the next chapter claims affinity with Zimmermann, whose compositional achievements are worlds above my own. Comparison is not the point. I very much want to end this collection of essays which center on representation in music with a reflection on its contraries and to reaffirm, via my personal witness of the countercurrents as a composer, that musical semiotics must be as alert to the loss of meaning as to its construction. The particular that I want to emphasize is the role of a fascination with musical logic, with the *sensory* logic of music as a determining factor both in the meaning of music and in its loss of representation. Representation yields to play, a turn that belongs to semiotics and provides the theme of Danuta Mirka's *The Game of Music*. For the professional musician with access to a score—be he or she the composer, the performer, or the critic—this fascination can be explicitly accounted. For other auditors it may be entirely intuitive. I insist that explicit and intuitive apperceptions can be aesthetically equivalent. My position in listening to *Northwest Passage* is not very much privileged by my access to a score. Yet, even if the auditory experiences have some equivalence for all who share the music, the composer's reconstruction (ultimately untrustworthy as any personal memory must be) might still be distinctive as a mode of explanation. I indulge my own fascination with syntax here as an exhibit pertinent to the brief.

15 Replaying My *Voice Mail*

I am a composer who was slightly diverted from composing for a number of years by a theoretical project. For most of the years when I studied problems in semiotics and, eventually, wrote and published my *Elements of Semiotics* (1999), I thought of my semiotics and my own composing as unconnected with each other except by their competition for time. *Elements*, after all, is not even a book about *musical* semiotics. It concerns *general* semiotics. *Voice Mail*, a suite, twenty-five to thirty minutes long, of thirteen short pieces for solo piano, is among the first compositions I wrote after *Elements* was published, and it was the first of my own compositions on which I brought semiotic contemplation to bear. If the music offers witness to any semiotic doctrine, it might be simply this: A musician needs no consistent or constant stance toward representation. A composer might write program music on Monday, "absolute" music on Tuesday, expressive music on Wednesday, and abstract music on Thursday, and there is no reason why the same variability should not occur *within* one composition. It seems to me now that semiotic inconsistency, rather than merely a symptom of aesthetic theory, is and must be a symptom of the fine arts themselves. The karma of the fine arts is to continually renegotiate the fascination of perception itself and the subordination of perception to communication or practical use.

One of the objects of the present essay is to demonstrate this symptomology in a particular case. I think of *Voice Mail* as "pretend" program music, as asserting textural, topical, and stylistic affiliation with suites of musical pieces focused on images and characters (less so stories). But *Voice Mail* unfolds a design which, in the end, resists its programmatic gambits. If it means something, it means something that the thirteen titles don't add up to. Like much other music—sometimes, I even think, like all music that is meant as foreground music, not background music—*Voice Mail* moves from image to abstraction. I tell my story as an instance of this general case.

The two objects of representation I will be most concerned to discuss in this essay are representations of tonality and representations of topics. I will describe syntactic relations and semantic elements of the composition in leisurely detail, especially the syntax, reserving my argument about their integration for a final section which also discusses performance.

Music hosts a three-way competition among the material attractions of sound, the fascinations of structural elaboration, and engagement in reference, or, we

An earlier version of this essay appeared in *Ex Tempore* in 2001 as "Resisting Temptation" (*Ex Tempore* X, no. 2: 16–38). The publisher of *Voice Mail* is Patchwork Publishing, Toronto.

might say, among sensation, syntax, and semantics. If we are careful, we must keep it in mind that the distinction between syntax and semantics can be problematic. Chomsky demonstrated in *Aspects of Syntax* (1965, pp. 148–63) that choosing to describe a linguistic regularity as syntactic or semantic may be arbitrary. In computer science the distinction can be formulated relative to a *level of interpretation;* in *Elements* I treat it as relative to the delineation of a *text* and/or the presumption of an abstract *grammar.* Although a "commonsense" or rough-and-ready understanding should be good enough here, it is important that the domains have interchanges.

Usually we think of tonality as a syntactic aspect of music, and the representations it requires are syntactic representations (for example, when a chord of the sixth degree or an inversion represents a tonic function). *Voice Mail* extensively represents tonality, but tonality does not provide very much of its syntax. Tonality is represented as a semantic content, as a topic. The difference is not pure. Tonality is not dialectal in *Voice Mail,* but tonal elements, oblivious of any tonal rules, do participate in idiolectal patterning.

15.1. Sound Structure

Thematic Forms

In its competition for attention (with reference and sensation) structure weighs in with a heavy display of thematic forms. They were one of my chief delights in composing *Voice Mail,* and I hope they add to the entertainment of listening to it. With the exception of numbers I, XII, and XIII, each piece broadcasts a distinct pattern, and the exceptions, as exceptions, contribute to the same sport:

I.   Freely unfolding melody with (quasi-Alberti) accompaniment
II.   Developing variation on a motive with climax and then a suggestion of reprise
III. AA′ with a quick turnaround in between
IV.   Theme and free transformations (melodic contours preserved)
V.   A rigid two-part invention
VI.   Theme with four strict variations
VII. Song–Development–Song (short-long-short); the development progresses in rhythm, not in harmony
VIII. AA′A″ or three verses; unlike III, where the model and its repetition differ only in a few selected details, the repetitions here are systematic "modal transpositions," as explained below
IX.   ABCB′: B′ repeats the rhythm of B on a static chord
X.   Fugue by augmentation (ABA′)
XI.   Imitation chorale prelude
XII. A parody of a well-known piece, loyal measure for measure
XIII. Potpourri of motives from previous numbers in free fantasia style.

These forms are aurally straightforward and blatantly different. Strangely, I can't bring to mind much repertoire in which the contrast of *forms* (not contrast of *genre* or contrast of *style*) is the main engine of a little suite. There is a big element of this in *Agon,* as part of much else. Berg amused himself and musicologists with a play of Neoclassical forms in opera, but surely it is secondary to the drama. Here it is in the center ring.

Harmonic Design

Charles Wuourinen refers admiringly to evocation of tonal idioms in Stravinsky's late style as "punning."[1] In *Voice Mail,* tonal idioms are too prevalent and sometimes too systematic to call puns, but the elements of tonality induced provide more color and imagery than logic. Features which evoke or *refer to* tonality include sonority types (triads, sevenths, etc.), voice-leading relationships, imitations of harmonic progressions, and, although with a very haphazard distribution, some dissonance resolutions.

Tonal grammar has an aural authority which is not annulled by simple fiat. *Voice Mail* is able to absorb extensive tonal reference only because its vocabulary is severely limited. Economy of vocabulary, if sufficient, can match tonality in its force of appeal to an intuitive sense of order. This is a simple principle and not a new one. A development passage limited in its motivic vocabulary to one cell and its variants can leap any harmonic distance in a single bound, and we follow happily. In Debussy's style repetition often serves to delimit a vocabulary so clearly that it becomes independent of its conventional harmonic interpretation. In both of those cases, vocabulary limitation enables music to escape tonal constraints or tonal interpretations. In *Voice Mail,* this common principle serves in the absence of any a priori tonal framework. The limitation is harmonic but not tonal. *Voice Mail* is made out of thirteen unordered pitch-class (pc) sets that are (with one exception) never transposed or inverted or otherwise altered. The pc set organization is perceptually salient—unusually so, I believe. Much of the time these sets, twelve pentads and one trichord, are either heard one at a time or kept separate from each other by rhythm and/or register. More often than not they occur complete. The identity and perseverance of the pc sets is sometimes enhanced by motivic relations and registral limitations. Tonal elements in *Voice Mail* may offer the comfort of familiarity, but those elements only rarely add up as complete structures. The pc sets are ultimately more prominent and establish a sense of order which becomes firmer and firmer as the music unfolds.

I feel half a *poseur* adapting this jargon, "pc" sets. Given the simplicity of the method and the results, would it not be plainer and truer to say "modes"? Perhaps it is worth looking at the connotations of these terms. "Mode" should imply that the pitch collections have a tonic. Possibly the case here and there, but not consistently. On the other side, to speak of "pc sets" suggests much by association that is not legally implied: a stylistic tendency that makes living a long time in a

---

1. Lecture at the Toronto Royal Conservatory of Music, April 2001.

small, recurring collection of pitch classes more the exception than the rule, a stylistic tendency that maintains a wary eye on octave duplication and registral com-
pactness, a possible bad conscience if closure of the full chromatic aggregate is
neglected—in other words, a stylistic tendency that doesn't deploy "pc" sets the way
we typically deploy scales and modes. But, of course, these are only informal associations. *Voice Mail* is not unique as a context where they do not apply.

The sound world of *Voice Mail* is highly chromatic but not homogeneously so.
Its harmonic world does not suggest symmetry. The design which distributes the
pc sets in *Voice Mail* (and which also contributes to their construction, but with
considerable dilution) is a *Fano Lattice* or *Fano Geometry*. Before getting to par-
ticularities of its realization in *Voice Mail*, I will describe the Fano lattice. To sim-
plify the demonstration, I describe this lattice as a finite geometry and *as if* it were
simply a design for constructing pc sets. Please note that as I mentioned, in *Voice
Mail*, the more important application is actually the *distribution* of pc sets, not their
construction.

The Fano Lattice

The world may not need to hear yet another design for pc sets, but I confess,
having toyed with this occasionally for over twenty years, that I want to tell about
it. The Fano lattice can be defined as a geometry, a collection of points and lines.
For the moment, think of the points as pc's, and think of the lines as unordered
sets. The design encompasses $n^2 + n + 1$ points, that is 3, 7, 13, . . . points for $n =$
1, 2, 3, . . . The cases of seven and thirteen elements are all we need. A reasonable
projection of the seven-element geometry can be drawn in two dimensions, as in
Figure 15.1, but the geometry is not really two-dimensional. The lines *appear* to
cross at several points on paper only because the picture flattens them onto its surface. One line would be in front, one behind. For this diagram we must adopt the
understanding that lines do not intersect except at the dots as well as that straight-
line segments are equivalent to circles. Each line segment or circle corresponds to
a set of three points (dots). Every dot lies on three lines.

In abstracto, this design is richly symmetrical, but symmetry is not a danger in
its musical application to constructing pc sets. The design for seven has application
to any seven-note scale, but within twelve-tone equal temperament, no seven-pc
scale is symmetrical. As I realize it with twelve pitch classes, the design for thirteen
comes out with a hole or a joker. No great danger of symmetry there, either. In
Figure 15.2 I show three distributions of the diatonic collection that correspond
with the seven-element design. Apart from their diatonic transpositions, these and
their three inversions are the only distinct designs of pc classes that realize this
geometry within that scale.[2] The first of these is entirely trivial (in the case of a

---

2. I first learned about this design in an introductory course in finite mathematics which I had the
pleasure to attend ca. 1978 with Morton Abramson. I wrote a paper for the course which enumerated
the distinct ways of labeling the vertices of a seven-point Fano geometry with the pc's of one diatonic
scale. Sometime after that I permanently loaned the paper to a student.

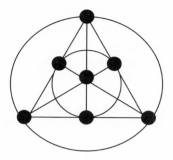

Figure 15.1. Seventeen-point Fano geometry projected on two dimensions.

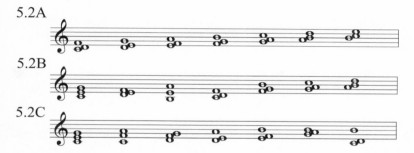

Figure 15.2. Collections of pc sets in diatonic collection determined by Fano geometry.

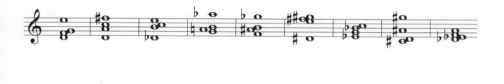

Figure 15.3. Pc set collection from thirteen-point geometry (Sonata for Violin and Piano).

diatonic collection), and the second is at least partly trivial.[3] The third may seem trivial to some readers, but I am fond of it.

The notes which follow are written as if we had thirteen distinct pc's to work with—I don't; some people do!

   a. Each pc of seven belongs to *three* sets (or with thirteen pc's, *four* sets).
   b. Each set out of seven includes *three* pc's (or with thirteen, *four* pc's).

---

3. The all-interval tetrachords provide similarly trivial realizations in a thirteen-note scale.

c. Any two sets have exactly one pc in common.

d. Every interval (not interval class) occurs just once.[4]

e. For the seven-design, the *complements* of any two sets have *two* pc's in common (for the thirteen-design, *five*).

f. Every set has *two* pc's in common with each of the complements of the other sets (for thirteen, *three*).

g. For the thirteen-design, the intersection of any two set complements is a subset of the union of the other two sets that share their one common pc (trivial with seven, a compositional resource with thirteen).

h. A full lattice is uniquely determined when each element has been inserted in one position.

i. The homogeneous distribution of common tones determines that the union of any two sets in the seven-design is a five-pc set, but the cardinality of a union of three sets is either six or seven, depending on whether the three share one common tone or not. Parallel, messier relations obtain for thirteen.

My twelve-note application of the thirteen-note design, simply leaving a hole, provides nine mutually overlapping tetrads that also overlap four mutually disjoint trichords. (Associating the four three-pc sets with an ordered row does *not* provide a simple key to ordering the thirteen sets. Proof withheld.)

Figure 15.3 shows the pc set system of another composition of mine, *Remembering Major Dreaming of Minor,* a sonata for violin and piano. In this system the pc's are arranged strictly to correspond to the Fano geometry with one "point" unassigned—hence the four trichords.

Figure 15.4 shows the *distribution* of pc sets among the thirteen numbers of *Voice Mail.* One point in the geometry of thirteen corresponds to one set, not one pc. This distribution also corresponds strictly to a Fano geometry. There are four sets in each piece. Any two pieces have one set in common.

The design is compositionally and perceptually consequential. One consequence is that each piece has the potential to recall harmonic or melodic characteristics of any of the previous ones; the thirteenth number, though composed of four sets like the others, quotes motives from all the preceding pieces "at pitch." The recurrences of sets across the suite may or may not strike the attention of the listener—who knows what someone will notice!—but they are palpable enough to be strongly determinative of an overall harmonic character. There is a kind of resonance in memory that builds up from the long-range repetitions of the never transposed sets, and at least a sense of logic—if not closure—that emerges as less and less that is entirely new (harmonically) occurs. The harmony of the thirteen pieces surely sounds more rational than the harmony of any one or two of them; yet the limitation of vocabulary in each single piece contributes to its own unity and identity, just as a rather uniform density of the harmonic vocabulary unifies pieces across

---

4. I don't think I perceive closure in the full exposition of the lattice as an acoustic event, but formally the presentation of the full set of pc (or other element) *pairs* here is analogous to a presentation of the full aggregate in a tone row.

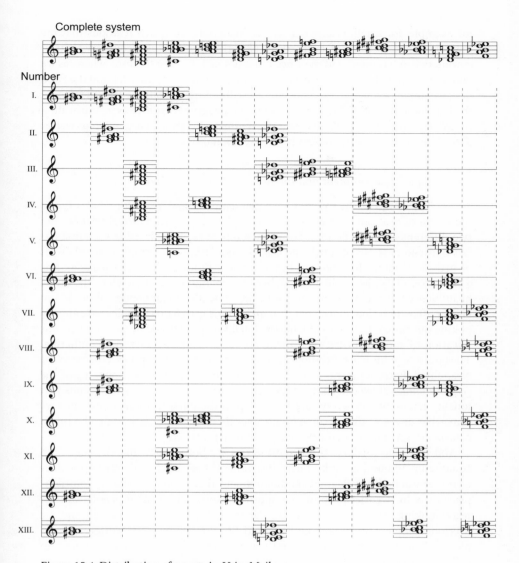

Figure 15.4. Distribution of pc sets in *Voice Mail*.

the suite. In the composing out, recurrences of sets in different numbers are some-times linked motivically. I don't think the fact that, by the end, every possible pair of two sets has occurred in just one piece is audibly salient, but this is a property of the syntax that ensures fresh harmonic combinations in each number. (As I or-der the pieces, the thirteenth set to appear enters in the seventh piece. But no mat-ter how the pieces might be reordered, the tenth piece would be the last one that might possibly introduce a new set.)

My fetishization of the Fano geometry responds to a number of personal tastes, for example, for small, unordered sets as "materials," for pitch relations that my memory can keep track of fairly easily. Non-transposition as a counterweight to chromaticism has interested me since I first noticed it in Liszt's *Tasso,* where, as we noted in Chapter 4, one of the principal themes is never transposed. I find the Fano design complex enough to hold my interest without transpositions or with few, and the harmonic vocabulary it provides is quite manageable for memory. Above all, it is favorable to materials which defeat the symmetry of the equal-tempered twelve-note scale in a chromatic context by recalling tonality.

Equal Temperament and the Representation of Tonality

The sound of the twelve-tone equal temperament heard for what it is and the sound of that same system when it is deployed *to represent* tonal relations are two different sounds. The sound of equal temperament displayed as such first enters music in passages of quick and casual modulation like complete, rapid cycles of fifths in Chopin (for example, in the E-major Etude or the A-flat Ballade). It is a pretty sound. We hear it in all of Webern's serial music and in much of the music he influenced. It goes hand in hand with the principle of complementation. When Haydn offers us a slow movement in E major for a quartet in E-flat, we are already poking our nose into that world, for the tonalities, placed side by side with no implication of movement between them, are truly supplementary, not conflicting. The opposite holds when Beethoven, in adjacent phrases, transposes a theme to the Neapolitan. Equal temperament takes some of the sting out of the opening of the *Appassionata,* but we can compensate because we know the acoustic tensions that tonality represents. When we are caught up in the tonal relations *represented* we somewhat discount the tiresome homogeneities of the chromatic scale, the rough consonances, compromised dissonances, and symmetries.

And make no mistake, those symmetries are both pretty and tiresome. Full equal-tempered tuning for keyboard instruments took hold gradually in the nineteenth century. When flagrant modulation and then atonality became commonplace early in twentieth-century composition, some sharp-eared people were already looking for a way out—Partch, Harrison, the quarter-tone people, and the overtone people. Others seek an exit (and I'm not convinced it works) in complexity. The way out that I like best was also the way in, via *representation.* In college, in theory class we used to sing:

This   is   real-ly not D min - or,   it is a tone row.

Figure 15.5. Schoenberg, Op. 37.

And, really, it isn't D minor, but the surface invocation of D minor is vitally important in offsetting the tendency of the chromatic scale toward excessive symmetry.

Tonal References in Voice Mail

My recurrent engagements with the Fano design have been motivated in part by its facility in paraphrasing tonal effects, but *Voice Mail,* deploying pentads instead of tetrachords, greatly exaggerates the effect. How the pentads were individually constructed is almost peripheral. I did start with a Fano lattice analogous to Figure 15.2, but enriched it with notes added by arbitrary procedures. It may seem silly to have announced all this theory and then to report a cooked collection, but the distribution of the sets is my excuse for the theory, not their construction. Yet even the cooked sets retain the feature that any two have a common tone (now *at least* one common tone, not *exactly* one common tone). And the cooked system still represents all pc intervals at least once, though not exactly once. There are eight |A|'s, not surprising if it sometimes sounds like a tonic, and five each of the other pc's. (I use the bars to indicate the class, not a pitch.) In Figure 15.4 the sets are listed in the order of their first appearance. Some pieces introduce one pitch (generally isolated) that is not included in any of their four sets. These exceptions take nothing from the audibility of the system, and I doubt that much more extensive exceptions would need to. My brief for the system is not a defense of purity. Beyond a certain point, the purity of any musical procedure is only a labor-saving device or a private amusement.

An anomaly of the particular system of sets in this composition is that one pentad type, the pentatonic scale, appears twice. Two of the sets, sets 10 and 11 in Figure 15.4, are pentatonic scales (B-pentatonic and A♭-pentatonic). It is also this one pentad that is once further transposed, to E-pentatonic, in Number 12.

Besides the two pentatonic pentads, three other sets lie wholly within diatonic scales. The fifth, suggesting A minor, the twelfth, suggesting B-flat major, and the sixth, suggesting G major, do also, as does the first, the trichord. The second suggests E minor, and the eleventh can be accommodated in B-flat minor. The five others are near misses, with at least one subset of four pc's compatible with a major or minor scale. This aspect of the system is haphazard. Allusions to scales in the various sets rarely cooperate. The sets, individually, are deployed registrally and rhythmically in ways that make other harmonic allusions than those mentioned. Where sets or parts of sets overlap, still other harmonic associations are evoked. This said, what I would emphasize is that the tonally suggestive content of the sets is not repressed as it might be, for example, in a style that discouraged proximate octave duplication. The two numbers which come closest to observing a closed tonal syntax are Number 8, which I describe in some detail later on, and Number 12, which is a special case because built in parody technique. One can readily hear Number 8 as "in" a blotchy G-sharp minor and the following piece as a vagabond A-flat major. Number 12 really has a tonic (or good imitation) with a functional IV and a "dominant prep" on the lowered sixth. Most other keys are local color patches, though sometimes persistent.

Note that the requirements of the set distribution dictate in this case that seven of the thirteen numbers will deploy a pentatonic scale, three with A♭, three with B, plus one with both. The one with both is Number 4. At its beginning,

Figure 15.6. Incipits of principal fugal entrances in *Voice Mail,* No. 10, "Per Augmentationem."

Number 4 quotes a traditional pentatonic tune in its entirety with a pentatonic accompaniment—a passage of some extent that is entirely diatonic. In Number 10 extended passages are confined to the "A minor" pentad. In both these cases the quasi-tonal passage is interrupted by an interjection which makes no tonal sense whatsoever. These interjections sound familiar when heard in the context of the whole suite as they repeat prior harmonic material. I estimate that they sound arbitrary out of context, but the context is fixed in my mind.

It is because the presentation of the pentads is often so relaxed and redundant that my instinct is to say "mode" instead of "pc set." I will point out in a fuller analysis of Number 8 how another logic becomes syntactically and perceptually predominant, ultimately resisting the representation of tonality. For a first preview of that logic, Figure 15.6 shows entrances of the subject of Number 10, the fugue.

The question what tonality becomes when it reappears in post-serial or elaborated minimalist styles has been in the air for a few decades, and I don't think we have a standard toolkit for describing it. Perhaps we have not adequately appreciated how diverse a phenomenon tonality was before 1900. My own quick remark above, that tonality in a strong sense of the term is a rule system, shortchanges the problem. Functional harmony entails rules about complete, ordered sequences of chords, but there are lots of other manifestations of tonality. Tone centricity is an element often mentioned. Fields of connotation are elements more often neglected. The *Tristan* chord is not enough to imply tonality by itself, but the opening measure and a half of the *Tristan* Prelude, played well, with suggestive dynamic phrasing, certainly is enough. References to vernacular styles associated with tonality can prejudice our hearing and interpretation of harmonies that, in themselves, offer minimal grounds for a tonal reading. Perhaps that is the case in Number 8, Tango. A hint of tango rhythms and tango gesture might be enough to encourage interpretations of the harmony in relation to minor and even to establish a positive valence for its suggestion of flat-second degrees.

The full score is reproduced as Figure 15.7. Figure 15.8 shows the first of the three, strictly parallel seventeen-measure verses analyzed by lynes on the underlaid staves. Except at mm. 14 and 15, I think it is evident that the segmentation of the verse by pc sets largely corresponds with obvious gestalt boundaries.

No need to catalog all the elements of a potential tonality. To remark just a few, the 4/3 resolution to G-sharp minor at the opening is repeated in the last measure of the Coda. There is a full-fledged V^7–I progression in B-flat at m. 13. The parallel sixths at m. 7 add by their connotation of popular styles to the impression there of E minor. The F♮ with which E-major elements are associated throughout does not weaken the centrality of E because the flat second degree, a characteristic of some Spanish vernacular styles, was imported to the Argentine tango. If the first verse, mm. 1–17, is taken in isolation, then I think the play of tonal suggestions, disorganized as it is, can appear the governing unity. But play through Figure 15.9, which brings together mm. 14–16 with its corresponding transpositions in the second and third verses. Notice that the E-major triad of m. 14 disappears through mm. 31 and 48. The chromatic cluster which has replaced it in m. 48 needs some elegance of touch from the pianist to hold its place, but granted that delicacy, the notes sound "correct" because of the constancy of the set. Note also that the one foreign body, the C, is invariant except that it moves up one octave. These are simple relations. The whole Tango proceeds by nearly systematic modal transposition of this sort. Since the structure of verses makes it easy to compare parallel passages, I leave it to any interested reader to extract other examples. I think it will be clear if the piece is studied as a whole that these modal transpositions (or rotations) establish an aural organization sufficiently forthright to dominate the more chaotic tonal references. The effect of this logic is stronger over the whole Tango than in a seventeen-measure excerpt, and it is enhanced further by resonance with other numbers. Figure 15.10 samples figures in pc set 2 from each of four numbers where it appears.

As the set class identities gain force across the suite, gaining stability and accessibility, the tonal indications, though salient, are revealed as ephemeral. G-sharp minor frames the Tango, but to see that this tonality has been represented without really taking hold, I think it is sufficient to play the Tango (ideally omitting the six high-register C's) substituting a *tierce de Picardy* at the end. By the time we get to the Coda, the "dissonant" bass notes which respond to the triads in mm. 52 and 53 sound like right notes—one recognizes the local closure when the pentad is completed. But a B♯ substituted in the last chord sounds like an intrusion from another universe.

Passionate, impulsive & with no fear of exaggeration

Figure 15.7. *Voice Mail,* No. 8, "Tango."

Figure 15.8. Measures 1–17 of *Voice Mail*, No. 8, analyzed by pc content.

Figure 15.9. Measures 14–16, as above with parallel figures (modal transpositions).

Of course, the flicker of competing triads has as much to do with representing "tango" as with representing "key." Genre stylization injects color. Like tonality, genre also encounters resistance from the rigidity of the pitch system.

15.2. Topics, Gestures, and Genres: *Voice Mail* as Program Music

Voice Mail plays with programmatic titles and allusions to genres. In contemplating the game, I would hope we would recall the idea of imagination in early-nineteenth-century music. "Imagination" is not a synonym for "invention" or "creativity." Coleridge investigates imagination as the special faculty that produces and elaborates "image." *Voice Mail* offers grounds for imagining but often twists or undercuts its images. Such irony was not at all foreign to Romantic aesthetics, but I believe it was then a countercurrent, a reaction to the foregrounded ideal of the image as a transcendent symbol. In *Voice Mail*, features that either resist or distort representation are quite pervasive. The harmonic techniques already described support this tendency. Early-nineteenth-century music depends on the hallucinatory power of smooth and sensuous tonality, an effect foregrounded by the development of the piano. The harmonic system of *Voice Mail* encourages various

Number 1

Number 2 -- *Adagio*

Number 9 -- *Fast Rock*

See also Figure 15.8

Figure 15.10. Examples of second pc set from three other numbers.

grating and abrupt transitions that make no straightforward contribution to the development of its initial images. The overall quality is not dreamlike, unless it be of a dream recurrently interrupted, perhaps dreams of bucolic idylls littered with pop cans and styrofoam. Such a metaphor illustrates an ambiguity inherent in resistance to reference. Almost inevitably, the interruption itself or any other twist or distortion permits further interpretation as an elaboration or ornament, or as what Hatten (1994) calls a trope. One might give up pastoral dreams because of the beer cans, or one might dream the cans, too.

One kind of resistance can be understood as a contest of *topic* and *texture*. (I have pointed out earlier that topic methodology requires historical discipline. By exercise of my composer's license, I am using the idea informally.) Titles and program notes must be part of the game in any account of topics. It is quite possible that hearing *Voice Mail* in complete ignorance of its titles would be a better musical experience. My personal reactions regarding those alternatives with other music are inconsistent. In *Voice Mail* I have by now forfeited my choice, and I stick to the original agenda. Here, again, is the table of contents, but this time with a view for reference, not thematic form:

1. "Invocation—To Mnemosyne and Amnemosyne," or to the goddesses of Memory and Memory Slips, if you will. The melody of Number 1 is a fake. Like a first assignment in a composition class, its notes are |A|, |G♯|, and |B| throughout. I think it depends *as a form* on evoking associations with the melodic rhetoric of other styles of music. At the climax the melody is reduced to one note over pseudo-arpeggios. The strain between the rhetoric and the repetitious, contrived pitch

240 *Resisting the Representation*

constraints are like brackets or scare quotes around the "melody" thematizing, with a little help from the title, a topical reference to memory, but if that signal is too subtle, the quotation ending the piece, from Schumann, Op. 78, ought to do the job.

2. "Midnight Skyscape" is representationally straightforward even if the texture has turned inside out before the end. The musical syntax is orderly. Any listener so inclined can make up a picture or a story, though I don't have one; the music does not resist. Representationally *straightforward* does not mean representationally *definite*. In combination with a mounting song and culminating fireworks, the title invites the pathetic fallacy: nature as a metaphor for soul.

3. In "Pas de deux" the principal topic suggested by the title and by the tune should be "ballet." The somewhat static, seven-quarter-note measures (or phrases) are poised. The predominant foot—♩♩♩—a dactyl accentually or an anapest quantitatively is the same as the Sugar Plum Fairy's foot in *The Nutcracker*, but much too fast. Accidents ensue. This representation is arbitrarily disrupted by a muddy outpouring, *fortissimo*, in the lowest register. In the written-out repeat, the wound is repaired. A trope or a hole in the canvas? As I remember, the composer, when composing, only wished to fool with the sound and neutralize its semantic character, but by the time he came to write program notes, he had figured out a literary interpretation (which I will spare the reader).

4. The fourth number, "Traditional Song (Anglo-American)," the number that presents both of the pentatonic scales, includes a folk song that is more than a topic as it is quoted fully and needs no quotation marks. There is no doubt in my mind what my representational intentions were here, right from the start. I learned and loved the "Riddle Song" when I was a young child, and years later, not yet an adult, but then a camp counselor teaching it to campers, I suddenly understood it as a song about stillbirth:

> I gave my love a cherry, that had no stone
> I gave my love a chicken, that has no bone
> I gave my love a ring, that has no end
> I gave my love a baby, with no cryin'
>
> How can there be a cherry that has no stone?
> How can there be . . . etc.
>
> A cherry when it's bloomin', it has no stone
> A chicken when it's pippin', it has no bone
> A ring when it's rollin', it has no end
> A baby when it's sleepin', there's no cryin'.

The program notes, which include the verses and the remark I paraphrased above, set up the music to sound sad. Perhaps, without a program note, it would not sound sad. (There is no way for me to know.) I had no intention of opacity or irony; yet, I have a special reason to mention this representation in the present discussion of resistance.

The melody itself is presented with slight irregularities of rhythm that, to my ear, compensate for the rhythmic nuance words would afford in a sung performance (*parlando* style, the topic of "speech"). As the number proceeds, phrases are increasingly separated by isolated and angular interjections (gesticulations, "speechlessness"). A tiny elf pulling at the composer's left ear complained of the maudlin result. It was absolutely necessary to oppose representation, to return for an instant to pure sensory listening. My solution (not motivically irrelevant) was the measure shown in Figure 15.11.

Surely, if one measure of music in isolation can mean nothing, this one should. But resistance to a force does not cancel it. Resistance attests its object. We look at a cathedral and see gravity made visible. Sails let us see the wind. I can't say no one will find the song too sentimental or that everyone will find it sentimentally effective, but I think I can say that, in this case, resistance enhances representation. In music and in persons, we sometime identify most with emotion held back. If you accept the logic of my demonstration, examples of the same principle in standard repertoire may come to mind.

5–6. The fifth and sixth numbers, the two most suggestive of twentieth-century Neoclassicism in style, don't participate readily in the free-ranging imagery of the others. Number 5, the two-part "Invention," is faithful to its genre, and this study in imitative counterpart may have no topics outside musical style history itself. The subject, fixed by rhythm and contour, is a type known from Bach, fugal subjects in the manner of a gigue. The counterpoint opposed to it invokes the athletic pointillism of a more recent era. Until toward the end, where things speed up and fragment, the texture formed by the contrasting lines is merely an exaggerated example of a contrapuntal strategy already familiar from Bach and Scarlatti. The sixth piece, "Variations," makes no particular references that I know how to specify, even though I am privately aware of some sources.

7. "Opera Song (Male Voice)," on the other hand, is elaborately representational. The bass line is complicated enough to suggest both a persona and a developed rhetoric. The three sections of the aria are separated by a quiet figure blurred by pedal that I had thought of as changing stage lights, until another pianist told me they were actually the off-stage choir. The representation goes awry, and I don't think you will find a story or a trope that can undo the semantic nonsense. The song's development proceeds through a series of rhythmic mutations that have more to do with *kriti* than *bel canto*. It isn't worth the ink it would take to figure out whether the result is semantic or anti-semantic; suffice it that the question is on the table.

8. The "Tango" was meant to sound like a tango and be played like a tango. But it is (another pianist pointed out) a cubist tango. The roughed-up rhythms and disjointed phrasing might either enhance or endanger the reference. At a detailed level, its genre is not consistent, for there are, I believe, elements of two distinct traditions, the sung tango and the danced tango. "Tango" is a loaded topic evoking images of sexuality, violence, and, for the sung tango, complaint. (The typical lyrics are about the woman who did me in.) None of these themes are evoked consistently, but perhaps all are available to the pianist in fragments.

Figure 15.11. Measure 32 of *Voice Mail,* No. 4.

Figure 15.12. Measures 1–3 of *Voice Mail,* No. 1.

9. "Party Song" is fast rock. The topic is, depending on your taste in semiotic theory, either resisted or troped by long and short un-rocklike silences and extra and missing half beats.

10. I think of "Per Augmentationem," the fugue, as the most abstract number of the whole suite; yet it is not like Numbers 5 and 6 in this respect. The Invention and the Variations are both busy and more insistent on focusing attention on stylistic logic. Number 10 is slower and in any reasonable interpretation, the calmest of the pieces. The syntax of *Voice Mail* is largely patent, but the relations of augmentation here are perceptually liminal, a characteristic that seems to me to participate in evoking a more diffuse state of consciousness and blurring the boundary between representation and sensation.

There are both pro-genre and anti-genre elements. Anti: The action stops for an exposition of the subject in inharmonic similar motion at registral extremes—a moment of contrapuntal nonsense. Pro: The counterpoint then resumes in a pianistically enriched texture that, despite ugly little blotches, is right out of the tradition of keyboard fugue.

11. Per Organo Pleno. Dense over-pedaled chords represent the organ, and a plodding melodic rhythm represents chorale style. But in the middle, the image turns inside out, pedal off, doubling off, meter awry. Once again, whether that reversal is an interruption of reference or a trope on it, I will not try to figure out.

12. . . .
13. . . .

This is data enough. I must now explain in what sense none of this matters and in what sense I think it does.

15.3. The Semiotic Character of *Voice Mail*

There is no story, no argument, no plan organizing the collection of programmatic and generic references, or at least none that I've noticed. There is a stylistic *prise de position*, but no integrating logic of discourse. Like the tonal structures that are broached but rapidly discarded within several of the numbers, the fairly rich splatter of semantic pointers offers color and variety but contributes little to coherence. Furthermore, for all the talk of topics in classical music, the same balance often holds there. Topics bring life to an abstract design, provoking greater identification and involvement with its parts but not accounting for the sense. The sense is the syntax. In the present design, the Fano lattice space is gradually saturated. As that happens there is an irregular but still palpably directional enrichment of pianist means (for example, richer pedal effects in the eleventh and thirteenth pieces than elsewhere). The strongest genre contrasts are in the second half. Music can be abstract in its overall conception and nevertheless very dependent on reference to sustain the vivacity of its character. Music lives as an abstract medium when it is abstracted *from* something. Pure design without the coloration of referential suggestions is sometimes of great interest to us, but overall, I think it forms a rather minor part of music—I would say even a rather minor part of *abstract* music. The refusal to pin down ultimate references is not a flight from semiotics. What I advertise here is no more than Suzanne Langer declared when she defined a sign as "anything we use for abstraction."

Notation permitted European music to develop a wonderful division of responsibilities between composition and performance. I have argued, especially in Chapter 5, that the basis of this division is not a European invention and does not depend on writing. The consequence of separating composition from performance is largely to alienate composition from the deepest, plainest, and most prevalent determinants of musical meaning, the nuances of rhythm and color that convey gesture and tone of voice. Those are the responsibility of performance.

How I understand that responsibility can be shown with the opening three measure of the first number (Figure 15.12). The diacritical markings (which are more graph than notation) are more elaborate here than in most of the suite. A simple double turn is repeated with an indication of a swell. The swell is contra-metrical, so if one is inclined toward meter one might want to do more. Consider the possibilities of accenting the first note or the last note, much or little, in either m. 1 or 3, the possibility of playing them the same way or playing them to contrast. Performance makes gesture, not composition. The gestural intentions of the performer establish a choice among diverging worlds.

But that is merely the pianist's right hand. More is at stake in the left hand in realizing meter, which will itself become more representational when it is firmly embodied and less representational when it is disembodied. I know my own taste in this regard. The gates of music opened for me so that there was no turning back when, as a child, I first encountered the rollicking bass octave ostinatos in the musette of Böhm that J. S. Bach copied out in the notebook for Anna Magdalena. I never outgrew it. I still sometimes feel like a child reaching out for Mr. Böhm's hand, to catch his beat. But what does the score tell us of this with its sometimes persistent, sometimes changing, sometimes obvious, sometimes contradictory metrical structures? The pianist, Lidov, now plays parts of *Voice Mail* with a bouncing measure that the composer, Lidov, never had in mind. The semiotician, Lidov, finds this entirely as it should be.

When I was a young composer I heard much talk of a need to liberate music of the Western Classical tradition from its dependence on the score. That discourse was salutary then, but the thesis was false. A better thesis would have been that performance needed to be liberated from the score. The first half of the twentieth century suffered the convergence of at least three tendencies that inhibited imaginative performance. In composition, expressionism gave rise to a style of notation which seemed to aim to be fully determinative of performance, as if it were the performance that was to be notated, not the composition. In music historical studies, progress in documenting the theories of style of various epochs as well as their performance practices undermined the assumption that composers' intentions could be best discovered by the performer's development of his or her personal intuition. And, to provide the new performance style authorities with proper police services, we elaborated the art of sound recording, which ensures that we live with our mistakes and exaggerations.

The problem of constraint on performance has somewhat healed itself in recent decades because of experimental notations, renewed interest in improvisation, more subtle historical reconstructions, and even a fluidity of recording that robs the record/tape/CD of monumentality. My thought when composing *Voice Mail* was that we have a ways to go. We can see an older attitude in the questions and injunction with which Josef Lhévinne concludes the penultimate chapter of his slender but very thoughtful book, *Basic Principles in Pianoforte Playing* (1972):

1. Do you express the *composer's* thought and mood?
2. Do you express what *you* feel and wish?
3. Whatever it is, by all means express something!
   (emphasis in the original)

This will not quite do for us. We know that the score is not sufficient evidence by itself of the composer's thought and mood. But what if the composer's mind had never settled this matter to begin with? May I presume, as the composer in this instance, to assert that my intentions in composing, if there were any, should be irrelevant to the performer? I never renounced my own intentions; I simply used them up. I used them for choosing notes, knowing full well that the notes could not capture all the intentionality with which they were, fleetingly, invested in my imagination.

My technique in *Voice Mail* aims to arrange musical notes in such a manner that the performer will have specific incentives (topical clues, traces of gesture, hints of voice and rhetoric, evocations of memory) to assign intentions to the music and will have space to realize them. The page is neither blank nor fully colored in. Option 1 above is rejected outright for most of *Voice Mail*. (I don't want to pretend that my stance is pure or radical. I certainly did mean, for example, that the "Tango" should sound like a tango. I hope the score provides grounds for the hesitations and violence that I love in tangos.)

But option 2 is also rejected. The score is not a blank book for the pianist's self-expression. If it does not specify mood, the score does suggest a way of making sense. The only acceptable manner to realize option 3, heartily endorsed, is by making sense of the score, *as if* it had consistent intentions. The pianist ought to play as the only one who, by special privilege, knows the composer's exact thoughts. One might posit that attitude for any music, but in many cases there would be no specific grounds for it. Here this disposition is implied by everything I have reported about structure and representation in *Voice Mail*.

The irresponsible performance is the performance that does not aim at interpretation. The task of the composition was to suggest but ultimately to resist representation. The responsibility of the performance is to overcome the resistance.

References

Adorno, Theodor W. 1973. *Philosophy of Modern Music.* Translated by Anne G. Mitchell and Wesley V. Blomster. New York: Seaburg Press.

Amrom, Simcha. 1969. "Essai d'une notation des monodies à des fins d'analyse." *Revue de musicologie* 55: 172–216.

Babbitt, Milton. 1972a. "Remarks on Recent Stravinsky." In Benjamin Boretz and Edward Cone, eds., *Perspectives on Schoenberg and Stravinsky.* New York: W. W. Norton.

———. 1972b. "The Structure and Function of Music Theory." In Benjamin Boretz and Edward Cone, eds., *Perspectives on Contemporary Music Theory.* New York: W. W. Norton.

Bach, C. P. E. 1974 (1762). *Essay on the True Art of Playing Keyboard Instruments.* Translated by W. Mitchell. London: Eulenberg.

Bartha, Dennis. 1971. "On Beethoven's Thematic Structure." In Paul Lang, ed., *The Creative World of Beethoven.* New York: W. W. Norton.

Barthes, Roland. 1967. *Elements of Semiology.* Translated by Annette Layers and Colin Smith. London: Cape.

Barzun, Jacques. 1943. *Classic, Romantic and Modern.* Toronto: Little, Brown.

Berlioz, Hector. 1975. *Beethoven by Berlioz.* Edited and translated by R. De Sola. Boston: Crescendo.

Blum, Stephen. 1985. "Rousseau's Concept of *système musical* and the Comparative Studies of Tonalities in Nineteenth-Century France." *Journal of the American Musicological Society* 37, no. 2: 349–61.

Brogan, T. V. F. 1993. "Abstract Poem." In Alex Preminger and T. V. F. Brogan, eds., *The New Princeton Encyclopedia of Poetry and Poetics.* Princeton: Princeton University Press.

Busoni, Ferruccio. 1962. *Sketch of a New Esthetic of Music.* In *Three Classics in the Aesthetic of Music: Monsieur Croche the Dilettante Hater,* by Claude Debussy and Ferruccio Busoni. New York: Dover.

Casini, Claudio. 1985. "*La Traviata, ein Melodram?*" In Casini, *Verdi.* Königstein: Taunus.

Chavez, Charles. 1961. *Musical Thought.* Cambridge, Mass.: Harvard University Press.

Chomsky, Noam. 1965. *Aspects of the Theory of Syntax.* Cambridge, Mass.: MIT Press.

Chomsky, Noam, and Morris Halle. 1968. *The Sound Pattern of English.* New York: Harper and Row.

Churchill, Ward, and Jim Vander Wall. 1988. *Agents of Repression: The FBI's Secret War against the Black Panther Party and the American Indian Movement.* Boston: South End Press.

Clynes, Manfred. 1989 (1976). *Sentics: The Touch of Emotions.* New York: Doubleday.

Coker, Wilson. 1972. *Music and Meaning.* New York: Collier-Macmillan.

Colapietro, Vincent. 1989. *Peirce's Approach to the Self.* Albany: SUNY Press.

Cooke, Deryck. 1959. *The Language of Music.* London: Oxford University Press.

Cowell, Henry. 1996. *New Musical Resources with Notes and an Accompanying Essay by David Nicholls.* Cambridge: Cambridge University Press.

———. 2001. *Essential Cowell: Selected Writings on Music.* Edited by Dick Higgens. Kingston, N.Y.: McPherson.

Cumming, Naomi. 2000. *The Sonic Self: Musical Subjectivity and Signification.* Bloomington: Indiana University Press.

Dahlhaus, Carl. 1970. *Analysis and Value Judgement.* Translated by S. Levarie. New York: Pendragon.

———. 1985. *Realism in Nineteenth-Century Music.* Translated by Mary Whittall. New York: Cambridge University Press.

———. 1989. *The Idea of Absolute Music.* Translated by Roger Lustig. Chicago: University of Chicago Press.

Darwin, Charles. 1873. *The Expression of the Emotions in Man and Animals.* London: John Murray.

Davidson, Archibald T., and Willi Apel. 1949. *Historical Anthology of Music.* Vol. I. Cambridge, Mass.: Harvard University Press.

D'Indy, Vincent. 1909. *Cours de composition.* Paris: Durand.

Dougherty, William. 1993. "The Play of Interpretants: A Peircean Approach to Beethoven's Lieder." In Michael Shapiro, ed., *The Peirce Seminar Papers: An Annual of Semiotic Analysis.* Vol. I. Oxford: Berg.

———. 1994. "The Quest for Interpretants: Toward a Peircean Paradigm for Musical Semiotics." *Semiotica* 99, nos. 1–2: 163–84.

———. 1996. "Musical Semiotics: A Peircean Perspective." In Raymond Monelle, ed., *Musica Significans: Proceedings of the Third International Congress on Musical Signification, Edinburgh (1992).* London: Harwood.

———. 1999. "Mixture, Song, and Semiotic." In Ioannis Zannos, ed., *Music and Signs: Semiotic and Cognitive Studies in Music.* Bratislava: ASCO Art and Science.

Dumas, Alexandre. 1902. *Camille: A Play in Five Acts.* Translated and adapted from the French with a critical introduction by Edmund Gosse. New York: P. F. Collier.

———. 1963. *La dame aux camélias.* Paris: Calmann-Levy.

Eco, Umberto. 1976. *A Theory of Semiotics.* Bloomington: Indiana University Press.

Erickson, Robert, and John MacKay. 1995. *Music of Many Means: Sketches and Essays on the Music of Robert Erickson.* Lanham, Md.: Scarecrow.

Friedlaender, Max. 1922. *Brahms' Lieder: Einführung in seiner Gesänge für eine und zwei Stimme.* Berlin: Simrock.

Gal, Hans. 1916. "Die Stileigentumlichkeiten des jungen Beethoven." *Studien zur Musikwissenschaft* 4: 45–117.

Garvin, Paul. 1964. *A Prague School Reader on Esthetics, Literary Structure and Style.* Washington, D.C.: Georgetown University Press.

———. 1981. "Structuralism, Esthetics and Semiotics." In Wendy Steiner, ed., *Image and Code.* Ann Arbor, Mich.: Horace H. Rackham School of Graduate Studies.

Gavoty, Bernhard. 1974. *Frédéric Chopin.* Paris: Grasset.

Goodman, Nelson. 1968. *Languages of Art: A Contribution to the Study of Symbols.* New York: Bobbs-Merrill.

Grauer, Victor Grauer. 1981. "Modernism/Postmodernism/Neomodernism." *Downtown Review* 3, nos. 1–2: 3–7.

———. 1988. "Mondrian and the Dialectic of Essence." *Art Criticism* 11, no. 1: 1–26.

———. 1996. "Toward a Unified Theory of the Arts." *Music Theory Online* 2, no. 6: http://boethius.music.ucsb.edu/mto/issues/mto.96.2.6/mto.96.2.6.grauer.html.

Greimas, Algirdas-Julien. 1984. *Structural Semantics: An Attempt at a Method.* Translation of *Sémantique structurale: Recherche de méthode.* Trans. Daniele McDowell,

Ronald Schleifer, and Alan Veleie, with an introduction by Ronald Schleifer. Lincoln: University of Nebraska Press.

Groos, Arthur. 1995. "'TB Sheets': Love and Disease in *La traviata.*" *Cambridge Opera Journal* 7: 233–60.

Grove, George, 1962. *Beethoven and His Nine Symphonies.* New York: Dover.

Gurney, Edmund. 1967. *The Power of Sound.* New York: Basic Books.

Hantz, Edwin. 1985. Review of Fred Lerdahl and Ray Jackendoff, *A Generative Theory of Tonal Music. Music Theory Spectrum* 7: 190–202.

Hatten, Robert S. 1993. "Schubert the Progressive: The Role of Resonance and Gesture in the Piano Sonata in A, D. 959." *Intégral* 7: 38–81.

———. 1994. *Musical Meaning in Beethoven: Markedness, Correlation, and Interpretation.* Bloomington: Indiana University Press.

———. 2004. *Interpreting Musical Gestures, Topics, and Tropes: Mozart, Beethoven, Schubert.* Bloomington: Indiana University Press.

Hepokoski, J. A. 1989. "Genre and Content in Mid-century Verdi: 'Addio, del passato' (*La traviata,* Act III)." *Cambridge Opera Journal* 1, no. 3: 249–76.

Higgins, Thomas, ed. 1973. "Notes toward a Performance with References to the Valldemose Autograph." In Frédéric Chopin, *Preludes, Opus 28: An Authoritative Score, Historical Background, Analysis, Views and Comments,* ed. Thomas Higgins. New York: W. W. Norton.

Hjelmslev, Louis. 1943. *Prolegomena to a Theory of Language.* Translated by Francis J. Whitfield. Madison: University of Wisconsin Press, 1961.

Hopkins, Pandora. 1977. "The Homology of Music and Myth: Views of Lévi-Strauss on Musical Structure." *Ethnomusicology* 21: 247–63.

Hornbostel, Erich Moritz von. 1975. *Opera Omnia.* Edited by Klaus P. Wachsmann, Dieter Christensen, and Hans-Peter Reinecke in collaboration with Richard G. Campbell et al. The Hague: Nijhoff.

Huneker, James. 1966. *Chopin: The Man and His Music.* New York: Dover.

Jackendoff, Ray. 1987. *Consciousness and the Computational Mind.* Cambridge, Mass.: MIT Press.

Jakobson, Roman. 1960. "Closing Statement: Linguistics and Poetics." In *Style and Language,* ed. Thomas A. Sebeok. Cambridge, Mass.: Technology Press of MIT.

———. 1967. "Visual and Auditory Signs." In *Selected Writings,* vol. 2. Paris: Mouton.

Johnson, Mark. 1987. *The Body in the Mind: The Bodily Basis of Meaning, Imagination and Reason.* Chicago: University of Chicago Press.

Keiler, Allan H. 1983. "On Some Properties of Schenker's Pitch Derivations." *Music Perception* 1, no. 2: 200–28.

Keller, Hermann. 1965. *Phrasing and Articulation: A Contribution to a Rhetoric of Music.* Translated by Leigh Gerdine. New York: W. W. Norton.

Kimbell, David R. B. 1981. *Verdi in the Age of Italian Romanticism.* Cambridge: Cambridge University Press.

Kristeva, Julia. 1974. *La révolution du langage poétique.* Paris: Editions du Seuil.

Langer, Suzanne. 1953. *Feeling and Form: A Theory of Art.* New York: Scribner's Sons.

———. 1957. *Philosophy in a New Key: A Study in the Symbolism of Reason, Rite, and Art.* Cambridge, Mass.: Harvard University Press.

Leibowitz, René. 1975. *Schoenberg and His School.* Translated by Dika Newlin. New York: Da Capo.

Lerdahl, Fred, and Ray Jackendoff. 1983. *A Generative Theory of Tonal Music.* Cambridge, Mass.: MIT Press.

Lester, Joel. 1986. *The Rhythms of Tonal Music*. Carbondale: Southern Illinois University Press.

Lévi-Strauss, Claude. 1966. *The Savage Mind*. Chicago: University of Chicago Press.

———. 1970. *The Raw and the Cooked*. New York: Harper and Row.

Lewin, David. 1986. "Music Theory, Phenomenology, and Modes of Perception." *Music Perception* 3, no. 4: 327–92.

Lhévinne, Josef. 1972. *Basic Principles in Pianoforte Playing*. With a new foreword by Rosina Lhévinne. New York: Dover.

Lidov, David. 1975a. "Between Insight and Explanation." *Linguistic Association of Canada and the United States*, Toronto, 1975: LACLXS Forum, no. 2: 619–26.

———. 1975b. "On the Musical Phrase: No. 1." *Monographies de sémiologie et d'analyses musicales*. Montreal: Faculty of Music, University of Montreal.

———. 1980. *Musical Structure and Musical Significance—I* (Working Paper). Toronto Semiotic Circle [First] Monograph series. Toronto: University of Victoria in the University of Toronto.

———. 1992. "The '*Lamento di Tristan.*'" In M. Everist, ed., *Music before 1600: Models of Musical Analysis*. London: Blackwell.

———. 1995. "Toward a Reinterpretation of Compositional Theory." In Eero Tarasti, ed., *Musical Signification: Essays in the Semiotic Theory and Analysis of Music*. Berlin: Mouton de Gruyter.

———. 1998. "Musical Semiotics—Science, Letters, or Art?" *Integral* 10: 125–45.

———. 1999. *Elements of Semiotics*. Toronto: St. Martin's Press.

Lidov, David, and James Gabura. 1973. "A Melody Writing Algorithm Using a Formal Language Model." *Computers in Humanities* 4, no. 314: 138–48.

Liebowitz, René. 1975. *Schoenberg and His School*. Translated by Dika Newland. New York: Da Capo.

List, George. 1963. "The Boundaries of Speech and Song." *Ethnomusicology* 7, no. 1: 1–16.

London, Justin. 1997. "Lerdahl and Jackendoff's Strong Reduction Hypothesis and the Limits of Analytical Description." *In Theory Only* 13, nos. 1–4: 3–28.

Martinez, José Luiz. 1997. *Semiosis in Hindustani Music*. Imatra: International Semiotics Institute.

Matejka, L., and I. Titunik. 1976. *Semiotics of Art: Prague School Contributions*. Cambridge, Mass.: MIT Press.

McClary, Susan. 1991. *Feminine Endings: Music, Gender and Sexuality*. Minneapolis: University of Minnesota Press.

McKay, J. 1977. "The Bréval Manuscript: New Interpretations." *Le Cahiers Debussy* 1, nouvelle série. St. Germain-en-Laye: Centre de documentation Claude Debussy.

Messiaen, Olivier. 1966. *Technique de mon langage musicale*. Paris: Leduc.

Meyer, Leonard B. 1957. *Emotion and Meaning in Music*. Chicago: University of Chicago Press.

———. 1973. *Explaining Music: Essays and Explorations*. Chicago: University of Chicago Press.

———. 1989. *Style and Music: Theory, History, and Ideology*. Philadelphia: University of Pennsylvania Press.

Mickiewicz, Adam. 1976 [1821]. *Switezianka*. Translated by R. Pietraz. In *Poesiealbum* No. 109, ed. B. Jentzch. Berlin: Neues Leben.

Mirka, Danuta. 1997. *The Sonoristic Structuralism of Krzysztof Penderecki*. Katowice, Poland: Music Academy.

———. In preparation. *The Game of Music*.

Molino, Jean. 1975. "Fait musical et sémiologie de la musique." *Musique en jeu* 17: 37–61.

Monelle, Raymond. 1997. "Binary Semantic Opposition in Debussy." In Raymond Monelle, ed., *Musica Significans: Proceedings of the Third International Congress on Musical Signification, Edinburgh (1992)*. London: Harwood.

———. 1999. "Music's Transparency." In *Les Universaux en musique: Actes du 4ème Congrès international sur la signification musicale, Paris, 1994*, pp. 20–29. Paris: Publications de la Sorbonne.

———. 2000. *The Sense of Music*. Princeton, N.J.: Princeton University Press.

Morris, Charles. 1938. "Foundations of the Theory of Signs." In *International Encyclopedia of a Unified Science*. Chicago: University of Chicago Press.

Morris, Charles William. 1970. *The Pragmatic Movement in American Philosophy*. New York: G. Braziller.

Mursell, James Lockhart. 1937. *The Psychology of Music*. Westport, Conn.: Greenwood Press.

Nattiez, Jacques. 1973. *"Densité 21.5" de Varèse: essai d'analyse sémiologique*. Montreal: University of Montreal, Groupe de recherches en sémiologie musicale.

———. 1975. *Fondements d'une sémiologie de la musique*. Paris: Union Général d'Editions.

———. 1982. "Varèse's 'Density 21.5': A Study in Semiological Analysis." Translated by Anna Barry. *Music Analysis* 1, no. 3: 243–340.

———. 1990a. *Musicologie générale et sémiologie*. Paris: Christian Bourgois.

———. 1990b. *Music and Discourse: Toward a Semiology of Music*. Translated by Carolyn Abbate. Princeton, N.J.: Princeton University Press.

Noske, Fritz. 1977. *The Signifier and the Signified: Studies in the Operas of Mozart and Verdi*. The Hague: Nijhoff.

Peel, John, and Wayne Slawson. 1984. Review of Fred Lehrdahl and Ray Jackendoff, *A Generative Theory of Tonal Music*. *Journal of Music Theory* 28, no. 2: 271–94.

Peirce, Charles Sanders. 1955. *Philosophical Writings*. Edited by Justin Buchler. New York: Dover.

Pierce, Alexandra, and Roger Pierce. 1989. *Expressive Movement: Posture and Action in Daily Life, Sports, and the Performing Arts*. New York: Plenum.

———. 1991. *Generous Movement: A Practical Guide to Balance in Action*. Redlands, Calif.: Center of Balance Press.

Persichetti, Vincent. 1961. *Twentieth Century Harmony: Creative Aspects and "Practice."* New York: W. W. Norton.

Polanyi, Michael. 1969. *Knowing and Being: Essays*. Chicago: University of Chicago Press.

Powers, Harold S. 1980. "Language Models and Musical Analysis." *Ethnomusicology* 1: 1–60.

Rahn, Jay. 1983. *A Theory for All Music*. Toronto: University of Toronto Press.

Ratner, Leonard. 1980. *Classic Music*. New York: Schirmer.

Reich, Willi. 1971. *Schoenberg: A Critical Biography*. Translated by Leo Black. London: Longman.

Riemann, Hugo. 1903. *System der musikalischen Rhythmik und Metrik*. Leipzig: Breitkopf und Härtel.

Riethmüller, Albrecht. 2001. "Wunschbild: Beethoven als Chauvinist." *Archiv für Musikwissenschaft* 58: 91–109 (English version in *Beethoven Forum*, forthcoming).

Rousseau, Jean-Jacques. 1970. *Essai sur l'origine des langues, ou il est parle de la mélodie et de limitation musical*. Edited by Charles Porset. Bordeaux: Ducros.

Ruwet, N. 1972. *Language, musique, poésie*. Paris: Le Seuil.

———. 1975. "Théorie et méthodes dans les études musicales: quelques remarques rétro-spectives et preliminaries." *Musique en jeu* 17: 11–36.

Said, Edward W. 1991. *Musical Elaborations*. New York: Columbia University Press.

Samuel, Claude. 1967. *Entretiens avec Olivier Messiaen*. Paris: Belfond.

Saussure, Ferdinand de. 1915. *Course in General Linguistics*. Edited by C. Bally and A. Sechehaye. New York: McGraw-Hill, 1966.

Schaeffer, Pierre. 1966. *Traité des objets musicaux*. Paris: Seuil.

Schenker, Heinrich. 1954. *Harmony*. Translated by C. Jonas. Chicago: University of Chicago Press.

Schiff, David. 1983. *The Music of Elliott Carter*. London: Eulenberg.

Schmitz, A. 1978. *Das romantische Beethovenbild*. Darmstadt: Wissenschaftliche Buchgesellschaft.

Schnebel, Dieter. 2001 (1979). "Die schwierige Wahrheit des Lebens: zu Verdis musikalischem Realismus." 2nd rev. edition. In *Musick-Konzepte* No. 10. Munich: Richard Boorberg.

Schoenberg, Arnold. 1951. *Style and Idea*. London: Williams and Norgate.

———. 1965. *Collected Letters*. Edited by E. Skin. Translated by E. Wilkens and E. Daiser. New York: St. Martin's Press.

Scruton, Roger. 1980. "Possible Worlds and Premature Sciences." *London Review of Books* (February 7): 14–16.

Seeger, Charles. 1975. "On the Moods of a Music Logic." In *Studies in Musicology 1935–1975*. The Hague: Mouton.

Selleri, Franco. 1989. *Quantum Paradoxes and Physical Reality*. Edited by Alwyn van der Merwe. Dordrecht: Kluwer.

Sitwell, Osbert. 1949. Liner notes for William Walton and Edith Sitwell, *Façade*, Columbia Records ML 2047. Frederick Praunitz, conductor; Edith Sitwell, reader.

Spencer, Herbert. 1970. *Literary Style and Music, including Two Short Essays on Gracefulness and Beauty*. London: Kennikat Press.

Stiller, Andrew. 1985. *Handbook on Instrumentation*. Berkeley: University of California Press.

Stockhausen, Karlheinz. 1961. Liner notes for K. Stockhausen, *"Zxylus," "Refrain."* Phono-recording. New York: Time-Life.

Stone, Elsa, and Kurt Stone, eds. 1977. *The Writings of Elliott Carter: An American Composer Looks at Modern Music*. Bloomington: Indiana University Press.

Stravinsky, Igor. 1947. *Poetics of Music in the Form of Six Lessons*. Cambridge, Mass.: Harvard University Press.

Tarasti, Eero. 1979. *Myth and Music*. The Hague: Mouton.

———. 1994. *A Theory of Musical Semiotics*. Bloomington: Indiana University Press.

Tenney, James. 1964. *Meta+Hodos: A Phenomenology of Twentieth-Century Musical Materials and an Approach to the Study of Form*. New Orleans: Inter-American Institute for Musical Research, Tulane University.

Tovey, D. 1935. *Essays in Musical Analysis, I*. London: Oxford University.

Weintraub, Wiktor. 1954. *The Poetry of Adam Mickiewicz*. The Hague: Mouton.

Zimmerman, Walter, ed. 1985. *Morton Feldman Essays*. Kerpen: Beginner Press.

Index

Page numbers in *italics* indicate illustrations.

Schoenberg, Arnold, 29, 73, 188–190, 194–195, 203–208, 213; *Erwartung,* 205; *Moses and Aaron,* 208; *Pierrot Lunair,* 205; *Second Quartet, Op.* 10, 205–207; *Third Quartet, Op.* 30, 207; *Fourth Quartet, Op.* 37, 208, *233*
Schubert, Franz, 33, 122, 145, 195, 210, 213; *Sonatas for piano,* D. 959, 138–140; D. 960, 37, *38–39*
Schumann, Robert, 12, 145, 158, 207
Schweitzer, Albert, 89
Scruton, Roger, 7
Seeger, Charles, 156, 199
Segmentation, 16, 94–101, 106–121
Semiotics, 2–3, 13, 79–83, 101–103
Sentic form, 133–137, 160, 168
Sign classifications, 6–14, 29, 125, 146–149
Sitwell, Dame Edith, 209
Sitwell, Osbert, 211
Spencer, Herbert, 8
Stiller, Andrew, 197
Stockhausen, Karlheinz, 192, 195, 214
Stravinsky, Igor, 145, 188–190, 212–213; *Le sacre du printemps,* 95; *Requiem Canticles,* 210; *Symphony of Psalms,* 96; *Variations,* 210
Structural levels, 167
Structuralism, 15–23, 188
Symbol. *See* Sign classifications

Tarasti, Eero, 11, 22, 72, 151, 181
Taxonomy. *See* Paradigm and syntagm; Segmentation
Technology, 126
Tenney, James, 16, 109, 113

Texture, 187, 189, 193
Time spans, 114–120
Tinctoris, Johannes, 29
Tonal hierarchy, 107
Topic, 7–14, 160, 187, 192–193
Topos, 165
Toscanini, Arturo, 55
Tovey, Donald, 41
Transformative discourse, 143–144

Universality in music, 2

Verdi, Giuseppe: *La Traviata,* 165–175
Varèse, Edgar: *Density 21.5,* 100–101, 199
Visual art. *See* Plastic and musical art
Visual perception, 114

Wagner, Richard, 80, 138, 166, 172, 190; *Tristan,* 155
Weintraub, Wiktor, 158
Wertheimer, Max, 16
Westergaard, Peter, 116
Whitman, Walt, 215
Wuourinen, Charles, 227

Xenakis, Xanis, 194, 210

Yeston, Maury, 116

Zimmerman, Walter, 129n., 202, 221–224; *Patience and Opportunity (Geduld & Gelegenheit),* 224; *Randonnée No. 1, Northwest Passage,* 221–223

DAVID LIDOV is a composer, born in the United States and resident in Canada since 1966, whose theoretical investigations were an early and influential source of the musical semiotics movement of recent decades. He studied at Columbia University in New York and teaches at York University in Toronto.